C000276379

What was wrong with that then, umps?

The diary of a recreational cricket umpire

About the Author

Matthew Stevenson was born in Amersham in 1963. He played club cricket for thirty years, for Chalfont Saints C.C. from 1978-92 and for Chalfont St. Peter C.C. from 1993-2007, before retiring as a player and taking up umpiring in 2008. His other interests include all sports - especially football, rugby and tennis - long-distance walking and the countryside, British and maritime history, and current affairs.

Matthew Stevenson

What was wrong with that then, umps?

The diary of a recreational cricket umpire

Olympia Publishers
London

www.olympiapublishers.com
OLYMPIA PAPERBACK EDITION

Copyright © Matthew Stevenson 2016

The right of Matthew Stevenson to be identified as author of
this work has been asserted in accordance with sections 77 and 78 of the
Copyright, Designs and Patents Act 1988.

All Rights Reserved

No reproduction, copy or transmission of this publication
may be made without written permission.
No paragraph of this publication may be reproduced,
copied or transmitted save with the written permission of the publisher, or in
accordance with the provisions
of the Copyright Act 1956 (as amended).

Any person who commits any unauthorised act in relation to
this publication may be liable to criminal
prosecution and civil claims for damage.

A CIP catalogue record for this title is
available from the British Library.

ISBN: 978-1-84897-746-4

First Published in 2016

Olympia Publishers
60 Cannon Street
London
EC4N 6NP

Printed in Great Britain

Foreword

There was certainly a sound. But what was it? Bat on ground? Bat on pad? Or bat on ball? And if it was the ball, did it carry cleanly to the keeper? Or was it a bump ball? Let us face it – any umpire at any level knows what it is to be unsure. Convention allows the batsman the benefit of any doubt, but the fielding side have that triumphant look that says they don't share your doubts. And you know the bowler may have been unlucky the previous over when you judged a straight one to be going just over the top. In any case, the batsman's benefit can become a coward's refuge – if it was out, you ought to have given it out. Such uncertainties and the mental agony that accompanies them will be familiar to those officiating at any level. For those on the international panel, the truth will be there on camera to haunt them – and those umpires may be coming back for the next four days!

For the mere recreational umpire doing his best in a Saturday league game, there is only the post-match inquest to sour the taste of his pint before he can escape. Perhaps the recriminations continue or perhaps he will be lucky. "It's part of the game – I don't let it worry me." I well recall the words of a captain I had apparently erroneously triggered in the opening over of a match. Such generous sentiments and his prompt departure from the crease that day are a welcome part of a game in which those who make mistakes galore with bat or ball can too often expect no error from the appointed umpires. "If I made no mistakes, I'd be wasted at this level," I have often said, only too aware that even at the very highest level an official has been known to clock up three wrong decisions by lunch on the first day.

Matthew Stevenson's book is all about life as an umpire at club level. In many ways his experiences of Saturday league cricket and Sunday friendlies will mirror those of members of the ICC's elite panel, but in other respects the challenges he describes will be radically different. A correctly marked pitch can be taken for granted at Lord's and they won't be searching for six stumps that match. The arrival of the lady kindly doing teas will play no part in determining the intervals. There will be experienced scorers, knowing what is expected of them and working as a team. And they will certainly not be expecting to hear that one of the captains "should be here very shortly" or that "we've only got six so far", all too familiar words to social match umpires as the starting time passes with the toss still to take place.

The recreational game can also be marked by knowing nothing of one's colleague for the day. Will he turn up the prescribed 45 minutes in advance? Will he be one for wearing the once *de rigueur* tie or will he have moved with the times to the open-neck favoured by those at the top of the game? Will he be a stickler for procedures or an old-school grump who has no time for the notion of working together to count the balls? Will he laud his greater umpiring credentials or will he accept that the two officials are equal partners on the day? Above all, as at first-class level, will he be good company for the match?

It was as an umpiring colleague that I first encountered Matthew in the Thames Valley League, of which he is now secretary. I am probably identifiable in his diary of the past four seasons to most of those who have stood with me, and I was one in whom he confided that he was maintaining a diary of his experiences. Having encouraged him to keep going and been privileged to see an early draft of his book, I have no hesitation in commending it to anyone involved in any way with the greatest of all games, one where the pleasures of officiating far outweigh the occasional sadness when its behavioural standards lapse to those of Premier League football, where a Level Four fracas is under way on the screen even as I pen these words.

Douglas Miller

Introduction

This diary recounts my experiences as an umpire in recreational cricket over five English seasons, 2011 to 2015. It focuses on the practical application of the laws of the game, the assorted characters who play, officiate and administer it, and the various local grounds that I have visited along the way. I have tried to make it entertaining and irreverent, and hope that it will appeal to the umpiring fraternity, other cricketing enthusiasts and even some non-cricketing aficionados. I also hope that it will convey to all cricketers and cricketing enthusiasts just how hard it is to umpire a cricket match well.

I have always kept a record of the cricket matches I have participated in, progressing from the mediocrity of my batting statistics to notes about the mistakes I have made as an umpire – the latter in the hope of not repeating them! This diary is the result of these notes. For each diary entry, I have given the team names, the type of match and the score to add context, but have deliberately not mentioned the names of any players or colleagues.

It is interesting how the diary has developed over the five years. During the first two seasons, in 2011 and 2012, I was still in full-time employment and, aside from the occasional Sunday or midweek junior match for my club, broadly only umpired once a week in Saturday league matches. In 2013 I found myself out of work and started to pick up appointments from the Buckinghamshire ACO, including junior and senior county matches and club cup matches. Then in 2014 I started picking up more social, friendly and school appointments. In 2011 and 2012 I umpired 22 and 20 matches respectively; in 2013 I stood in 43 matches; and then in 2014 and 2015 in 63 and 61 respectively. In total I stood in 209 matches over the five seasons, with 106 different colleagues and at 78 different grounds.

All the events described in this diary are true. That said, I have subsequently edited it in two respects. Firstly, where the same incident has occurred in multiple matches I have amalgamated my comments into one diary entry to improve readability. Secondly, I have added in the occasional anecdote or story where it was relevant to the topic I was discussing or, more tangentially, to the ground I was standing at.

Reading back through my diary I have observed three notable recurrent themes: how the professional game and television coverage impacts on recreational umpires; the increased use of the win/lose format in the recreational game; and whether or not umpires should keep the score. My views on the first two subjects are strong and have remained consistent; on the latter, I have moved from one side of the argument to the other and continue to waver.

Matthew Stevenson
October, 2015

The 2011 season

I retired from playing at the end of the 2007 season at the age of 44 due to a combination of a bad back and poor form. From 2008 to 2010, I umpired for my club, Chalfont St. Peter, as a 'club' umpire. The latter travel around with their club and, like the players, scorers, tea ladies, supporters, friends and family, are part of this wider family. But this is the problem. During the match, as an umpire one needs to cease being part of one's club, and to become detached and completely impartial. One has to not only be fair but also be *seen* to be fair. By last season I was beginning to find the latter tiresome.

So, I have decided to join the Thames Valley Cricket League panel this season. Panel umpires are neutral (of course, all umpires are by definition neutral, but what I mean is that they are not associated with either of the clubs involved in the match) and are assigned to matches by the TVCL. I expect the umpiring to be easier in some respects and harder in others; the former because I will just call it as I see it and will not give any thought to being *seen* to be fair, the latter because the standard of cricket will be higher and the players will have higher expectations of me. Socially, I fear that it will be less enjoyable, and that I will miss my club and my old cricket friends.

Stoke Green C.C., Saturday, 30th April, 2011

Friendly (40/40). Stoke Green 135 (37.2), Chalfont St. Peter 136-7 (30.3). Chalfont St. Peter won by 3 wickets.

This match felt quite strange, like it was my last one as a club umpire, and my last one for my club as well. Of course, I will no doubt be umpiring the odd friendly or junior fixture at/for Chalfont in the future, but I will not be doing any more of their TVCL matches. There is one Chalfont batsman who I will not miss. He's a lovely chap, but he's a walking LBW. He plants his front foot, plays around it – and as soon as he misses he's a dead man walking. And I'm afraid he misses quite a lot! Today, to the relief of my right index finger, he was out caught before LBW came into play.

Stoke Green is not in truth one of my favourite grounds, primarily because there is a busy and rather noisy road running along one side. The playing area has long straight boundaries and rather short square ones. If you are playing on the left hand side of the square as you look out from the pavilion then hitting a six over midwicket is little more than a short wedge in golfing terms (or, to the off side, a sliced drive, which is more analogous to my golfing ability!) It also has absurdly low showers; as if they were designed for people no more than five foot tall. I am 5' 11" and today I had to bend uncomfortably to wash my hair – for a man with a bad back this was not good!

Kew C.C., Saturday, 7th May, 2011

TVCL Division 3B. Kew II 247 (50.1), British Airways 250-7 (47.4). British Airways won by 3 wickets.

This was my first match as a TVCL panel umpire. I was nervous beforehand. I had umpired TVCL matches for my club but this was different, a step up. I gave four LBWs, which is unusual for me – I have a reputation as a 'not outer'. I should have given five – I turned one down towards the end of the match and immediately afterwards felt that it was the wrong call. Did I turn it down because I'd already given four? If I am honest, yes. I must learn from this: ignore all that has gone before and give each decision on its merits; be thick-skinned and have the courage of my convictions.

I made one other mistake today. Late in the match, one of the BA batsmen played no shot, the ball struck his body and ran off towards fine leg, and he and his colleague then ran two. When they had finished running, I called and signalled dead ball – but I should have done so after the first run had been completed.[1] The Kew bowler was even more ignorant of the laws than me – he asked why I did not call dead ball straight away. I told him so that his team might have the chance of a run out! "Oh. Good call, umps!" he said.

I also made a dress code *faux pas* today, or to be more accurate my colleague, a club rather than panel umpire, bowled me a googly and tricked me into one! I wore navy flannels, a collared white shirt, an ACO tie and a white blouson. My colleague wore (smart) black jeans, white shirt without a tie and a cricket jumper – close, but no cigar! On reflection, I think that if he was not going to dress up to match me then I should have dressed down – an ECB ACO polo shirt without a tie would have been better.

Changing after the match was an interesting experience. The umpires' room at Kew (an afterthought, like in all except the most modern pavilions) is on one side of the pavilion,

---

[1] Law 26.3, 'Leg byes not to be awarded'.

with the players' changing rooms and showers on the other, and the bar in the middle. I contemplated moving the mountain to Mohammad (carrying my kit bag to the shower), or crossing the bar with a towel around my waist, but eventually decided that extra deodorant would be my best option!

Kew has many of the best attributes of the traditional English cricket club: passers-by watching the cricket, a nice tea, good beer, old team pictures and memorabilia in the clubhouse, church bells, friendly members, banter. There are even red buses going up and down the A205, which would please Henry Blofeld. It is just a shame about the tarmac path, which cuts across part of the outfield and the aeroplanes, which are especially annoying here when they are landing at Heathrow from the east.

Chiswick & Latymer C.C., Saturday, 14th May, 2011

TVCL Division 3A. Beaconsfield II 264 (51.3), Chiswick & Latymer 265-5 (39.0). Chiswick & Latymer won by 5 wickets.

This was one of those days when you cannot make it up.

My colleague, another club rather than panel umpire, was late. We are supposed to be there at least 45 minutes before the start of play[2] to inspect the ground, do the administration, talk to the captains, supervise the toss etc. I did all this alone. It was agreed that I would do the bowler's end at both ends – something I dislike due to the extra

---

[2] Law 3.1, 'The umpires – appointment and attendance'.

intensity and concentration required – and that a player from the batting side would stand at square leg. After about an hour's play my colleague finally arrived and entered the fray. Dressed in (black) jeans and a white polo shirt, he told me that he'd had a bad day, and would have to leave by 6.00pm latest. Gobsmacked, I asked him if he thought it might be better to not stand at all, but he was adamant, and informed both captains of his plans. I hoped that they would decline his offer to stand part-time, but not having to find volunteers for square leg duty clearly trumped any wider concerns. At 6.00pm, half way through the second innings, he gave his apologies and left. "Thanks for coming ..."

Then came the saga of the injured batsman with a runner. Chiswick needed 266 to win and were well placed at 130–1, up with the run rate and with wickets in hand. The opening batsman was on about 60 and had so far scored his runs almost exclusively in boundaries and singles. Then he went down with cramp and asked for a runner. I thought he could be pulling a fast one but agreed to his request (my part-time colleague had by now departed). Over the next twenty minutes it became clear that Chiswick, maliciously or not, were gaining advantage from the situation. Firstly, the runner started scampering singles, and turning ones into twos, which the injured batsman had certainly not been doing. Then the injured batsman's cramp seemed to stop inhibiting him. Beaconsfield complained bitterly and asked me to intervene. I felt isolated and alone, and could not remember whether or not the laws allowed an umpire to reverse the decision to allow a runner. By now I was also again standing at the bowler's end all the time so I had no time for any quiet contemplation, or even for a quick check of the laws! I decided that I could not reverse my decision (correctly as it turned out as there is nothing in the laws which permits me to do this[3]), and the batsman with the runner duly steered his team close to victory, getting out only when the result was no longer in doubt. The atmosphere after the match was tense, to say the least, and matters then took a further turn for the worse: there was a wedding reception in the clubhouse so there was no opportunity for all the protagonists to sit down together and have a beer!

I think the main lesson for me to learn from this experience is to exercise caution before agreeing to a request for a runner. If it is not clear, I will tell the batsman that I will observe his movements over the next over or two and then make a decision. This is a variation on the theme of walking to square leg and consulting with one's colleague in order to buy time to think. If only I'd had a colleague to consult ...

Chiswick play at the former Old Latymerians ground. The pavilion faces the wrong way (for cricket), the straight boundaries are very short, and the square boundaries are open, which means that on a hot day the ball runs away for miles. And, like Kew, it is on the Heathrow flight path. If there is a faint nick while an aeroplane is passing overhead then the umpire has no chance of hearing it, none whatsoever! I have always found coming here a bit odd. In the early 1990s Old Lats had several bowlers who bowled off the wrong foot! It was Pythonesque, a Ministry of Silly Bowling Actions!

---

[3] Law 2.1, 'Substitutes and runners'.

Burnham C.C., Saturday, 21st May, 2011

TVCL Division 2B. Burnham II 232-9 (52.0), Kidmore End 54 (17.3). Burnham II won by 178 runs.

This was a fairly remarkable match. Burnham batted first and made a good score; and then their overseas player, a left-arm quick with late in-swing, destroyed Kidmore. He bowled from my end and it was a pleasure to watch. He took the first nine wickets, five clean bowled and four LBWs, all stone dead from my point of view. I turned down several other appeals and some of them may well have been out? The batsmen were (not unreasonably) planting their front foot just inside what they thought was the line of the ball, and then being undone by the late in-swing. My colleague denied the bowler (and me) a 'ten-for' by upholding an appeal against the last batsman at the other end.

I made a bad mistake today, or more precisely embarrassed myself. Kidmore End's spin bowler asked me to stand right up to the wicket. I really hate this because it makes it even harder (than it already is) to transfer my vision from the bowler's feet to the batsman's end. Discomfited by this, I then had a conversation with the bowler about where his feet were landing, and almost immediately realised that I was talking complete nonsense.

I also lost count of the balls in the over a couple of times today. Counting to six should be one of the easier tasks for an umpire and, once you have established a good routine, it is. My routine is to click my counter as soon as I consider the ball to have become dead (unless of course it is a no ball or a wide, or the bowler has aborted before releasing the ball etc.) The one thing which still sometimes throws me, though, is when a wicket falls or there is an appeal that I turn down; once the adrenalin of the incident has passed, I often cannot remember whether I have clicked my counter or not. Fortunately, I was working well with my colleague today – a fellow panel umpire for the first time! – and signalling after the fourth ball of each over, so he put me right when I erred.

Tring Park C.C., Saturday, 28th May, 2011

TVCL Division 3B: Wooburn Narkovians 146-9 (52.0), Tring Park II 147-2 (34.5). Tring Park II won by 8 wickets.

Tring Park has always been one of my favourite grounds, so it was great to get an appointment there today. It has a modern purpose-built clubhouse with a great view from the first floor balcony, and the ground itself is large and spacious but enclosed on three sides by a beech hedgerow and elegant mature trees. It's also an attractive drive to Tring through the rolling hills of the Chilterns from my home in Marlow.

The hospitality today was superb. I was offered a cup of tea and a biscuit on arrival, the tea was excellent and the chairman brought a pint of beer into the dressing room after the match. It makes a big difference when you visit a club as a stranger to be treated like this. I also had a good game, no mistakes as far as I am aware. We had several delays for rain, and even when we got started again the clouds were low, dark and threatening – we did well to get the match completed!

There was one incident today that could have been tricky. One of the Wooburn batsmen skied the ball up in the air, and immediately began shouting, very loudly, "f***, f***, f*** ..." The catch was duly taken and he trudged off disconsolately. After the match, I sought him out and told him that, if the fielder had dropped the catch, and the opposition had appealed for obstructing the field, then I would have given him out.[4]

Naming the ten different ways that a batsman can be dismissed is a good quiz question. I separate them into the common ones (bowled, caught, LBW, run out and stumped) and the obscure ones (hit wicket, hit the ball twice, handled the ball, obstructing the field and timed out). With regard to the latter, I have seen hit wicket a few times, but have never personally seen a batsman dismissed in the other four ways in thirty odd years of involvement in the recreational game. I do remember a famous story, however, from Chalfont Saints in the early 1980s, of a footballer making up the numbers and playing his first game of cricket – and being given out for obstructing the field. He struck the ball to midwicket, called for an impossible run, his partner sent him back and, as he turned to make his ground, the fielder lobbed the ball back towards the wicketkeeper over his head; seeing the ball in the air, and realising that he was about to be run out, the footballer swung his bat at the ball and swiped it to the square leg boundary! This was followed by, in turn; silent incredulity, laughter, indignation – and a walk back to the pavilion for the batsman!

---

4 Law 37.1, 'Out obstructing the field'.

Over rates are an issue at Level 3 and below in the TVCL. In Levels 1 and 2 clubs are docked points for slow over rates, which means that the matches rarely finish much later than the scheduled close of play time of 7.30pm. This is not the case in Level 3 and below, and the umpires can do little more than politely encourage teams to bowl their overs at the required rate. Some players moan about late finishes but spend the afternoon dawdling around and chatting. Today, Tring bowled their overs at 20 an hour, and we finished in good time to watch the Champions League Final in the clubhouse, Manchester United v. Barcelona.

Chalfont St. Peter C.C., Sunday, 29th May, 2011

TCSL Division 1 (40/40). Chalfont St. Peter 205-8 (40.0), Tiddington 206-3 (37.1). Tiddington won by 7 wickets.

I returned to my own club today to umpire a Sunday league match – and immediately found myself conscious again of the need to be *seen* to be fair! I do not feel like this when I am a 'neutral' umpire, and am already, interestingly, finding that I much prefer being on the TVCL panel to umpiring Chalfont every week! What happened today is that there were two close LBW appeals for me to consider. I gave a Chalfont batsman not out in the first innings and then a Tiddington batsman out in the second. Both decisions were marginal but I gave them in good faith. The reaction of the Tiddington players was exemplary in every possible way, but I nonetheless felt that I may have been silently perceived as Chalfont's twelfth man. After I had given the Tiddington batsman out I thought to myself, "I hope there isn't another one to give ..." I am stubborn and thick-skinned enough that

I would have raised my finger if appropriate, but I just feel inhibited about doing so when my own club is involved.

There was one incident today, which had the potential for controversy. A catch was taken on the deep midwicket boundary, aka 'cow corner'. The Tiddington batsman momentarily stood his ground, unsure whether or not the fielder might have stepped over the boundary in taking the catch, before leaving the field voluntarily. I do not think that the Chalfont fielder did overstep, but then my view was no better than the batsman's. I have been in this situation once or twice as an umpire, and indeed once as a batsman. It is not always possible to tell whether or not a fielder or ball has crossed the boundary from 50 or more yards away, and in these circumstances I think that you have to accept the fielder's word. The only possible variation on this is if there happens to be someone else nearby with a better view. In that case, I am always happy to take their advice, which is usually communicated to me by them signalling a four or a six, or out, and then by me to the scorers by my repeating their signal. It's a cricketing version of semaphore!

I also made a silly mistake today that, fortunately, nobody else noticed. While in play, the ball struck a close fielder on his protective helmet and then ricocheted into space. I immediately, and incorrectly, called and signalled 'dead ball'.[5] The batsmen could have taken a single but obviously declined to do so after my call. I knew immediately that I had made a mistake – the ball was not dead and I was mistakenly thinking of the law which precludes a catch being taken after

---

[5] Law 23.3, 'Umpire calling and signalling dead ball'.

the ball has struck a protective helmet[6]! – but nobody said anything, either at the time or later. My colleague at the time was a player umpire and he was certainly unaware of anything amiss.

The Chalfont Park ground has an attractive setting, although sadly it has gradually lost its peace and tranquillity since the A413 dual carriageway was built and has got ever busier! It was also more attractive before the conifers were planted on the golf course along the second fairway. (I do not like conifers; or, more precisely, I do not like them, from an aesthetic point of view, in the English countryside.) The various clubhouse developments have not really improved matters, either. The second (wooden) clubhouse was sited ideally in the corner of the ground; then an ugly squash court building was appended to it in the early 1970s; and then, when a fire burnt down the wooden structure in 1999, the brick squash courts were converted into a new clubhouse – not unattractively, but the building is in the wrong place, inside what should be the wide mid off/long leg boundary! But it's still my club and I have a deep affection for it.

Chiswick & Latymer C.C., Saturday, 4th June, 2011

TVCL Division 3A. Chiswick & Latymer 108 (33.5), Cove II 112-3 (17.2). Cove II won by 7 wickets.

I had a sense of foreboding about today's match, primarily because I thought that I would probably be standing with the same colleague as four weeks ago. As it transpired, he surpassed himself this time by not turning up at all.

---

[6] Law 32.3, 'A fair catch'.

As the only qualified umpire present, it was incumbent on me to stand at the bowler's end at both ends throughout the match[7] with players from the respective batting teams standing at square leg, usually on a ten over rota. I think that this is probably right in a league match, but it is nonetheless far from ideal. I do not believe that the umpire at the bowler's end can concentrate properly, for the full duration of the match, without the relative relaxation of square leg duties every other over – and I was mentally exhausted at the end of today's match even though it was fairly one-sided and finished early. Moreover, I think that most player umpires see their, say, ten over stint in the white coat as a chore, even more so when they are limited to square leg duty, and this is a shame; I think that they should be encouraged to take full responsibility and to try to enjoy their umpiring stint.

One thing that I found especially hard today was counting and scoring. I made at least two counting mistakes and at one point completely lost track of the score. The latter is a real bugbear for me; I find it difficult to keep score at the best of times, let alone when I do not have a colleague.

Gerrards Cross C.C., Saturday, 11th June, 2011

TVCL Division 3A. Maidenhead & Bray II 249-2 (52.0), Gerrards Cross II 228-9 (48.0). Match drawn.

I arrived at the ground early today, more than an hour before the start, put my kit bag in the dressing room and

---

7 Laws 3.1, 'Appointment and attendance of umpires' and 3.2, 'Change of umpire'.

then went out to have a look at the ground. Neither my colleague nor the opposition had arrived yet but the home team's opening bowler was practising on the strip next to today's pitch. I was astonished, especially as he could have moved one strip further across and been perfectly within his rights. I walked over and explained to him that you cannot practise either on the pitch or on either of the ones adjoining it on the day of the match (you can practise elsewhere on the square up to half an hour before the start of play).[8] He was apologetic and thanked me for explaining the law to him, so I decided to use Law 43[9] and let the matter pass without further action.

My colleague arrived shortly afterwards. He is a very nice chap and a good umpire, but he has a rich West Indian accent and a mild speech defect, so understanding what he is saying is not easy. Mid-pitch consultations before tea were difficult. Matters improved a little thereafter when I started watching his lips closely, but there are only so many times that one can say pardon before it starts to become embarrassing!

Bray had a good opening bowler today – a little chap with a fast arm. But he did not bowl many overs, primarily, I think, because he was running in at full pace for about 25 yards on every delivery. Has he not heard of Richard Hadlee? Twelve paces, 400 Test wickets. I think that if he had been able to bowl a more effective second spell at the end of the Gerrards Cross innings then he would have won the match

---

[8] Law 17.1, 'Practice on the field'.

[9] Law 43 is an umpiring euphemism; there are 42 laws of cricket, so 'to use Law 43' essentially means to use common sense to resolve an exceptional or unforeseen problem.

for Bray. Most tail end batsmen *dob* out for a draw by pushing forward, head over the ball – but not if they fear that it might end with a painful (and expensive) visit to the dentist!

The Dukes Wood ground at Gerrards Cross is attractive. It is located away from the village centre and therefore lacks the atmosphere provided by spectators and passers-by, but it has a well-designed, modern clubhouse, an excellent square and outfield, and is surrounded on three sides by elegant 'stockbroker' gardens. My only criticism would be that the clubhouse is in the wrong place. It is sited behind the bowler's arm and, as often as not, the sightscreens block the view from both the bar and the attractive terrace, which leads out onto the ground.

Cove C.C., Saturday, 18th June, 2011

TVCL Division 1. Cove v. High Wycombe II. Match cancelled.

Rain, rain, rain! I had a frustrating day today. I was originally supposed to be umpiring at NPL Teddington but that game was abandoned in the morning before I set off. I was then diverted by the TVCL appointments officer to Cove for a Division 1 match against High Wycombe II, which would have been a really interesting challenge. However, by the time that I arrived at the ground, and after having got lost a couple of times, this match too had been cancelled. It was the first time that I had been to Cove and it is an attractive ground – hopefully, I will get to return one day in better weather!

So I drove back home to Marlow and spent the rest of the day listening to *TMS* on the radio. It was the third day's play in the Test Match between England and Sri Lanka at the Rose Bowl, Southampton, and it sounds like the paying spectators had a day of frustration to match my own, with changeable weather leading to stop-start play. They were no doubt phlegmatic, as all cricket fans, especially in England, must be about such matters. However, what did anger them was that the tea interval was apparently taken during perfect playing conditions. This really is utter madness. It is one thing for there to be no play due to weather conditions, but quite another for there to be no play, after long delays, just because the good weather happens to coincide with a scheduled break. Rod Tucker, one of the umpires, later admitted that an early tea could have been taken when they came off after one of the rain showers. I think that professional cricket is too preoccupied with fair playing conditions and the match rules – it needs to give more priority in its thinking to its paying customers!

I remember something similar happening when I was a spectator at Headingley on the first day of the fourth Ashes Test Match in 2001. There was a long delay after overnight rain, finally we got about half an hour of play – and then everyone went off, in brilliant sunshine, for a scheduled break. The paying spectators were furious, and rightly so.

Maidenhead & Bray C.C., Saturday, 25th June, 2011

TVCL Division 3A. Hillingdon Manor 226-9 dec. (49.5), Maidenhead & Bray II 215-9 (50.0). Match drawn.

There was an interesting incident today with a replacement ball. The straight boundary at the river end of the Bray ground is not the longest, and balls are sometimes hit over the netting and into the gardens that back onto the ground – and *de facto* lost. During one of my first matches as an umpire a couple of years ago I made the mistake of consulting the two captains (the batting captain was at the crease at the time) about the replacement. It should be the umpires' decision alone but, my having given them the opportunity to do so, the two captains then predictably disagreed over the replacement. Anyway, lesson learnt, and today I sent the players away when the box of spares was brought out.

However, the ball that my colleague and I selected proved problematic, and it soon became clear that it was too heavy, and that the batsmen were having trouble hitting it off the square. The fielding team soon worked this out and were clearly happy with developments. This put me and my colleague in a tricky position. Should we replace the replacement? The argument in favour was that it was obviously not like for like; the argument against was that it is the home team which supplies the box of replacement balls and, as it was they who were batting, they were arguably the victims of their own negligence in providing poor quality spares. This ball was also the only one in the box of spares which had looked of comparable usage. However, all of a sudden and much against the odds, the original was found, and normal service was resumed. Maybe there is a god after all?

One of the Bray batsmen was dismissed while the rogue spare ball was in use. He had a ready made excuse for his demise, and spent the next ten minutes walking round the outfield clucking like an old hen! The Hillingdon fielders were amused by his discontent, and made a few comments in his direction. Bad workmen blame their tools was the gist of it.

I was offered tea and biscuits before the match, served on the patio, which overlooks the attractive Bray ground. It is genteel and posh, similar to Gerrards Cross and very Home Counties. I sat there and pondered the contrast between this club and Barnsley – the other club associated with the Bray president, Michael Parkinson, which I have visited once or twice over the years. I wonder whether they have ever played against each other? That, I imagine, would be a bit of a culture clash!

Winchmore Hill (Bucks) C.C., Friday, 1st July, 2011

BCB Under 15 (20/20). Chalfont St. Peter 129-5 (20.0), Winchmore Hill 97-7 (20.0). Chalfont St. Peter won by 32 runs.

I always associate this ground with evening knockout cup finals in the 1980s and 1990s. It is a classic small village cricket club but is surrounded on three sides by high trees, which means that the light is often a problem in evening matches. Fortunately, the weather tonight was fine and it was also high summer, so there was no such problem.

I had a dilemma today with a young player bowling back foot no balls, i.e. his back foot was not completely inside the return crease.[10] To call him or not to call him? The argument in favour was that it is my job to apply the laws; the argument against was that, frankly, he really wasn't very good, and he certainly wasn't troubling the batsmen. So I decided against, and settled for telling him and his manager/coach after the match.

NPL Teddington C.C., Saturday, 2nd July, 2011

TVCL Division 3B. NPL Teddington 225-8 (52.0), Teddington Town 227-2 (37.1). Teddington Town won by 8 wickets.

Bushy Park and recreational cricket are synonymous. The four grounds within, Hampton Hill, Hampton Wick Royal, Teddington Town and Teddington, are all attractive venues with people milling around, stopping to watch the cricket and continuing with their walks or family games. However, NPL is a bit different: it is a private ground on the edge of the park, so it has better facilities than the aforementioned but less atmosphere. Funnily enough, I only ever played at NPL once and was out to the first ball of the match, so it was nice to return today for a 'local derby' and have a better game from a personal perspective.

I made two good and slightly unusual decisions today. Firstly, I gave an NPL batsman out LBW when the ball clearly hit his pad before striking his bat; I was concentrating well and saw exactly what had happened. The batsman

---

10 Law 24.5, 'Fair delivery – the feet'.

walked off waving his bat, but this was not the point. The bowler (unsurprisingly) and non-striking batsman (gratifyingly) both commended me on a good decision. Later, in the second innings, I gave a Teddington Town batsman not out when he gloved a ball to the wicketkeeper having previously taken his hand off the handle of bat. Both decisions went against the same NPL player, the first time as a batsman and the second when he was bowling. "Have we crossed swords somewhere in the past?" he asked, wryly.

There is a player whose name I have often seen in the result sheets scoring runs for NPL. Today I saw him bat for the first time. He came in at five or six, plonked his front pad down the track and played round it, nudged balls into gaps, rotated the strike, tucked away boundaries. All afternoon I was thinking that if he misses then LBW will be in play. He didn't miss. 80 odd not out. Good player.

Aesthetically, I was standing at the wrong end of the ground today, with my back to three elegant Poplar trees behind the bowler's arm. Like Monet I am fond of Poplar trees, especially on a hot day at a cricket ground; I like the way they sway gently in the breeze, cooling the mind if not the body.

In the bar after the match there was an interesting cricketing debate: was Ian Botham a great or just a good cricketer? I am not sure quite how we got onto this subject, but there were some good arguments put forward both for and against. My twopennyworth is that an analysis of his record against the greatest team of his generation, the West

Indies, would suggest that he fell some way short of greatness.

RAF Vine Lane, Saturday, 9th July, 2011

TVCL Division 3A. Beaconsfield II 277-6 dec. (45.0), Hillingdon Manor 216-8 (55.0). Match drawn.

I nearly went to the wrong ground today. I played at Hillingdon many times over the years: nice club, nice people, not really the nicest of grounds. Fortunately, I chanced to mention to a friend a couple of days ago that I was going to Hillingdon this week. "Oh", he said, "well, at least no dog s*** and church bells these days!" Thus I discovered that Hillingdon Manor 1st XI now play at the RAF ground in Vine Line and only the lower teams still play at Coney Green. Incidentally, I have nothing against church bells; in fact, I like them in moderation and at a reasonable distance. But there wasn't much of either of these on the boundary edge on 'wedding Saturdays' at Coney Green!

I always used to field in the covers or at midwicket, or on the boundary. This was perhaps because I was reasonably athletic, fairly quick and had a decent throwing arm; more likely it was because I couldn't catch close to the wicket. I remember playing a match at North Maidenhead in 1995 and the captain, an old friend, flustered in the heat of battle, moved me to second slip. "Made it at last", I said. "Don't flatter yourself", was his reply. I mention all this because, while I was normally happy enough to disappear to the boundary and pass the time of day with spectators, this was not the case at Coney Green, or at least not until the bell ringers had called it a day!

Anyway, all good, I went to the right ground – and what a very nice ground Vine Lane is! It has an attractive pavilion dating back to 1949 with many interesting photographs inside, and a good tea, good beer and a good match made for an excellent day. I wonder whether playing here will enable Hillingdon Manor to attract better players?

I had a couple of difficult LBW calls today. The first one involved a Hillingdon batsman with a penchant for flicking to leg. Viv Richards used to hit off-stump half-volleys through mid-wicket with unerring consistency but there are no batsmen of his calibre playing in the TVCL. When I see a batsman like this, I take particular note of where his feet start and where they move to, how close to the stumps the bowler gets, the angle of his delivery and, crucially, the line of the ball as it strikes the pad. The Beaconsfield captain shrewdly left a big gap between mid-on and square-leg to tempt this batsman and he duly obliged by missing one. He was struck on what I thought was middle and off stump, and I did not think the ball was going down, so I gave him out.

A later Hillingdon batsman was playing in a completely different style, thrusting his pad at the ball, sometimes playing a shot, sometimes not, as he tried to play for a draw. There was a huge shout for LBW against him. He was playing a shot this time, and although I thought that the ball was hitting middle and off stump, I think that he may also have just got outside the line, so I said not out. Two very tight calls. I may have got them both right, or both wrong. I would love to see my decisions played back on the DRS, it would be fascinating!

An umpire will sometimes get 'judgement calls', fifty/fifty decisions which must be called one way or another. One team will be disappointed, so a thick skin is essential. I am generally a 'not outer' and will usually give the batsman the benefit of the doubt. While this is in itself fine, and I would say that most recreational players prefer this approach, it is important for me that I do not hide behind this and duck difficult calls. If the batsman is out then my finger must go up. I like to talk about my decisions with the players afterwards. Not all my colleagues agree with or are comfortable with this, and I respect that, but I think it is very beneficial all round. Players like an explanation, regardless of whether or not they accept it, and, I think, respect you more for taking the trouble to communicate with them; and umpires can also learn from players. Of course, not all players stay behind for a beer, and not all of those who do are sociable with the umpires. I stayed late today talking cricket with some of the Hillingdon and Beaconsfield players, and it was both enjoyable and informative.

There were two other notable incidents today. During the Beaconsfield innings, having bowled a decent spell of five or six overs at my end, the Hillingdon opening bowler had a tantrum. Not with me, or with the batsmen, or with his captain. It wasn't really clear with whom he was so upset or indeed why, but I think it involved one of his teammates? Various people tried to calm him down, and the captain took him off and sent him down to fine leg, where, like a bear with a sore head, he just got more and more angry, stomping around and gesticulating wildly with both arms, like Basil Fawlty when his car wouldn't start. And then all of a sudden the red mist evaporated and he was fine, and that was that. It was very odd and, I have to admit, rather amusing.

Then, during the Hillingdon innings, a young spin bowler was putting in a tidy if somewhat unthreatening spell at my end. The Beaconsfield captain, with runs to play with, came over to speak to him several times and implored him to give the ball more flight, to toss a few up and try to buy a wicket. But the youngster just couldn't do it, and kept bowling flat, good-length balls. Over-coaching, perhaps? Maybe he has learnt the game with runs conceded prioritised over taking wickets? Exasperated, the captain had to take him off and put himself on to open the game up.

Monday, 25th July, 2011

I usually go to at least one day of every Test Match at Lord's but missed this week's match against India because I was away on holiday. The DRS is the hot topic of conversation at the moment. India do not like it, and have rejected its use for LBW decisions in this series. I think they are wrong. Opinions are divided about the DRS: some see it as diminishing the role of the on-field umpire, but I am strongly in favour for a number of reasons. Firstly, I think it is better to get the decision 'right' (I accept that LBW almost always, and caught quite often, will always be subjective decisions, but run out and stumped are fairly definitive with the use of slow-motion replays) if one can. Secondly, the terms of reference for the DRS is to eliminate howlers, no more no less, and this is what it does if used properly;

marginal decisions will remain marginal, *plus ça change.* Thirdly, I think it protects rather than undermines the umpires; if they make a howler then their decision is reversed and does not have a major impact on the outcome of the match, and although their humiliation is very public, it passes quickly. Fourthly, cricket is a game which can naturally accommodate the DRS delay, although I do think there should be a principle that if a decision cannot be made within, say, 90 seconds, then it should be given not out and the match continued. Finally, I think the DRS review is educational for everyone watching on television and can only enhance understanding of the Laws of Cricket.

Today, Stuart Broad had Sachin Tendulkar stone dead LBW but Billy Bowden gave it not out, presumably because he suspected a faint inside edge? When it was played back on Hawk-Eye there was no inside edge and the ball was shown to be hitting middle stump. It was a big moment: if Tendulkar had gone on to make a hundred then India may have saved the game. As it was he was out soon afterwards so it did not really matter, but that is not the point.

One final observation about the DRS – for now! I remember watching some television highlights of the 'Laker match' at Old Trafford in 1956 and wondering why the bowler's end umpires were standing right on top of the stumps leaning noticeably down and forward? (N.b. I would not last five minutes in this posture with my bad back!) I assume that it was partly because of the old 'back-foot' no ball law, which remained in place until 1962? However, I have also heard that Hawkeye predicts the trajectory of a delivery from stump high at the bowler's end, so maybe the lower eye position of the 1950s umpires was better than ours – for decision-making if not the health of their backs? A recent Hawkeye experiment has apparently shown that umpires sitting in chairs, i.e. with a lower eye-line, make better LBW decisions, so perhaps it is reasonable to conclude that 'vertically challenged' umpires are better placed to make good LBW decisions *vis-à-vis* height?

Hartley Wintney C.C., Wednesday, 27th July, 2011

I have never played or umpired at this ground but in recent years have often passed by it *en route* to and from work, so today when I saw that there was a match in progress I decided to stop and have a look round. It has an attractive setting and an elegant modern pavilion full of old cricket photographs dating back to the 1870s. There was also some history to read about as well: the club and this very ground dates back to the 1770s; and in the 1980s two clubhouses were raised to the ground in two years, the first by a fire and the second by the great storm of 1987.

It was a 20 overs per side evening match with two player umpires officiating. I did not stay for long but as I walked round the boundary I observed them make an absolute horlicks of an overthrow incident. The ball was struck out towards deep extra cover; the batsmen ran one and turned for a second; the fielder released his throw long before they had crossed for a second time; but it was a wild throw which evaded everyone and went for a boundary four. The correct action would have been to inform the scorers that five runs had been scored.[11] There are no official signals for this, so

---

[11] Law 19.6, 'Overthrow or wilful act of fielder'.

some sort of verbal communication is usually required. The player umpire signalled boundary six. This rightly caused some consternation. After some discussion he then signalled boundary four – without having reversed his previous signal. There then ensued more discussion, and then the game resumed. As I had not been paying attention to the score before this incident I have no idea whether or not they eventually got it right?

Wooburn Narkovians C.C., Saturday, 30th July, 2011

TVCL Division 3B. Tring Park II 210-8 (52.0), Wooburn Narkovians 160 (45.4). Tring Park II won by 50 runs.

An umpire's relationship and interaction with his colleague is important. A 'not outer' and 'the fastest gun in the west' do not make a good combination. Today, I did not uphold any appeals because I was not absolutely sure that any were out. At the other end my colleague gave five or six, including an LBW from the first ball of the match which, from square leg, I could see was clearly too high. As the match progressed, the bowlers were choosing umpire rather than end.

There is a case for standing with the same colleague every week: people of like-minded temperament, similar decision-making mind-set, and socially compatible should in theory work well together. On the other hand, it is nice to meet a different colleague each week – and you can always learn new tricks from new people. Although I can see the merits of the former, I prefer the latter.

Golden ducks are bad enough. They are even worse when it is the first ball of the match. You walk off humiliated, 0–1 after 0.1, all over before it has even started! I suffered this grim fate five times during my career, and three of them, especially, stick in the memory. The first was plumb LBW in a BSCA Under 13 Final for Dr Challoner's – undone by 'the old straight one', as a late friend of mine was wont to say. The second was bowled shouldering arms for Chalfont Saints – time stood still for a while! And the third was at Chalfont Park and involved a West Indian chap ordering a double rum and coke before the match, then another one, then opening the bowling, then starting with two huge wides – and then bowling me neck and crop with his third delivery! At least this one did not actually feel like a golden duck, and I did not walk off with the score at 0–1, but it was still technically a first baller!

Wooburn is a nice club. They need a new clubhouse, but a project to that end is apparently underway. It has a nice rural setting with green hills on both sides, but the ambience is dependent on the vagaries of the Heathrow flight path. If the aeroplanes are taking off to the west then they pass directly overhead. Today, unfortunately, they were thundering over relentlessly.

Horspath C.C., Sunday, 31st July, 2011

TCSL Division 1 (40/40). Horspath 206–3 (40.0), Chalfont St. Peter 207–3 (39.1). Chalfont St. Peter won by 7 wickets.

This was my first visit to Horspath. It was a pleasant drive from Marlow, although the ground itself was nothing special.

During the day the 'Bell incident' occurred in the Test Match between England and India at Trent Bridge. It was interesting that the umpires used Law 43 to resolve it. Ian Bell struck what he thought was a boundary four off the last ball of the afternoon session and then promptly walked off the pitch, assuming that the ball was dead. However, the Indian fielder had actually stopped the ball, even though he himself also thought that it had crossed the boundary, and therefore just lobbed it casually back to the captain and wicketkeeper, M.S. Dhoni. However, Dhoni had his wits about him. He had seen what had happened on the boundary, and he had also observed that the bowler's end umpire had neither signalled boundary four nor called over and time, i.e. the ball was still in play. So he promptly removed the bails and appealed for a run out – and the appeal was duly upheld. Bell was half way off the field when he was given out, and Dhoni then walked off to a chorus of boos from the crowd. I think this was rather unfair on him, because the root cause of the problem had been Bell's carelessness.

It was what happened next which was of particular umpiring interest. Once Bell had left the field of play it was technically too late for Dhoni to withdraw his appeal.[12] However, during the tea interval discussions between the umpires and the captains obviously took place and, when play resumed, Bell had been reinstated. Once Dhoni had agreed to withdraw his appeal, the umpires used Law 43 to resolve the issue. While this was, I think, a sensible course of action, I wonder what would have happened if England had

---

[12] Law 27.8, 'Withdrawal of an appeal'.

not been so strongly on top in the game? Say they had been 150–5 in the fourth innings chasing 200 to win. Law 43 is a useful tool for umpires but it is easier to apply it when there is nothing at stake.

Hayes C.C., Saturday, 6th August, 2011

TVCL Division 2A. Windsor 228-7 (52.0), Hayes 83 (32.5). Windsor won by 145 runs.

There is nothing particularly attractive about either Hayes or its cricket ground, except that it is a proper cricket club. The bar is always buzzing, the people are friendly, there is cricket memorabilia everywhere, including some fascinating old photographs, and I like going there.

The umpires' room is small – there is quite literally not enough room to swing a cat! "Do you want to come out before I come in," my colleague said to me when he arrived. Like at so many clubs it is clearly a pragmatic afterthought. In this case, space has been stolen from the away dressing room, or maybe one of the showers has been taken out? With my club rather than my umpiring hat on, I have every sympathy with Hayes and other clubs in a similar predicament: panel umpires, and private changing facilities for them, post-date most cricket pavilions! And it is not as if your average cricket club is flushed with funds to make structural improvements!

Windsor's opening bowler, an extrovert Australian, gave a running commentary during his spell on what type of ball he was going to bowl next, in-swinger, out-swinger, off-cutter, quicker one, slower one. I am not sure whether it was for my benefit or the batsman's – maybe both? I must say, however, that he metaphorically put his money where his mouth was, and bowled Hayes out. Then, in the bar after the match, aka Fred Trueman, he held court, telling the batsmen whom he had dismissed what they had done wrong, and me which decisions I had got right and which wrong. He was tremendously good company.

My colleague today was not the most smartly dressed umpire whom I have stood with. Maybe he didn't have enough room to smarten up? Most umpires seem to prefer not to wear a tie; I am happy to go with the flow, although I do think that an ECB ACO tie looks smart. To adapt the old adage about playing: even if you can't umpire, at least look as though you can.

There was an interesting conversation in the bar after the match about the standing ovations that Sachin Tendulkar is getting before every innings he plays at the moment. He must be privately embarrassed by them, not least because he is not scoring any runs. Someone said that he deserves the ovations because of his impeccable sportsmanship and for being such an outstanding role model over many years; someone else said that he deserved them for being the greatest player of his generation. I agree with the former but not the latter. How many great match-winning innings has he played? Certainly not as many as, say, Brian Lara.

Kidmore End C.C., Saturday, 13th August, 2011

TVCL Division 2B. Boyne Hill 159-9 (52.0), Kidmore End 160-3 (42.1). Kidmore End won by 7 wickets.

Kidmore is one of my favourite grounds, especially as they now have a spanking new clubhouse. It is a nice drive through the lanes from Marlow and it has an attractive rural setting. The umpiring facilities in the new clubhouse are the best that I have experienced: it was from the sublime to the ridiculous after Hayes last week, or the other way round to be precise.

There was an incident today when my colleague inadvertently put me in a difficult position. He was at the bowler's end and a low catch was taken by first slip. He walked over and consulted with me. He asked if I thought the ball had carried, and I said yes, I think it did. He then said that he wasn't sure and that, on reflection, he felt that he should say not out, which he duly proceeded to do. All this was, to a degree, fine. It was his call, and although he had asked my advice he was under no obligation to take it. He had considered his position while walking over to speak to me, and had decided that there was enough uncertainty to say not out. All fine. The problem was that all the fielders assumed that he had declined to uphold the appeal on my advice, and some of them subsequently made a few comments to this effect; nothing unpleasant or foul-mouthed, but clearly intended for my ears. Not wishing to undermine my colleague, I ignored them and said nothing, and did not discuss it with anyone after the match either. Umpiring can be a lonely job sometimes.

Later on, with the match decided, I had a more light-hearted exchange with a bowler, which went something like this:

"What was wrong with that, then, umps?"
"Missing leg stump."
"Really?"
"Yes, and maybe another set."
"Right you are. I'll get my coat."

Teddington Town C.C., Sunday, 14th August, 2011

Today I had lunch with a friend in Teddington. She is Russian. In the afternoon we went for a walk in Bushy Park and stopped for a while to watch a gentle Sunday match being played on the Teddington Town ground. I made a brief (and futile) attempt to explain the Laws of Cricket, and it reminded me of when I once took an American work colleague to a cricket match in which I was playing some years ago. As I came out of the changing room he approached me with a worried look on his face – and told me that the opposition, "had the same kit as us".

I have many fond memories of playing at this ground, including one of my best ever innings in a Sunday match and on another occasion taking two catches at third man off our quickie – it was always a fast track and the straight boundaries are short. I also remember it for two amusing incidents. The first one must have been in the late 1990s. The boundary markers on one side were for many years rusty iron girders, and I remember an accident-prone Chalfont fielder chasing the ball to the boundary and crashing into one

45

of them at pace – and then going down like a horse in the Grand National. Not funny for him, of course, but I'm afraid it was for everyone else! Funnily enough he did the same thing a couple of years later at Rickmansworth, but for iron girders read wet concrete! The other occasion was more recently, in the early 2000s. I was batting and struck a boundary four, and the ball disappeared into the overgrown long grass beyond the iron girders. To my surprise, several fielders – rather than the usual reluctant one – then promptly chased after it enthusiastically. I didn't really know what was going on, but it transpired that there were some naturist sunbathers (female, young ...) nearby. I was concentrating on my batting – I'm sure that Geoffrey Boycott would have approved!

The standard of play in the match was not high, and a few wickets fell in quick succession to a 'toss it up and hit me' bowler. Most batsmen at this level are, by definition of the standard they are playing, constrained by ability; as long as they are presented with 'proper' bowling they will generally try to play 'properly', but when the toss it up and hit me comes on they are either unable to resist the temptation to hit him out of the ground, or alternatively feel egotistically obliged to do so even though they know that it will probably lead to their demise. The toss it up and hit me himself needs to be shameless and thick-skinned; most of his wickets will come from catches in the deep, and he will get no respect from teammates or opponents alike – his only solace will come from his tally of wickets at the end of the season.

Tring Park C.C., Saturday, 20th August, 2011

TVCL Division 3B. Tring Park II 244-8 dec. (41.0), NPL Teddington 167-9 (49.0). Match drawn.

I made a mistake today which cost Tring a victory. I turned down an appeal for caught behind against one of the NPL batsmen. The Tring fielders were disappointed and gave the batsman some stick, telling him that it is the done thing to walk in such circumstances. The batsman made a comment in response, which made it clear to me that he had nicked it. Although I obviously got this decision wrong, in a sense, as an umpire, I also got it right. The umpire can only give what he sees and hears, and it's better to say not out if in doubt than to raise one's finger speculatively.

The NPL batsman went on to make 70 odd and batted until nearly the end. After the match the Tring captain and players were not reproachful to me for denying them a victory, and that is much to their credit. My 'mistake' today, and the players' reaction to it, is also indicative of why I have enjoyed being a panel umpire more than a club one: I may or may not be a good umpire, but nobody doubts my integrity.

My colleague and I had a GWL (ground, weather and light) issue to deal with today.[13] It was a damp, miserable day and there were a couple of heavy showers, one before the match started and one just after. In the end we subtracted ten overs and played a 90 over match, and everyone seemed happy.

---

[13] Laws 3.8, 'Fitness of ground, weather and light'; 3.9, 'Suspension of play for adverse conditions of ground, weather or light'; and 7.2, 'Fitness of the pitch for play'.

North Maidenhead C.C., Saturday, 27th August, 2011

TVCL Division 3B. Tring Park II 213-2 dec. (47.0), North Maidenhead II 216-5 (29.4). North Maidenhead II won by 5 wickets.

When I arrived today I felt like I had just stepped aboard the *Mary Celeste*: the clubhouse and dressing rooms were open, the pitch was marked and the stumps were out, but there was not a soul anywhere. This surreal experience continued for about five minutes. Then Tring (the away team!) arrived, followed by my colleague and, finally, some North Maidenhead players.

The main item of umpiring interest today was Tring's young opening batsman repeatedly wandering yards out of his crease at the non-striker's end. He was not trying to steal a run or gain an unfair advantage – he was just in a world of his own. I felt sure that the opening bowler would notice but he did not. Then first change came on, but he didn't notice either. Then the young man was caught behind and that was that. I was wondering whether the bowler would warn the batsman – he is expected to do this within the spirit of the recreational game but is not obliged to do so by the laws – or just run him out? I sought out the Tring captain afterwards and told him what had happened, and he said, "Oh, yes, we've spoken to him about this several times already!" I suspect that he will have to learn the hard way, but an opposition bowler will need to spot it first!

I have sometimes wondered whether the increasingly common pre-match team bonding and practice sessions improve the chances of said team playing good cricket and winning? Today, Tring practised and warmed up diligently, batted steadily, bowled and fielded okay – and were soundly beaten; by contrast, some of the North Maidenhead players did not even arrive at the ground until just before the start, let alone practise or warm up. I am not sure what this proves? My (unscientific) opinion is that the aforementioned pre-match sessions do give teams a little bit extra, maybe five or ten percent, in terms of fielding and team spirit, but are nonetheless no substitute for old-fashioned cricketing skills.

British Airways C.C., Saturday, 3rd September, 2011

TVCL Division 3B. Wooburn Narkovians 197 (52.0), British Airways 167 (42.4). Wooburn Narkovians won by 30 runs.

British Airways C.C. is not a traditional English cricket ground. It has excellent playing, changing and clubhouse facilities, but they are all geographically disparate; it is very open and the ball runs away for miles when a boundary is struck; and it is sandwiched between the M4 and the Heathrow runway – so quiet and peaceful it is not.

Today, I had a personal disaster. I arrived at the ground, parked my car, opened my boot and took out my kit bag. Well, I would have done if it had been in there! To my horror, it was not! There wasn't enough time to go home and collect it, so I had to borrow from my colleague and the home club. It was embarrassing. Fortunately, I think I had a good game, so I recovered a little bit of pride, at least.

To go with the flow or apply the laws, that is the question. Today, BA began the match with ten players. Their eleventh man and opening bowler did not take the field until twenty minutes had passed. After what I calculated to be a further fifteen minutes he started making preparations to come on to bowl. I was at square leg at the time so I walked across to talk to my colleague. He was uncertain about the timings so we agreed to go with mine, and told the bowler that he could not bowl for another five minutes. (If a fielder has been off the field for 15 minutes or longer then he cannot bowl on his return for the same number of minutes that he has been absent.[14]) At this point, one of the Wooburn batsmen sportingly intervened and said that he would be quite happy for said bowler to bowl straight away which was, unsurprisingly, well received by the BA players. My colleague and I decided to go with the flow, and duly let the bowler bowl straight away. However, I found the whole thing unsatisfactory. As an umpire it is my job to apply the laws. I have no doubt that the Wooburn batsman's intervention was well intentioned, but it made me appear pedantic. It is always a moot point whether or not the laws should be applied to the letter. Ultimately, it is the players' game, and (in the recreational game at least) if they are all happy then it is probably best to just go with the flow.

The BA captain today was what I would call a mobile phone 'junkie'. Every time I spoke to him, before and after the match, he seemed more interested in his phone than me. I thought this was rather rude but I do not think that he meant any offence. He was just addicted to it, completely unable to tear himself away. I actually felt sorry for him in the end and,

---

[14] Law 2.5, "Fielder absent or leaving the field".

after I had signed the result sheet, I left him to his private cyber world and sought out someone who might like to do something old-fashioned, like have a pint and a chat about the game. I realised that he and I actually have polar opposite feelings towards our mobile phones: he *wants* his to ring or bleep, craves it almost, lives for the interaction; whereas I *resent* mine doing likewise, and see it as an intrusion of my private space. He's young, I'm middle-aged ...

Eastcote C.C., Sunday, 4th September, 2011

Today I watched the last overs of a Sunday match at Eastcote with a friend and then had a pint of beer in the bar afterwards. It is an attractive ground surrounded by mature trees, passers by stop for a while and watch, and the clubhouse is full of cricketing memorabilia. British Airways yesterday seemed miles away.

One of the umpires today was an elderly gentleman. Very elderly. And he did not look terribly spatially aware. He obviously enjoys still being involved, and has no doubt been a great servant to the game. But can he really see and hear well enough? Would he be able to take evasive action quickly enough? If the ball struck him would it be life threatening? I think the doddery old umpire is now becoming a cricketing anachronism. Is this progress (raising standards) or taking something from the character of the game?

A few young players walking round the boundary passed behind us at one point and they were talking, with a degree of reverence, about 'Swanny' (Graeme Swann), who was in the wickets again last week at The Oval after a quiet (by his recent standards) summer. I would say that he is the most revered English cricketer of his generation *amongst young cricketers*. This is partly because of his affable and jovial character but primarily, I think, because of his talent. Most English cricketers, batsmen and seamers included, have tried to bowl off-spin at some point or another – and have realised how fiendishly difficult it is to spin the ball in the first place let alone do so and retain control of line and length.

Wormsley, Sunday, 18th September, 2011

Today I watched the last couple of hours of the ECB Over 50s final between Derbyshire and Kent at Wormsley. It was a good match – Derbyshire won by six runs – and the standard of play was high. As the game was moving towards a climax, a throw from a Derbyshire fielder broke the wicket, which led to an overthrow. I have always thought that this law is deeply unfair. My rationale is that if the fielder has the skill to send in an accurate throw, which breaks the stumps, then he should not be penalised for his skill! I think that as soon as the wicket is fairly put down at either end it should be dead ball.

The Wormsley ground is magnificent, perfect in almost every way. It was built from scratch by John Paul Getty Jr. I must say that, having spent a short time working in the United States, I can understand how one might become an Anglophile. Baseball, for instance, is essentially poor man's cricket. There are different balls that the pitcher can deliver, but not as many variations as the bowler in cricket – the mere fact that the pitch in cricket comes into play adds a whole new area of interest; the striker can hit to the left or the right, and can attempt either a home run or a positional strike to get players on the other bases home, but he cannot play a late cut or a glance to leg; and it is full on all the time, always a winner and always a loser, very American, no concept of a gentlemanly handshake, honours even, match drawn.

Postscript to the 2011 season

So that is it for another season, my first as a panel rather than club umpire. On balance, and somewhat against expectation, I must say that I have preferred life as a panel umpire. I have missed my own club and my old cricket friends, but it has been nice to meet lots of new cricket people and the umpiring has definitely been more challenging and enjoyable.

At the beginning of the season I wrote about how I was beginning to find the need to be *seen* to be fair as a club umpire tiresome. Club umpires can be perceived as 'their' team's 'twelfth man' and, sometimes, when I turned down an appeal against one of 'my' team, fielders would make comments like, "we're up against twelve today", "we need to hit the stumps today" or "we'll need to take eleven or twelve today". On occasions, I felt that there was some malice in these comments – a 'cheap dig' at me camouflaged as 'encouragement of their team' - but always let them pass, accepting them in good humour with the thick skin that one needs as an umpire. As a panel umpire this season, I did not hear any such comments. Panel umpires may or may not be deemed competent by players, but their impartiality is not questioned.

The 2012 season

This year I found myself looking forward to the new season more than for many years. I think this is because I felt so comfortable as a panel umpire last season and actually enjoyed it socially much more than I had expected to. My feelings now contrast with the trepidation that I was feeling this time last year when I had just joined the panel for the first time.

Last year I was allocated mainly to Level 3 matches, although I was promoted to do various higher matches as the season progressed. This year most of my appointments are for Level 2 matches – so a higher standard of cricket and almost always a fellow panel colleague to stand with.

Slough C.C., Saturday, 12th May, 2012

TVCL Division 2A. Slough II v. Finchampstead II, Match cancelled.

It was very wet this morning and it was no surprise to receive a call from Slough at about 11.00am to say that the match was off. I never quite know what to do with myself when my cricket is rained off. Normally, if it is raining, then I just get on with something else indoors. But if it's a cricket day and I've been rained off then I invariably find myself at a loss, and completely unable to do anything constructive or worthwhile. It is completely irrational but always the case. It is the opposite feeling to when it snows and one suddenly, unexpectedly, has a day off work.

There are some really lovely grounds in the TVCL but Slough is not one of them. I used to enjoy playing at their old Chalvey Road ground, which had a nice town centre atmosphere and a superb track (not that I ever scored any runs there!) The club sold this ground for housing development ten or twelve years ago, and built a magnificent new out-of-town ground. But I find the new ground a cold and empty, and rather characterless place. It could do with a few mature trees, but this of course takes time. So, if I had to lose one of this season's appointments to rain, this may have been the one that I would have chosen!

Windsor C.C., Saturday, 19th May, 2012

TVCL Division 2A. Eversley 209-5 (52.0), Windsor 151-7 (48.0). Match drawn.

Windsor is a visually appealing ground set in Home Park with the castle in the backdrop. It is just a shame about the aeroplanes. It is better when they are taking off to the west because, although noisier with their engines on full blast, they pass over more quickly and sometimes veer off north or south without passing directly overhead; when they are landing from the west it is just a continual whining racket all afternoon. Today, however, was a more romantic aeronautical day. The Queen's Diamond Jubilee was being celebrated, and the modern jets were grounded for a while as the Battle of Britain Memorial Flight (a Lancaster, a Spitfire and a Hurricane) did a flypast, which was then followed by an exhibition by the Red Arrows. We put the start back ten minutes to watch the spectacle.

My colleague today forgot his spectacles. As someone who is also afflicted by occasional absent-mindedness, and remembering my own catastrophe at British Airways last year, I felt great sympathy for him. He managed to get through the game without any obvious major incident, and I do not think that he informed either of the captains (perhaps wisely as it may have undermined the players' confidence in him?) I wonder what level of vision he actually had?

I learnt an important lesson about body language today. The Windsor wicketkeeper decided to stand up to the wicket for the opening bowler towards the end of his spell. An Eversley batsman nicked one, and the bowler duly leapt in the air and turned to me to appeal – only for the wicketkeeper to juggle and then drop the ball, which then ran back along the pitch towards the bowler. At this point the bowler was facing me with his back to what had just happened, and was still imploring me to give the batsman out. I pointed at the ball on the ground and began to explain, but as soon as the bowler saw my arm coming up with my index finger raised he assumed that I was giving the batsman out and began his celebration. Confusion then reigned until the Windsor fielders put him right. I am not sure who felt more embarrassed – me or the wicketkeeper? The moral of this story, I think, is that an umpire should not use his index finger for anything other than giving a batsman out!

Tring Park C.C., Saturday, 26th May, 2012

TVCL Division 3B. Harefield II 217-8 (52.0), Tring Park II 218-8 (47.0). Tring Park II won by 2 wickets.

As an umpire you have the best seat in the house, and I have learnt more about the game in the last four seasons as an umpire than I did in thirty years as a player. Today, I watched one of the Tring batsmen play an innings, which was a reincarnation of my own inadequacy as a batsman. He cut, flicked and drove the quick bowlers well, especially when they gave him too much width, but was then rendered strokeless by an off-spinner. Just like me, his weight was falling to the off side, and he could not play the ball spinning into him; or, more precisely, he could not score off it. I knew how it was going to end – just like me, he was going to get frustrated, hit out, and either miss a straight one or be caught at mid-on. The temptation for batsmen with this weakness is to open your shoulders, free the levers, and hit to cow corner. I now know that you should keep still and aim to hit straight through the V – even if the ball ends up at cow corner. One of the secrets of batting is, like umpiring, to forget what has gone before, keep your cool and think clearly. But when you are being strangled by an accurate bowler this is easier said than done.

The off-spinner nearly won the game for Harefield – and he may well have done so if I had upheld an LBW decision late on. It was a big decision, and with retrospect it may have been the decisive moment in the match. The batsman in question scored a few more vital runs afterwards and then the ninth wicket pair rather unexpectedly won the match for Tring. It was one of those 'judgement calls' which could have gone either way. The off-spinner was turning the ball sharply. Bowling round the wicket to a left-hander, he deceived him with an arm ball that struck him on the pad in line with middle, maybe middle and off, stump. I thought it was doing too much and said not out. As I thought about it as I drove home – I do this, I can't help myself! – I concluded that, on balance, I had probably got this one wrong.

My colleague today was once hit on the back of the head by an errant throw while standing at square leg in a match at Harefield (against Chalfont St. Peter) in 1993. He went down like a sack of potatoes and for a few moments there was much concern about his health, but fortunately all ended well. I wonder whether he remembers the idiot who threw the ball? I hope not – it was me!

Finchampstead C.C., Saturday, 2nd June, 2012

TVCL Division 2A. North Maidenhead 267-7 dec. (50.0), Finchampstead II 194 (48.2). North Maidenhead won by 73 runs.

Finchampstead is another of my favourite grounds and it was a pleasure to go there for the first time as an umpire today. As a player I never participated in a match on the main ground, so it was nice to do that as an umpire today. The ground slopes gently from top to bottom (rather than side to side like Lord's), the outfield is immaculate and it has a beautiful beech hedgerow separating the main and second grounds. And the teas are superb!

The main incident today concerned over rates. Finch had been deducted points the week before, and the skipper, one of the best known characters on the circuit, had a moan about it before the match to me and my colleague. Keeping wicket, he then proceeded to move his field what seemed like almost every ball! And when one of his key bowlers kept losing his run-up and aborting – he must have done this eight or nine times – Finch were getting into points deduction territory again. In the end, they just avoided a penalty.

After the match my colleague said that the drinks were on me.
"How so?"
"Because I won 3-1!"
He was talking (affirmative) decisions.
"I took an early lead with an LBW. You equalised just before tea with a caught behind. After tea I saw some dark clouds approaching and was pleased to move ahead again with another LBW. And then I clinched it at the death with that run out!"

Windsor C.C., Saturday, 9th June, 2012

TVCL Division 2A. Cookham Dean 119 (40.0), Windsor 114 (49.3). Cookham Dean won by 5 runs.

This was an exciting and tense game of cricket; low-scoring matches often are. Of course, in such matches the pressure on the umpires increases. However, I think that my colleague and I got all the key decisions right today. Irritatingly, however, I got caught out on the TVCL match rules when I gave the wrong information to the Cookham Dean captain about how and when the slow over rate penalties apply. He should have known the match rules himself as well but that is no excuse for my ignorance. Fortunately, my colleague knew the regulation and put us both right, and the captain duly speeded up his team and avoided a penalty. I hate getting caught out like this and will not sleep well tonight.

Cookham fielded an overseas player today, a chilled out gentleman of Caribbean origin. Neither I nor my colleague knew much about him. He came out to bat at 4 or 5, played a few airy-fairy shots, hit a couple of fours, could have been out several times – and then skied one up in the air and got caught. "He must be a bowler", we agreed, as he trudged off, rather nonchalantly. When Windsor batted, he did not bowl. Problems here, I think. Cookham will probably have paid his air fare, and someone will perhaps be putting him up free of cost. I think they will be expecting him to take his role as the club's overseas player a little bit more seriously.

An off-field distraction held up play for a few moments today but was quickly resolved. It reminded me of two occasions in my playing career when a match was held up in a similar way. The first was at North Maidenhead when a man with a grievance against the home club turned up on a motorised scooter and rode it round and round the field of play. Eventually, the police were called and he was moved on. The second was at Chalfont Park when an angry wife turned up at the ground while we were fielding and started shouting and gesticulating at her husband, demanding that he leave the field of play and come over to talk to her. He tried to ignore her but she continued shouting abuse at him. Attempts were made to continue the game but it was hopeless, so our captain suggested that the husband leave the field of play and try to placate his wife. "No", he said, "ignore her and she'll go away." She did, eventually. I do not think the marriage lasted long.

Wendover C.C., Sunday, 10th June, 2012

BCB Under 11 (20/20). Chalfont St. Peter 57 (18.4), Wendover 58-1 (13.3)

Wendover Cricket Club is an oddity. The main ground is in the centre of the town with a beautiful view from the clubhouse. Except that it is not the main ground – it is far too small and is only used for junior and 3rd XI matches. The main ground is actually about half a mile away, out of the town centre, large and spacious, but rather unfortunately situated right next to the busy A413 dual carriageway bypass. Why anyone would want to play here every other week is beyond me. Fortunately, the junior match today was at the 'town' ground, so I at least had a pleasant ambience to enjoy.

Technically, I volunteered to *umpire* this morning, but I was really needed to *manage*, because my club's regular Under 11 manager was away. In truth, a qualified umpire is not really needed for a club Under 11 match – my main roles were to ensure that the next batsman was padded up and adequately protected, to suggest bowling changes and fielding positions where appropriate, and to keep the score. The pleasure for umpires/managers in these matches is doing something for the greater (cricketing) good. And a trip to Wendover gave me the opportunity for a cracking walk over Coombe Hill in the afternoon.

Reading C.C., Saturday, 16th June, 2012

TVCL Division 2B. Reading II 164-9 (52.0), Bagshot 162 (47.1). Reading II won by 2 runs.

Reading is not one of my favourite grounds; it is just a bit too open for me. I have been there on hot days and roasted; today was the coldest day I can ever remember on a cricket field. People who know me will chuckle at this because I have a reputation for not feeling the cold. Today, I was cold, really cold, and of course these conditions are much harder for the umpires, who unlike the players do not have the opportunity to run around and get the blood circulating.

I made two mistakes today. One of the Reading openers got a very faint nick for a caught behind, which I missed. Later, I gave a Bagshot batsman out LBW and several people later confirmed that he had got an inside edge. As an umpire you know almost immediately when you have made these sorts of errors. The Reading batsman gave the game away with his body language, and my colleague later told me that he had heard two noises on the LBW. I have no problem with this kind of frankness – it is always better to know that you have made a mistake, it gives you a chance to think about what happened and why, and to store it in your memory bank for future reference. However, unlike last week at Windsor, I will not lose any sleep over these mistakes. I can only give what I see and hear.

At teatime we watched highlights of the England innings in the ODI against West Indies at the Rose Bowl, Southampton. Ian Bell made a hundred and a couple of times he played what I call the 'hip shot' – a short ball from a fast bowler which the batsman plays with an almost perpendicular bat through square leg. It can only be played if the bowling and pitch are both fast enough, and although common in the professional game I have never seen it played in club cricket.

Hayes C.C., Saturday, 23rd June, 2012

TVCL Division 3A. Hayes 231 (47.1), Royal Ascot 201 (48.0). Hayes won by 30 runs.

Anticipation is an important aspect of umpiring. Sometimes the hardest LBWs to adjudicate are when there is a new bowler or batsman involved. How close to the stumps is the bowler getting, and how is he shaping the ball? Where do the batsman's feet start and does he move across his stumps? The first over of a match is often hard as well, because one has not yet seen the bounce of the ball or the carry through to the wicketkeeper.

Today, I anticipated giving one of the Royal Ascot batsmen out LBW and then did so. Like the NPL Teddington player last season he was planting his front foot and playing around it, but unlike the aforementioned he missed, the bowler appealed and I put my finger up. Later on I heard him chuntering about my decision. I was tempted to walk over and ask him which stump he thought it was missing but decided that discretion would be the better part of valour. I do think it is good to talk through decisions after a game, but the player has to be receptive to such a conversation. This player needs to go to one of those indoor nets with a camera and watch his movements after the ball is released.

Eversley C.C., Saturday, 30th June, 2012

TVCL Division 2A. Cookham Dean 137 (50.1), Eversley 138-2 (22.5). Eversley won by 8 wickets.

To score or not to score? Some umpires feel that they should keep the score because they are ultimately responsible for its correctness.[15] Even though I dislike scoring I still incline to this viewpoint. The counter argument is that scoring detracts from the umpire's primary task of decision-making on the field of play; and scorers have scorebooks, coloured pencils and a colleague to liaise with, and are therefore more likely to be correct than an umpire with a clicker. However, against this, umpires do not always have the support of two competent scorers, and for an umpire to score reliably he needs to do so every time he officiates in order to establish a routine, and to thus make it second nature to update the score in the same way as counting balls.

Today, both Eversley and Cookham had a scorer. Well, they did at the beginning of the match. At some point unbeknown to my colleague and me, the Eversley scorer, a young lad of thirteen or fourteen, was 'poached' by their 4th XI, who had found themselves a man short on the adjacent second ground. This left the Cookham scorer on her own with an unfamiliar (electronic) scoreboard to operate. Then, to compound matters, an electrical fault caused the scoreboard to go blank for a dozen or so overs. My colleague and I kept the score, and eventually reconciled it with the scoreboard. In this case, it was a good job that we were both keeping score.

---

[15] Law 21.8, 'Correctness of result'.

I prefer the scoreboard to be updated consistently, i.e. after each run is scored or at the end of each over – but not a mixture of the two. As an umpire you need to have a routine, and you need to know what you are looking at when you look at the scoreboard. If it is being updated on an inconsistent or ad hoc basis then it can soon become confusing. And how many times do players contrive to stand in front of the scoreboard, sometimes for balls and overs on end? This turns me into Victor Meldrew!

Eversley is another of my favourite grounds. It has an attractive, rural setting but also a main (ish) road and pub along one side, which gives it a village feel with passers by pausing to watch. It also has a second ground and indoor school just round the corner, and there was a nice atmosphere and excellent food in the clubhouse after the match.

Little Marlow C.C., Monday, 2nd July, 2012

BCB Under 15 (20/20). Little Marlow 20-2 (5.0). Match abandoned.

Little Marlow is an attractive ground just to the east of Marlow. It has attractive mature trees around two sides of the ground, a great batting track and two nice pubs to socialise in after the match; its only downside is the proximity of the noisy A4155 road to the pavilion side of the ground. Unfortunately, tonight was a cold, wet evening, the game was soon abandoned and there wasn't even a chance to sit in one of the pub gardens and have a summer evening pint. Rain, rain, rain!

To play or not to play when it is cold and wet, and the forecast is for more of the same? It seemed right to try at the time, but with retrospect it would probably have been better not to have bothered this evening. GWL is the bane of a cricket umpire's life.[16] You want to play, of course, but you equally do not want anyone to get injured on your watch. The thing which an umpire does not factor into his decision-making process is the weather *forecast*. I think this may change in the not too distant future, given how accurate meteorology, even on a very local level, is becoming. This evening the forecast was poor – and accurate!

British Airways C.C., Saturday, 7th July, 2012

TVCL Division 3B. Falkland II 176 (51.3), British Airways II 113 (39.1). Falkland II won by 63 runs.

I remembered my kit bag this time! I still wake up in a cold sweat sometimes thinking about last September.

I think that I made a mistake today with a run out decision during the Falkland innings. I got into a good position. The ball had been struck out to deep mid-wicket, and the batsmen ran two before setting off for an unlikely third (it was late in their innings and they were taking chances). As the throw came in it looked for all the world as

---

[16] Laws 3.8, 'Fitness of ground, weather and light'; 3.9, 'Suspension of play for adverse conditions of ground, weather or light'; and 7.2, 'Fitness of the pitch for play'.

if there would be a run out. But the throw was not very accurate, the bowler fumbled the ball and then rather casually took off the bails. The batsman made a diving lunge for the crease and seemed to have got in, so I said not out. On reflection I do not think that he made it, because although his bat was past the popping crease he then had to make a downward movement to ground it. It all happened very quickly, so not out was the percentage call, but on reflection I think he was out.

I was at least in a good position to make the decision. Early on in my umpiring career I got myself into a very bad position for a run out. There was a batsman with a runner (all umpires hate this scenario!) and he (the runner) was running up and down on the line of the square leg umpire. I was at the bowler's end, and the ball went out to deep square leg. I moved to the same side that the ball was hit (which would have been the right thing to do if there had been no runner) and then, as the throw came in to my end, found myself between the runner and the stumps. Fortunately, the former got home safely so I do not think that anyone noticed. However, if there had been a run out appeal then, lacking eyes in the back of my head, I would have been in a hopeless position to judge it.

There were two other incidents today in what was actually quite a fractious match. At the beginning of the BA innings there was a possible ball tampering incident behind my back. I was unaware of anything untoward until the non-striking Falkland batsman suddenly started shouting at the bowler, "you can't do that, that's ball tampering", before turning to me and saying, "he can't do that, he was using his nails on the seam". I was immediately cross with the batsman – he should have drawn my attention to the matter before shouting out allegations. However, that aside, I then had to deal with the matter. I consulted with my colleague and we decided that, although a thread of the seam was hanging loose, there was no proof that this had been caused by a wilful action from the bowler.[17] I therefore cut it off with my scissors and the match resumed without any further issues concerning the condition of the ball.

Some readers may find it hard to believe that ball tampering occurs in recreational cricket. In truth, I think that such incidents are few and far between. However, a colleague once told me a story about an incident that he was involved in. The batting team was on top after some 20 overs of seam bowling. Standing at square leg, my colleague noticed one of the fielders bowl the ball hard into the ground on its way back from the wicketkeeper to the bowler. The same thing happened after the next ball, and the next again! At this point my colleague intervened and asked the fielder to desist from doing this. The fielder pleaded innocence and did as he was told. However, a few overs later he came on to bowl – spin. My colleague said that, had he known that said fielder was about to enter the fray as a spin bowler, then he would have replaced the ball and deducted five penalty runs (there are no warnings for changing the condition of the ball).[18]

Later, I got into a strange argument with a BA batsman about a no ball, which he thought I had missed. He was at the non-striker's end at the time, and one of his colleagues

---

[17] Law 42.3, 'The match-ball – changing its condition'.
[18] Law 42.3, 'The match-ball – changing its condition'.

was dismissed off the delivery in question. While the Falkland players celebrated and his colleague walked off, he challenged me and said, "that was a no ball, you missed it!" I said, "Let's discuss it after the match", and at the end of the game duly sought him out. I have no idea whether or not I did miss a no ball, but what was interesting was the feet position of the bowler in question. He was landing on his toes with his heel in the air; his toes were beyond the popping crease but his heel was behind it, although not grounded. This is a legitimate delivery.[19] The BA batsman accepted my explanation of the laws but remained adamant that I had missed a no ball.

My colleague today was a BA club umpire. At teatime the umpires are supposed to sit on their own, i.e. away from the players. I think this is sensible. I am very much in favour of a chat with the players before the match and of course being sociable afterwards, but I think it is generally best to keep one's distance *during* the game. Today, at teatime, rather bizarrely, my colleague went and sat with the BA players, leaving me on my own. I thought this was both improper and rather rude. He had a bad stutter, which I noticed had disappeared when he was with his friends, so maybe I should cut him some slack. But it was a bit like umpiring with Arkwright from *Open All Hours*.

"How many balls do you make that gone?"
"Ffffff ... two balls to go".

Chalfont St. Peter C.C., Friday, 20th July, 2012

---

[19] Law 24.5, 'Fair delivery – the feet'.

Friendly: Stuart Dalrymple XI 168-9 dec. (49.0), Chalfont St. Peter Club XI 133 (39.5). Stuart Dalrymple XI won by 35 runs.

Today I was back at my club for a memorial match for one of my best friends, who was given out prematurely in December last year at the age of 48. When I went to visit him at the hospice I cracked a rather poor joke about jug avoidance. He liked it; most cricketers enjoy a bit of banter, even if it's gallows humour. Today was a bittersweet day – happy memories, funny stories, absent friend.

I spent most of the day meeting and greeting rather than umpiring, but I did stand for the last hour of the match. This was fine today, in this sort of match, but I would not normally recommend an umpire taking the field mid-match or leaving before the end. This is essentially because of the need for consistent decision-making throughout the match, which is hard enough for the same umpire to achieve, but virtually impossible for multiple umpires.

Today's match involved largely middle-aged players, in other words, contemporaries. I retired at the end of the 2007 season at the age of 44 and am probably one of the younger umpires on the circuit. People often say to me that I retired too early; not, I hasten to add, because my cricketing talents are any great loss to the game but rather, I think, because I look young enough to still be playing. It is one of the ironies of umpiring in the recreational game that most people take it up only when they no longer have either the inclination or the physical capability to play.

So how does umpiring compare to playing? For me, there will never be any substitute for the latter: the pleasure of winning, or making runs well, in an important match; of timing a cover drive off a quick bowler; the camaraderie of the dressing room. However, umpiring does have its merits: you have the best seat in the house; there are new grounds to go to every week and new people to meet; and it is the next best thing to playing. The main difference is that you are on the go all day. I was a mediocre opening batsman and usually, sadly, had plenty of time after I was out to walk round the ground, admire the scenery and have a chat with teammates; as an umpire, you stand out in the middle for the whole duration of the match with just a short tea interval in between. The most interesting comparison, perhaps, relates to pressure and the fear of failure. Like all batsmen, I hated getting out, but usually got over it after about ten or fifteen minutes; however, as an umpire, a mistake haunts me for days afterwards, if not weeks. I think one explanation for this is that personal failure as a player can either be forgotten if your team wins or shared with your teammates if you lose; however, as an umpire, you have let down a player/team when you make a mistake, and there is nowhere to hide. Set against this, however, when I arrive at a ground as an umpire I am really looking forward to the match; as a player, and opening batsman, I usually began to feel mildly nervous as soon as I reached the ground.

Which way does one walk round a cricket ground? I always walked round anti-clockwise first, I think because I am a right-hander? In other words, I instinctively walked round the pitch watching the action in the middle as if I was still batting, i.e. over my left shoulder. Of course, you need to walk round both ways in order to appreciate all the different views.

Maidenhead & Bray C.C., Saturday, 21st July, 2012

TVCL Division 3B. Maidenhead & Bray 110 (41.4), Wooburn Narkovians 113-5 (39.5). Wooburn Narkovians won by 5 wickets.

I made an unfortunate error today with the ECB fast bowling directive for young cricketers. I was standing with a club umpire from Wooburn who was doing his first TVCL match. He was competent but he was not *au fait* with the finer points of said directive, so when the incident occurred I was effectively on my own.

The sequence of events was as follows: Bray batted first and got skittled out for 110; worse, their captain pulled a muscle while batting and was rendered *hors de combat* for the rest of the match. With a decidedly below par total to defend, Bray then opened the bowling with a 17-year-old, who bowled a good spell from my colleague's end and helped keep the pressure on Wooburn as they stuttered a bit in their run chase. According to the directive, a 17-year-old is only allowed to bowl a maximum of seven overs in a spell, and must then rest for the same number of overs he has bowled before returning to the attack. My colleague was unaware of this directive and did not intervene when the young man prepared to continue his spell and bowl his eighth over, so I walked across from square leg and told him and the acting Bray captain that, according to the directive, the bowler should now be removed from the attack. He (the acting Bray captain) then surprised me by saying that, as it was only a directive rather than a match rule, he was going to ignore it. At this point I should have told him to adhere to the directive but, flustered and unsure of my facts, I did no more than strongly recommend that he observe the directive. He did not take my advice and, with the match situation still tense, the young man bowled two more overs before coming off. Wooburn then got on top and eventually won the match fairly easily.

Why did I make this mistake? Partly, undoubtedly, because I did not understand the directive properly; partly, also, because I was flustered and did not have the help of an experienced colleague with whom I could have consulted. Umpiring is a considerably easier job when you are able to work as a team with your colleague.

There was a strong case for me reporting the acting Bray captain to the appropriate authorities after the match. I decided not to do so because I felt that I was partly to blame for *allowing* him to ignore the directive. I think I was also influenced by the fact that Wooburn won. To be fair to Bray, they were apologetic afterwards and promised that it would not happen again.

Boyne Hill C.C., Saturday, 28th July, 2012

TVCL Division 2B. Chesham 226-9 (52.0), Boyne Hill 227-5 (43.3). Boyne Hill won by 5 wickets.

This was a good match involving the top two teams in the division. I know a few bowlers who hate this ground because the slope plays havoc with their run-up, and it is also one of those grounds where the ball often gets lost in hedges and overgrowth. But, for all that, it has an attractive setting, a nice pavilion and a good atmosphere, and I was pleased to go there today for the first time as an umpire.

When I said hello to the Boyne Hill captain before the match it was clear that he did not remember me, even though I had umpired him the year before. He apologised. I said, "No problem. I must have had a good game!"

There was an interesting incident towards the end of today's match. It was clear that Boyne Hill were going to win – they had overs and wickets in hand, and their skipper and opening batsman was 70 odd not out. Chesham then brought back their opening bowler at my end. Tall and quick, he proceeded to bowl a series of hostile short-pitched deliveries. The laws state that the relative skill of the batsmen must be considered when deciding whether or not the bowling is dangerous and unfair.[20] I did not think that the skipper needed protecting although he had a right to be able to play normal cricket shots and one cannot do that when the ball is whizzing past your ears every time; I was, however, more worried about the number seven batsman who looked like he might get hurt. I consulted with my colleague and we decided that the bowling had become dangerous and unfair. I therefore informally warned the Chesham captain and bowler that if this continued I would no ball him and make a first formal warning.[21] The bowler then tested me in the next couple of overs before Boyne Hill passed Chesham's total,

---

[20] Law 42.6, 'Dangerous and unfair bowling'.
[21] Law 42.7, 'Dangerous and unfair bowling – action by the umpire'.

bowling one short-pitched ball an over and a series of rib-ticklers. I had decided that if he bowled a second ball in the over passing above the batsman's shoulder then I would take action; he did not do so, and the match ended quietly.

I am normally very self-critical, but I was pleased with how I dealt with this incident today. My mind went back to Wooburn last week and the ECB fast bowling directive; I got it wrong last week but right today. I think that the support of my colleague was arguably what made the difference today. We were able to discuss the incident and decide on an appropriate response.

Thursday, 2nd August, 2012

There was an extraordinary incident in the Test Match between England and South Africa at Headingley today. Graeme Smith edged a ball from Steve Finn to first slip and was caught. However, Finn had dislodged the bails at the non-striker's end with his knee and the umpire, Steve Davis, called dead ball. He later cited the dead ball law[22] and argued that Smith had been distracted by the breaking of the stumps at the non-striker's end. It also later transpired that Smith had previously complained to the umpires that Finn's habit of knocking into the stumps – it was the fourth time he had done it in this spell – was off-putting. The consensus of opinion seems to be that Smith bullied the umpire and landed a psychological blow against Finn – as well as gaining a reprieve. Finn broke the stumps twice more, and each time Smith struck the ball to the boundary, but to no avail as each

---

[22] Law 23.3, 'Umpire calling and signalling dead ball'.

delivery was also called dead ball. MCC has apparently been asked to review this law.

Sonning C.C., Saturday, 4th August, 2012

TVCL Division 2B. Yateley 197 (50.3), Sonning 121 (36.5). Yateley won by 76 runs.

Sonning's ground is situated barely a mile from its Reading counterpart. The former is small and friendly, enclosed by trees on three of four sides, and as a club is possibly punching above its weight in Level 2 of the TVCL; the latter is a big HCPCL club (they were actually relegated from the HCPCL last season but are presently winning the TVCL by a distance and are set for an immediate return), open and somewhat impersonal. I prefer Sonning.

When is a wide not a wide? During the Yateley innings a ball bounced over the head of the batsman so I called wide. My colleague later reproached me on this – the correct call would have been no ball.[23]

After the match we watched the Olympics in the clubhouse and there was a great atmosphere. It turned out to be Britain's golden evening, with three gold medals won in quick succession. Jessica Ennis and Sonning Cricket Club are now inextricably linked in my memory. The heptathlon/decathlon is my favourite Olympic event because, like cricket, it requires strategy and technical skill as well as physicality.

---

[23] Law 42.6, 'Dangerous and unfair bowling'.

Cookham Dean C.C., Saturday, 11th August, 2012

TVCL Division 2A. Cookham Dean 187 (51.5), Windsor 188-2 (40.4). Windsor won by 8 wickets.

By a strange quirk of the umpiring allocation system I today found myself officiating in the reverse fixture between Windsor and Cookham Dean. Cookham is an attractive ground on the top of a hill. It is a nice place to come on a hot, sunny day like today, especially when the aeroplanes are landing from the west (and thus not coming over Cookham).

There was one interesting incident today. During the Windsor innings, some of their players were walking round the boundary when the ball was struck out towards them. There were no fielders nearby and the batsmen just jogged a single as it looked likely that the ball would pass over the rope for a boundary four. However, at this point one of the younger Windsor players took it upon himself to advance several yards onto the pitch, pick the ball up and lob it back towards the Cookham fielder who was chasing it (I am fairly sure forlornly) to the boundary. I was standing at square leg at the time but immediately noticed some consternation amongst the Cookham fielders and thought that my colleague might have a problem. However, the Windsor captain, who was batting at the time and had struck the ball, immediately intervened and said that, in the circumstances, he would settle for a single. This was a sporting gesture, and saved my colleague (and me) from making a tricky call.

Gerrards Cross C.C., Saturday, 18th August, 2012

Gerrards Cross II 240-6 dec. (46.5), Maidenhead & Bray II 195 (50.3). Gerrards Cross II won by 45 runs.

There is a player in local cricket who has been winning matches single-handedly for years, originally with both bat and ball, nowadays just with the former as his fast-bowling days are over. His son presently opens the batting for England in T20s, and he amused me by explaining before the match that his kit now comprises largely of his (son's) cast-offs. Today, Bray dropped him early on, and some of their younger players apparently thought that this was funny? Silly boys. This is not a man to drop. He scored a ton.

Nothing much of interest happened today *vis-à-vis* umpiring. One of the Gerrards Cross batsmen declined to walk for an obvious caught behind so I had to send him on his way. Later on, I was pleased to hear his teammates giving him some stick about this during the tea interval. I think that there is an ambivalent attitude to 'walking' in the recreational game. It is still thought the thing to do, but although most players would, I think, agree that the presence of panel umpires has improved the game, it has also given those not keen on walking an easy excuse not to do so.

In a TVCL match that I stood in recently, a batsman walked and made a big show of it. However, an opposition fielder, standing next to me at square leg, said, rather pithily, and perhaps a little ungraciously, that the player in question was a selective walker. I think there was a bit of previous involving the two teams – and this player not walking. I respect the integrity of non-walkers in the recreational game – provided that they always accept the umpire's decision and do not complain when they get a bad one, because you cannot have it both ways! However, selective walking is morally ambivalent.

I participated in an interesting conversation in the bar afterwards about why South Africa are beating England in the current Test series. Hashim Amla is batting well, and their seam bowling prowess probably edges our more balanced attack. But the real difference between the teams, in my opinion, is that they have an extra player to us – this is what having a world-class all-rounder like Jacques Kallis in your team effectively equates to.

Eversley C.C., Saturday, 25th August, 2012

TVCL Division 2A. Datchet 40-1 (11.3). Match abandoned.

Today was a horrible wet day. I was actually quite nervous as I drove to the ground because I thought it was going to be a GWL nightmare.[24] I expected Eversley, the home team and second in the league table, to be very keen to play, and Datchet, top of the league, to be somewhat less so. I was correct about the former but delighted to be proved wrong about the latter – Datchet wanted to play and, in the words of their captain, "to win the league on the field of play". I thought this was a commendable attitude and it certainly made life considerably easier for my colleague and me. As it happened, half way through the afternoon, having already

---

[24] Laws 3.8, 'Fitness of ground, weather and light'; 3.9, 'Suspension of play for adverse conditions of ground, weather or light'; and 7.2, 'Fitness of the pitch for play'.

been on and off, there was a huge downpour and that was that.

There is only one thing worse than being rained off, and that is when the sun comes out immediately afterwards, as it did today, almost as if to emphasise nature's superiority over mankind and the game of cricket. I am a traditionalist and prefer declaration/time formats to win/lose matches, but I must acknowledge one major advantage of the latter, namely that it is easier to get a shortened match on by reducing the overs (and using D/L if possible).

Rained off, most of the players sat down and watched – and seemingly enjoyed – the T20 finals on television. I find this type of 'cricket' mind-numbingly banal. A vulgar mixture of slogging and diving around like goalkeepers. Where is the subtle balance between bat and ball? What happened to a batsman valuing his wicket? And as for the pyjamas and replica shirts, the blaring loud music and the drunken football chanting, ye gods, this is not my game. It is manufactured excitement for philistines. If this is the future of the game then count me out.

Merchant Taylors' School, Sunday, 26th August, 2012

Today I went to watch Old Merchant Taylors' play a centenary fixture against MCC at their new ground in Northwood. It is on the same site as the school and there are about seven or eight cricket grounds all side by side, each with covers, sightscreens and scoreboard. OMT have their own purpose-built clubhouse with three grounds alongside it – a major advantage for a TVCL club. I think that clubs with modern new clubhouses and multiple grounds on their main site will be in a strong position over the next ten or twenty years.

The OMT scorer was scoring online. In other words, he was using a laptop rather than a traditional scorebook, and each entry was updating a website. However, he was updating the electronic scoreboard separately, so still a little bit of integration required for the ultimate automated scoring solution.

When I go to watch cricket nowadays I tend to watch the umpires as much as the cricket itself. I observe mistakes and things that they could have done better, and also note the things they do well to incorporate into my own game. Today, one of the umpires gave two LBW decisions in the style of Steve Bucknor, waiting what seemed like an eternity before slowly raising first his arm and then the dreaded finger. I think that most batsmen, on balance, prefer a 'slow death' to the 'fastest gun in the west', because it at least gives them the comfort of knowing that their executioner has given the matter some thought. But there are limits and I thought that this chap today was somewhat overdoing it.

There are different styles when it comes to raising the finger, and I suspect that a psychiatrist could have a field day linking them to personality traits. I have noticed that the more officious umpires often tend to point at the batsman, like Alan Sugar firing an apprentice. This seems rather rude to me, as does Billy Bowden's crooked finger. I prefer to just raise my hand and finger upwards.

I am not quite sure what to make of Bowden. Is he a shameless exhibitionist, with his 'crumb-sweeping' wave of the arm to signal boundary four and his 'double crooked finger six-phase hop' for a boundary six, or one of the game's much-valued characters? He claims that he has to signal in this way due to rheumatoid arthritis but I think he also likes the attention his extrovert actions bring. My two pennyworth is that if an umpire is not noticed then he or she must have had a good game.

Reading C.C., Saturday, 8th September, 2012

TVCL Division 2B. Reading II 156-9 dec. (44.3), Boyne Hill 115 (36.5). Reading II won by 41 runs.

I thought that this was going to be quite an interesting day with Boyne Hill pushing hard for promotion. As it was they were soundly beaten by a mid-table Reading II team and the match finished early at about 5.45pm. I showered and changed, did the paperwork and had a beer with the captains, and left just as it was beginning to get quite dark.

Remarkably, the match on the second ground was still in play. I stopped on my way to my car and watched. Reading III were playing Eversley II in a Division 4B match that went the distance, with Eversley in the end winning in a tight run chase in distinctly fading light. There may have been another reason for the late finish but it was probably down to slow over rates. Without universal panel coverage below Level 2 in the TVCL, there are no penalties for teams that bowl their overs at below the required rate. This is one of the banes of the recreational game in the lower leagues.

Lord's, Saturday, 6th October, 2012

My final game of the season today, saving the best for last, was at the home of cricket. It was wonderful to walk through the Long Room and out onto the hallowed turf. Well, in my dreams! The reason for my visit was to attend the ECB ACO National Conference and it was an entertaining day. 'You vs. Hawkeye' looked fun, but demand far outstripped supply, unfortunately, so I did not get a chance to have a go myself.

Lord's looked as magnificent as ever today. To me, it looks as good empty as full. Sitting there on my own for a while, I realised how important the whiteness of the ground is – the seats, all the stands, the media centre etc. There is a symbiotic relationship between cricket and whiteness. Ditto Wimbledon. Why was the Olympic tennis an anti-climax after Wimbledon three weeks earlier? Several reasons, I think, including, amongst others, too much of a good thing, best of three sets matches, and not the biggest prize in the sport. But, above all, for me, the 'tennis pyjamas' were not aesthetically pleasing.

Postscript to the 2012 season

Overall, I really enjoyed the summer, with the exception of the match at British Airways in July. I umpired mainly in Level 2 of the TVCL, which meant that I mostly had a fellow panel umpire as a colleague, something that I much prefer. This was reflected in my respective experiences at Windsor, Boyne Hill and Maidenhead & Bray: at Windsor I got caught out but my colleague saved my blushes; at Boyne Hill my colleague and I worked together to diffuse a potentially tricky situation; but at Bray I had nobody to turn to when I needed a second opinion.

The 2013 season

My personal circumstances have changed since the end of last season: I am no longer in full-time employment. There are pros and cons to this situation for me, but the prospect of spending a whole summer outside in the fresh air, rather than just Saturdays, appeals. I have therefore made myself available for Sunday and midweek matches as well as for TVCL matches on Saturdays; the former are for the most part managed by my county association, the Buckinghamshire ACO, although other appointments sometimes come via networking and word of mouth. I have been offered various Sunday and midweek matches in the last two years since I joined the TVCL panel, but have only rarely accepted because I have generally preferred to keep Sundays free for other interests and did not want to use up my annual leave for midweek matches. Now I have all the time in the world, so am keen to get as many appointments as I can.

Windsor C.C., Saturday, 11th May, 2013

TVCL Division 2A. Finchampstead II 203 (51.4), Windsor 126 (38.4). Finchampstead II won by 77 runs.

Checking that young fast bowlers are bowling the correct number of overs as per the ECB Fast Bowling Directives is usually straightforward. You count the number of overs in the spell, and then make sure that they do not bowl again for the same number of overs. Today, the Finch captain was very enterprising, switching his bowlers (most of whom were young enough that the fast bowling directives applied) around regularly, using them in short spells and changing ends mid-spell as well. Keeping track of all this was challenging.

During a stoppage in play in my game today, I looked across at the match being played on the second ground (the old Windsor & Eton ground for those of us of a certain vintage!) and spotted a familiar bowling run-up and action. Sure enough, it turned out to be an old friend playing now for a different club, and we had a chat and catch up afterwards.

Burnham C.C., Sunday, 12th May, 2013

ECB Under 14 (40/40). Buckinghamshire 83 (36.5), Middlesex 84-1 (17.5). Middlesex won by 9 wickets.

This was my first county match for Buckinghamshire. As I have mentioned previously, compatibility with one's colleague is important. I have a quiet, understated, almost laid-back style and follow the old adage that if you are not noticed then you must be having a good game. Today I umpired with a colleague who had a somewhat different approach. "Get off the pitch!" he bellowed incessantly at the boys, like a cantankerous farmer telling ramblers to get off his land. Umpiring bedfellows we were not.

Burnham is an attractive new ground with excellent facilities – an impressive clubhouse and two good grounds. Today was a nice, sunny day and I passed the time of day between balls at square leg staring at the trees and the cloud formations. One of the nice things about umpiring a junior match is that one has time to do this. I know that most umpiring instructors would disagree with me here, and argue that you should always be concentrating, or at least be keeping your mind on the game. This is fair enough in theory, but junior matches are slower and the players more innocent, and one rarely has much to do at square leg.

Of course, an umpire stays at the same end for both innings of a single innings match, so choice of ends before the match is important. Well, it is to me – most of my colleagues do not seem to mind and let me choose my favourite end. I usually prefer to be able to see the scoreboard from square leg, because this is when I have extra time to check that I am in step with the scorers. However, I also factor in the most attractive views, the proximity of irritations like a noisy road and a general preference to not stand on a slope, upwards or downwards, at square leg (because I suffer from lower backache). Both the grounds at Burnham are flat and attractive, and, unusually, I do not have a preference for end on either.

Most umpires have a list of things that they say to the captains at the toss but I limit myself to two topics in TVCL matches. Firstly, I remind them that they are responsible for both the behaviour of their teams and their over rates (there are points deductions if they are slow in the TVCL); and, secondly, I encourage them to join me for a beer and a chat after the match, because this is the best environment for either party to air grievances. However, there are no over rate penalties in ECB junior competitions, behavioural issues (such as they are – I have never had any problems!) are managed by the coaches and parents, and there is no *après*-cricket!

I think that the match regulations (overs in match, overs per bowler, length of spells, fielding restrictions, competition rules for no balls and wides etc.) are the key things to discuss with junior captains at the toss. It is also a good idea to remind them about keeping off the pitch, the bane of my colleague today's life, it would seem.

One interesting aspect of ECB county junior matches is that each team has twelve players. Only eleven bat; and, while only eleven field at any one time, rolling substitutes are allowed and all twelve can bowl regardless of when they come on or off the field of play (Law 2.5 does not apply).[25] So the challenge for the umpires is to keep count of the fielders and ensure that there are no more than eleven on the field at any one time! (Interestingly, twelve player teams induce apoplexy in progressive scorers who use a computer, because cricket scoring software packages cannot cope with someone who is not on the list of batsmen coming on to bowl!) There are also two drinks breaks in each innings of these matches; they are called drinks breaks but are in fact used as 'coaching timeouts'.

Lord's, Friday, 17th May, 2013

I went to Lord's today to see the second day of the Test match between England and New Zealand. It was the coldest I have ever been at a cricket match – even colder, I think, than at Reading last season. I think it might be a middle age thing – I definitely feel the cold much more than I used to! It was so cold today that when the umpires took the players off

[25] Law 2.5, 'Fielder absent or leaving the field'.

in perfectly good light late on there was barely a murmur from the crowd. The floodlights were on and visibility was fine, but no doubt there is an obscure public-unfriendly ICC match rule that they were (correctly) following. I always feel sorry for the umpires in big matches when they get booed for suspending play due to bad light – this is a classic case of 'shooting the messenger!'

There was a surreal moment today when the ball was struck towards the Tavern boundary, where I was sitting, and two Joe Roots converged on it! It turned out that his brother, a near identical lookalike, is on the Lord's ground staff and was fielding as a substitute.

Bagshot C.C., Saturday, 18th May, 2013

TVCL Division 2B. Bagshot 194 (48.0), Chiswick & Latymer 86 (34.3). Bagshot won by 108 runs.

Bagshot is a nice well-run club. It has a small, intimate pavilion, a decent square and a ground set nicely between woodland, a pub and a main road. The latter ticks a lot of the boxes for an ideal location for a cricket club: the woodland gives shelter and shade, the pub atmosphere as passers-by watch the cricket, and the road visibility to passing traffic and thus free publicity. They field three teams on a Saturday now – a big improvement from when I played against them in the 1990s when they seemed to be struggling.

My colleague and I made one error today, which had only minimal effect on the match. The boundary rope was placed tightly around the (single) sightscreen, which would have been fine if everyone had bowled right-arm over. Unfortunately, they did not, and when a left-armer came on first change in the Bagshot innings I saw fielders moving the boundary rope prior to moving the sightscreen, which is not allowed.[26] So I stopped them and called the two captains together, and my colleague and I sought their agreement to redefine the boundary so that the sightscreen could be moved left and right without coming onto the field of play. Was I being pedantic? The Laws of Cricket are quite clear that the boundary must be set before the toss and not moved thereafter, so I think probably not. If my colleague and I had checked the boundary rope *vis-à-vis* the sightscreens before the match then this problem would not have arisen!

Chiswick's opening bowler had a complete nightmare today, bowling seven or eight wides in his first, and only, over. There is a slight slope on the Bagshot ground and later, when he was fielding at square leg, I asked him if this was what had caused him trouble. "No", he said, "I think it was the party last night ..." I have a tendency to over-analyse sometimes.

Tring Park C.C., Saturday, 25th May, 2013

TVCL Division 2A. Tring Park II 233-5 (52.0), Cookham Dean 189 (47.2). Tring Park II won by 44 runs.

Generally speaking, recreational cricketers do not know the Laws of Cricket as well as they should. Today I had a classic with the wide law. One of the Tring bowlers delivered several balls a yard or so wide of off stump, and I was ready

---

[26] Law 19.1, 'The boundary of the field of play'.

to call wide ball. However, the Cookham batsman kept taking a stride towards the ball and then shouldering arms – and then looking at me in disappointment when I did not call a wide. He got out shortly afterwards and left the field chuntering. I sought him out to explain the law after the match: a wide is judged from the nearest of *either* the stumps *or* the batsman's feet.[27] He thanked me for putting him right but then opined that, "you could have told me at the time". I said that I would have done so, discreetly, if he had happened to be at my end at a quiet moment, but also made clear that it is my job to apply the laws not to help one team or other make best use of them.

Burnham C.C., Sunday, 26th May, 2013

ECB Under 13 (40/40). Dorset 97 (39.3), Buckinghamshire 98-9 (39.1). Buckinghamshire won by 1 wicket.

This was an extraordinary game of cricket. Like the famous Headingley Ashes Test Match in 1981, it was rather dull until the end. Dorset did not seem to have got enough runs, then Buckinghamshire collapsed to 50–8 and it seemed game over – only for the ninth and then tenth wicket pairs to rally with some fine hitting and win the match dramatically, with overs as well as wickets running out. I do not think that the Dorset players could quite believe what had happened. They will learn.

There was a fascinating incident in the Test Match between England and New Zealand at Headingley today. Graeme Swann was bowling to Kane Williamson. The ball

---

[27] Law 25.2, 'Delivery not a wide'.

turned sharply into him, and Joe Root at square leg claimed the bat pad catch. The appeal was turned down, but Alastair Cook was convinced and reviewed. The DRS showed that there was no inside edge – but the ball was going on to hit the very top of leg stump, so Williamson was given out LBW. England will no doubt claim that they were appealing for LBW all along, but I really do not think that they were. This incident shows, simultaneously, how good the DRS is and how hard it is to umpire real time with the naked eye! Who would be an umpire?

I had not met my colleague today before, and he introduced himself by saying, "I'm an unconventional umpire." Well, he could say that again! His response to my question about the counting signals to be exchanged between us was illuminating:

"Do you signal on the fourth or fifth ball?"
"Neither. You count your balls and I'll count mine."

Burnham C.C., Saturday, 1st June, 2013

TVCL Division 2B. Bagshot 148 (44.1), Burnham II 152-2 (32.0). Burnham II won by 8 wickets.

This was a fractious and bad-tempered match, which did not reflect especially well on either team. There was a disciplinary incident during the Bagshot innings. I was standing at square leg. A short-pitched ball struck the batsman and there was a huge appeal for caught behind, which my colleague turned down. Unfortunately, the Burnham fielder at first slip continued his appeal, and to advance towards my colleague, after he had firmly and clearly said not out. This is completely unacceptable and my colleague and I had no choice but to report him.

I had quite a long (and amicable) chat with the player involved, his captain and several other Burnham players after the match. Burnham is a largely Asian club and the main thrust of their defence was that Asian cricketers are naturally more exuberant than their Anglo-Saxon counterparts and that no offence is meant by this exuberance. I understood the point that they were making. However, the Spirit of Cricket is clear: a player must not 'dispute an umpire's decision by word, action or gesture,' and nor must he 'advance towards an umpire in an aggressive manner while appealing'. The player today did both and will have to face the consequences of his actions.

Wooburn Narkovians C.C., Sunday, 2nd June, 2013

ECB Under 11 (40/40). Buckinghamshire 108-7 (40.0), Norfolk U11 109-5 (36.2). Norfolk won by 5 wickets.

Today was my first visit to Wooburn for two years. They now have a new pavilion, or a new shell round the old building to be more precise, and there were no (or at least not many) aeroplanes today, so all good for starters.

We needed a shorter boundary as it was an Under 11 match, but it had not been marked out. This was unfortunate but not the end of the world – we put markers out at fifteen-yard intervals and they did the job. This would have been a more serious problem if it was a senior match, or even an older junior one – and in that case I would have insisted that a line be marked or a rope found.

My colleague and I each made an error with waist height beamers today. I no balled a Norfolk bowler but forgot to give him a first warning[28]; this is important in case he bowls two more and needs to be removed from the attack[29], so one for my little black book. Later, a Buckinghamshire bowler bowled a beamer, which I thought passed the batsman below waist height, so I did not call it. However, to my surprise, my colleague called it from square leg. I let this pass at the time but reproached him after the match because it was my call. It is a good idea for the bowler's end umpire to look at his colleague and get a second opinion via hand signals, but it is his call and his call alone.[30] My colleague apologised; one for his little black book.

One interesting related point to the above is that some of the ECB junior competitions have match rules, which specify that any ball which passes above waist height, regardless of its speed, should be called a no ball. The Laws of Cricket state that a slow delivery should be called as a no ball only if it passes above shoulder height.[31] It is well worth checking the small print before the start of a junior match!

It was a baking hot day and when the match finished at 6.00pm what I really fancied was a swim in a nice cold pool rather than a pint. My colleague, unprompted, volunteered

---

[28] Law 42.6, 'Dangerous and unfair bowling'.
[29] Law 42.7, 'Dangerous and unfair bowling – action by the umpire'.
[30] Law 42.6, 'Dangerous and unfair bowling'.
[31] Law 42.6, '"Dangerous and unfair bowling"'.

the same thought, so that was that, off we went. I felt a bit sorry for the Wooburn chairman – he had opened the bar and everyone seemed to be heading off *post haste* after the match.

North Maidenhead C.C., Saturday, 8th June, 2013

TVCL Division 2A. Gerrards Cross II 201 (42.3), North Maidenhead 203-5 (47.2). North Maidenhead won by 5 wickets.

To score or not to score: some further thoughts. Today, the North Maidenhead scorer, an elderly gentleman, was either on his own or accompanied only by a variety of pressganged players, so I had the utmost sympathy for him. However, my colleague and I soon lost confidence in him as the total on the scoreboard started to go up and down like the Duke of York and his soldiers. It is one thing for the total on the scoreboard to be going up at a different rate, and in different increments, to one's own tally, but when it starts to come down periodically as well then alarm bells start to ring. It was chaos, but in the end North Maidenhead won easily so it was fortunately not a major issue.

I would say that having two reliable scorers is close to the top of my wish list when heading off to a match. It probably comes third, narrowly behind having a competent and temperamentally compatible colleague and a good tea. A decent pint of beer, i.e. bitter from a barrel, is probably fourth on my list.

When there is a problem with the score an umpire inevitably becomes more concerned about the acknowledgement of his signals. Properly trained scorers are nearly always very good at this, but player scorers often wave at you with one hand while simultaneously looking down at their book and writing. I do not think that they mean to be rude, or to implicitly say that they have seen what has happened (for instance, an obvious boundary four) and do not need you to tell them, but this is the effect of this action. I do not normally make a song and dance over this unless something out of the ordinary has happened. However, it is a different matter if I have multiple signals to make. Player scorers often seem not to understand that, just as the umpire has to make separate signals for each communication, they too are required to make separate acknowledgements of each signal. If I had a pound for every time I have made multiple signals to a player umpire and he or she has responded by continuously waving at me until I stop signalling ...

This reminds me of an amusing quiz question:

Question. Give an example of when an umpire has to make four separate signals to the scorer after the same delivery.

Answer. The bowler's end umpire calls and signals wide and, simultaneously, the square leg umpire calls and signals no ball; meanwhile, the ball beats both the batsman and the wicketkeeper and runs away for four byes. This requires the bowler's end umpire to make the following four separate signals:

i. reverse his original wide signal (this is because no ball always over-rides a wide[32]);
ii. call and signal no ball;
iii. signal byes (this is important because the scorer needs to know not to credit any runs to the batsman);
iv. and, finally, signal boundary four.

After the match one of the opening batsmen challenged me (politely) on the LBW decision that I had upheld against him earlier in the day. This is something that I like – I think it is helpful for all concerned to talk through decisions and increase mutual understanding. He thought that the ball was missing leg stump; I did not. Without the DRS to prove it one way or another, or even to shed light on it, we will never know. I then reminded him that the previous time I had umpired him (at Finchampstead last season) he had scored a ton. Of course, he remembered the ton but not that I was umpiring said match. I then said that, having spent all that afternoon at Finch watching him bat, I had no intention of doing so again! This amused his teammates and we parted on good terms. It is always good to have a social chat after the match.

Burnham C.C., Sunday, 9th June, 2013

ECB Under 11 (40/40). Buckinghamshire 167-8 (40.0), Oxfordshire 137 (39.5). Buckinghamshire won by 30 runs.

This was a rather slow match. Oxfordshire never looked remotely like chasing down Buckinghamshire's score, but nonetheless batted out all but one ball of their allotted overs.

---

[32] Law 24.10, 'No ball to over-ride wide'.

This match was a perfect illustration of my lack of enthusiasm for win/lose cricket. If the team batting second is not in the game, then the cricket becomes boring and pointless. Ten wickets are not needed for the fielding team to win, so the result is already clear. You might as well shake hands and retire to the bar. But nobody ever does. Everyone goes through the motions. The batting team looks for practice in the middle, the fielding team gives everyone a bowl and the fielders try to stay interested. There is no competitive edge or intensity to the play. But the poor umpires have to stay out in the middle for the duration. I believe that you should always have to bowl a team out to win a cricket match! Every ball must matter! And the captain must use his imagination to winkle out the tailenders. This is the game of cricket.

At least I was at Burnham, one of my favourite grounds, and was able to revert to staring at the trees and cloud formations to keep myself amused. I was also watching the aeroplanes taking off in the distance from Heathrow. Burnham is just far enough away to make the noise tolerable – three out of four turn away, either north or south, before they get to Burnham. And I must say that, visually if not orally, the way they curve away, brilliant white against the blue sky, and leaving a trail of white smoke in their wake, is pleasing on the eye. As I said, the cricket today was slow, very slow!

Chalfont St. Giles C.C., Tuesday, 11th June, 2013

BCB Under 12 (20/20). Chalfont St. Giles 99-6 (20.0), Chalfont St. Peter 34 (11.0). Chalfont St. Giles won by 65 runs.

I played all my senior cricket for two Chalfont St. Peter based clubs, Chalfont Saints until 1992, and then Chalfont St. Peter after the two clubs merged in 1993. And Chalfont St. Giles were always the great local rivals; so my memories of playing on this ground are of hard-fought local derbies, narrow victories and defeats and turgid draws. The afternoon matches were time rather than overs matches, and often finished with one team 'dobbing out' for a draw! The club has a strong local atmosphere, adjacent to Chalfont Wasps F.C. and at the heart of village life. It also has one of the best wickets in the local area, always hard and true, and coming on well. The only downside is that the ground is adjacent to an abattoir. I do not have a strong sense of smell, but even so...

I have one particularly fond memory of a match here in 1999. St. Giles had an 'old pro' who played against us every year. He gave little away with the ball and, batting second, liked coming in at about 6 or 7, and either steering his team home to a victory or ensuring that they did not lose. On this particular occasion I was skippering St. Peter, we had about 220 on the board, and St. Giles were about 130–5 with the last 20 overs about to start. So the old pro decided to dob out for a draw. Normally, he would succeed – he was both a good batsman and bloody-minded – but on this occasion I had an ace up my sleeve. We had an overseas player that season, a fast bowler, who I only used as a batsman on Sundays. However, when said old pro started dobbing out for a draw, I told him that I would bring the quickie on if he did not enter into the spirit of a Sunday cricket match. He didn't, so I did ... and, his bluff called, he clearly didn't fancy it! First ball he was a yard to the leg side. Second ball, two yards. Third ball same – and this time clean bowled. I then took the quickie off and we resumed our game of 'Sunday' cricket! It was one of those rare captaincy triumphs that you have every now and again.

Sadly, both the main protagonists in this story, old pro and fast bowler, subsequently died in unhappy circumstances, a salient reminder that cricket is 'only a game'.

Today's junior match was tame in comparison, and St. Giles ran out easy winners. It is easy to lose concentration in these matches, and I must admit that I was back in the 1970s and 1980s for most of the evening!

Sonning C.C., Saturday, 15th June, 2013

TVCL Division 2B. Thatcham Town 20-0 (7.0). Match abandoned.

Today's match only lasted for seven overs before it was rained off, but sadly it was long enough for me to make a howler. The Thatcham batsman played and missed, the wicketkeeper fumbled the ball, and the batsman scrambled a quick single. I signalled a bye. At this point it became clear that the batsman had nicked it, and the fumble had been a dropped catch. Complete humiliation for me. Umpiring can be a humbling experience sometimes.

There was a point of interest today re the laws with regard to how the match was called off. The umpires assume sole responsibility for GWL issues from the time that they arrive at the ground.[33] In practice, I have found that the captains often discuss the conditions with each other privately and then come to see the umpires, and this is what happened today. They came to the umpires' room and said that they were in agreement that the match should be abandoned. My colleague and I were surprised. We had been doing our calculations about the latest time that play could resume according to the TVCL match rules, and there was still another 35 minutes to go before this cut-off would be reached. However, we were happy to go with the flow, and shook hands and abandoned. Technically, though, my colleague and I should have made the decision on our own without any external input.

When the captains had left our room, I said to my colleague that I thought they had made a mistake, and he agreed with me. We changed and went into the bar to have some tea and a pint; by then, predictably, the sun had come out. Later, I noticed on the TVCL results website that a match had been completed a mile down the road at Reading. If either of these teams misses promotion or is relegated by a small number of points at the end of the season then I think they will regret today.

The changes to the GWL laws, which were introduced at the beginning of the 2011 season, are sensible. They have

---

[33] Laws 3.8, 'Fitness of ground, weather and light'; 3.9, 'Suspension of play for adverse conditions of ground, weather or light'; and 7.2, 'Fitness of the pitch for play'.

removed the farce of 'the light being offered to the batsmen' and all GWL decisions are now the sole responsibility of the umpires.[34] However, they have also inadvertently cranked up the pressure on the umpires, because mostly one team will want to play more than the other, or one will be in a winning position and the other a losing one. Today the captains were in agreement so, from the perspective of one's desire for an easy life, all was fine.

While we were off for rain my colleague told me about an incident in a Buckinghamshire Over 50s county match recently. The batsman skied a ball up in the air and the wicketkeeper settled underneath it to take the catch. He initially fumbled it, then grabbed it, seemingly gaining control in the progress, but almost immediately began showing off, juggling it from glove to glove and then on to each shoulder before losing control and allowing the ball to fall to the ground. The batsman stood his ground, so the fielders appealed and, after consultation with his colleague, the bowler's end umpire decided that the wicketkeeper had not had complete control over the ball and his movement and therefore turned down the appeal.[35] There was then an almighty kerfuffle during which the wicketkeeper lost his cool, threw the ball at some (partisan) spectators and was then told to leave the field by his own captain. I have never heard of a cricketer being 'sent off' before!

Amersham C.C., Sunday, 16th June, 2013

---

[34] Laws 3.8, 'Fitness of ground, weather and light'; 3.9, 'Suspension of play for adverse conditions of ground, weather or light'; and 7.2, 'Fitness of the pitch for play'.
[35] Law 32.3, 'A fair catch'.

ECB Girls Under 13 (35/35). Warwickshire 94-8 (35.0), Buckinghamshire 95-7 (33.2). Buckinghamshire won by 3 wickets.

Shardeloes is a stunningly attractive cricket ground, picture postcard beautiful from almost every vantage point: looking out from the pavilion; sitting on one of the benches at the top western end; looking at the pavilion and mature horse chestnut trees from the square. It is one of those grounds that you want to walk round in both directions. Several times.

That said, the elegant old clubhouse needs an upgrade and from a cricketing perspective the straight boundaries are too short. They could kill two birds with one stone if they built a new clubhouse and re-sited it at the same time (they have the space to do this), but that would no doubt cost a fortune. The shortness of the straight boundaries has been exacerbated by modern bats, which enable the ball to be hit harder and further than in days of yore.

The short boundaries were not a problem today for the 13-year-old girls but the changing facilities, a labyrinth of narrow passageways and unmarked doors, were. Or at least they were for me and my (male) colleague – we had to be careful when using the urinals and a post-match shower was completely out of the question!

This was my first girls match and the standard of play was high; in fact, I must admit that it was higher than I was expecting. In fact, it was comparable to boys cricket at this age group, and I do not think that there would be much in it if the boys played the girls. Some of the girls today were already quite tall and this really helped their bowling. Of course, the standard of boys cricket tends to rise sharply around the Under 14/15 age level when they reach adolescence and start to get bigger and stronger.

Bledlow Ridge C.C., Thursday, 20th June, 2013

BCB Under 15 (20/20). Chalfont St. Peter 122-9 (20.0), Bledlow Ridge 124-7 (18.4). Bledlow Ridge won by 3 wickets.

Bledlow Ridge is a beautiful village ground set in the Chiltern Hills just outside High Wycombe. I used to play here every year for Chalfont Saints in the Mid Bucks League, and it has mixed memories for me as the venue for perhaps both my worst and best moments on the cricket field. In 1988 I dropped an absolute dolly, a real sitter! The man I dropped went on to score a ton. And then to rub salt in my wounds I was out for a duck and we collapsed to an ignominious defeat! But two years later in 1990 I played my best ever innings here, 77 not out. We were chasing about 150 and got home easily by about five wickets! Mostly, during my career, my personal contribution had little effect on whether my team won or lost, but these two occasions were notable exceptions. Anyway, it was nice to return after maybe a ten or twelve year gap and to see the club and ground both looking well.

Having moved up the umpiring hierarchy in recent times, and become familiar with working with my colleague, it was odd this evening to have no interaction whatsoever with my colleague from the home club. He was simultaneously managing his team, ensuring that the next batsman in had a protector on and that someone was getting padded up, and keeping score with a book and pencil in hand; a cricket volunteer *par excellence*. But I found it hard to concentrate without an umpiring colleague working actively with me, even just signalling the fourth or fifth ball of the over, and the general lack of intensity in the play exacerbated matters. On one occasion I was miles away, watching some red kites swooping and climbing, and it took the sound of willow on leather to bring me back to the cricket! I wonder whether umpiring matches like this might get me into bad habits? I will need to be back on my mettle on Saturday.

Regarding the signals between umpires to keep count of the balls, the unofficial technique used to be a mutual movement of the arm to 45 degrees, with one finger pointed, after the fifth ball. However, the modern and, I think, better way is to signal four balls passed by touching your opposite arm with two fingers, and then to only use the fifth ball signal if one or other of you forgot after the fourth. (This happens more than you might think; counting, ostensibly the easiest of an umpire's tasks, often proves to be one of the most difficult!) Signalling on the fourth rather than fifth ball has two advantages: firstly, it is harder to lose count over four balls; and, secondly, and more importantly, if you do not agree with your colleague then you have more time to sort it out and prevent either a five or seven ball over!

Wokingham C.C., Saturday, 22nd June, 2013

TVCL Division 2A. Wokingham II 158-9 (44.0), Gerrards Cross II 92-9 (40.0). Match drawn.

Strangely enough, given my comments in the previous entry, today I had a difficult experience with a colleague in a TVCL match. When I arrived at the ground it was raining and there was some doubt about whether we would be able to play. My colleague was somewhat less than keen to start the game, which put him at odds with me, because I am always keen to play if at all possible; and then, during the match, when it started raining, he was again keen to come off at the first opportunity, even though I thought it was fine to continue for a while and so did the players. After the game, he told me that he was suffering some health problems at the moment but then rather bizarrely added that he had just umpired for nine consecutive days (he does school matches in midweek). I suspected that his recent schedule and health problems were the reason for his less than enthusiastic attitude. I think the players could see that we were not working well together as a team, and that this undermined their confidence in us.

I must admit that I was rather distracted during the build up to this match. I watched the first half of the first Wallabies v. British Lions Test Match in the clubhouse, but the second half began at about 12.30pm, just when I needed to be preparing for today's match. The intermittent rain showers were tantalising. Would they last long enough for me to see the climax of the match, and would the Lions win? No and yes, as it turned out.

I had a difficult 'judgement call' today. A Wokingham batsman edged to second slip. I was confident that the ball had carried and was surprised to see the batsman stand his ground. I walked over to my colleague and asked his opinion – he said that he had not been able to see because another fielder was blocking his view, and therefore could not give an opinion. I therefore went with my original conviction and gave the batsman out. Some of the Wokingham players later told me (very politely) that this was a bad decision, which I have no problem with at all. They were well positioned to see as the clubhouse at the new Wokingham ground is square to the wicket and that is where they were sitting. That said, the Gerrards Cross fielders were adamant that the ball had carried. As an umpire in these situations you cannot win. Even modern television technology sometimes struggles to prove definitively whether or not a catch has carried.

Wokingham had a young Indian boy, 14 years old, playing for them today. He was less than five foot tall and his voice had not yet broken. But he could bat. He came in at four and made about 12 or 15, effortlessly and with all the time in the world, including some lovely flicks through midwicket and a beautifully timed cove drive, before driving loosely and getting caught. I was rather disappointed when he got out because I had been enjoying watching him bat. The reaction of the Gerrards Cross bowler at my end to being played by this boy, prior to his dismissal, in such a disdainful manner amused me. I have umpired him before and he is normally quite aggressive (within the spirit of the game), but he obviously did not feel comfortable snarling and chirping at such a young boy so he just chuntered away quietly to himself. As soon as the boy was out, normal service was resumed. I have seen this sort of thing before, notably when there has been a lady batsman. It's almost like the players are slightly ashamed of their aggressive, macho behaviour when there are young boys or ladies involved.

One of my umpiring colleagues had marked my card with regard to the Indian boy and told me about an amusing incident when he had umpired him recently in a game against Windsor and 'Fred Trueman'[36]. Apparently the boy was putting Windsor to the sword and Fred, having been driven for four, walked back past my colleague and asked him if he had any ideas what he should bowl next. Indiscreetly, my colleague suggested that the boy had not yet had one 'up his nose', whereupon Fred delivered the perfect throat bouncer ... only for it to be majestically hooked for six. As a disgruntled Fred walked back to his mark, he said to my colleague, with a glint in his eye, "well, that shows how much you know about it, umps!"

This was my first visit to Wokingham's magnificent new ground. It is an increasingly common trend for town clubs to sell their grounds for housing development and then build a new out-of-town facility from scratch with the proceeds; in effect, they are swapping location for facilities. My concern for them as a club would be twofold. Firstly, over time, the people of Wokingham may forget that the ground and club is there, so they will have to work hard on marketing and publicity. And, secondly, I observed that, even though the facility is only a year or so old, there are some worrying signs of wear and tear, for instance, grass growing through the pavement in the car park. However, it is a superb facility, by

---

[36] See entry for Hayes C.C., Saturday, 11th August, 2011.

far and away the best I have ever seen in recreational cricket, and I wish them well.

After the match I went back to a social event at my club, Chalfont St. Peter, and heard an amusing story from today's 2nd XI match. A batsman was given out LBW. The ball had just clipped the top of his pad on the way through and he was indignant. "I hit that, umps", he said. "That's fine", said the (player) umpire, "in that case you're still out – caught at first slip!"

Windsor C.C., Saturday, 29th June, 2013

TVCL Division 2A. Marlow 243-5 dec. (50.0), Windsor 170-8 (50.0). Match drawn.

Windsor took a different line on the rugby to Wokingham last week, and their captain called in midweek to ask me if I had any objection to the start time being put back (by circa thirty minutes) so that everyone could watch the (climax of the) match. This put me in a difficult position. On the one hand, as a rugby fan, and remembering how frustrated I felt at Wokingham last week, I was delighted. However, I also had two concerns. The first one was that not all cricketers are rugby fans, and as it turned out nor was my colleague – and such an arrangement was thus rather unfair to them. The second was that delaying the start contravened TVCL match rules and was potentially unfair to other teams in the same division (for instance, if there was a delayed start then the later start time might enable a match which would otherwise have been abandoned to be completed). In the end, my colleague and the opposition, Marlow, were both happy with

Windsor's proposal, so I was happy to go with the flow (you will by now be aware that this is my default position in most circumstances!) So, in contrast to last week at Wokingham, this week I saw the rugby and the Lions lost. Hopefully, next week I will get both desired outcomes.

As it turned out, the rugby saved Windsor's blushes because it bought them some extra time to solve an embarrassing problem. I arrived just in time for the start of the rugby and found a good seat in the bar. I then overheard some rather interesting conversations. A misunderstanding with their new groundsman had led to a situation whereby a pitch had not been prepared for today's match. So, somewhat ironically, most of Windsor's players did not get to see the rugby after all – they spent the duration of the match preparing a cricket pitch!

I made an error on the last ball of the match today, for which the Marlow captain rightly reproached me. At the beginning of the last over Marlow needed two wickets to win the match and Windsor were holding on for a draw. It was very much game on. However, after the fifth ball had been safely negotiated by the Windsor batsman there was a tangible drop in the intensity of the Marlow fielders, and one of them encouraged the (fast) bowler to just bowl the last ball off a few paces and get it over with. This he duly did, but without his proper run-up he bowled a ball that I would normally have called wide. However, I sensed that everyone just wanted to get off and into the bar – after our late start it was by now 8.00pm – and therefore let it go, called time and thought no more of it. However, as we shook hands, the Marlow captain reproached me for not calling the wide because that would have given his team an extra ball and a chance of an extra bonus point. I acknowledged that he was quite right and apologised. In fact, the situation was worse than even he (the Marlow captain) realised. The next ball could have seen a run out off a no ball, which would have given his team a chance of an outright win. The wide and a subsequent boundary four would also have given Windsor an extra bonus point. I am really annoyed with myself and will not sleep well tonight. I must learn from this and always apply the Laws of Cricket to the letter in the future.

There was a slightly surreal moment as I came out of the shower. My towel was missing. I have a tendency to lose and mislay things, but I knew that I had brought my towel with me to the shower room because at Windsor this is something that you need to do to protect your modesty! There was another towel, not mine, on a hook, and a quick investigation established that one of the Windsor players had (mistakenly, and much to his embarrassment) used my towel rather than his own. He was apologetic. "No problem", I said, "mine's a pint of bitter!"

Dr. Challoner's Grammar School, Sunday, 30th June, 2013

ECB Under 15 (50/50). Buckinghamshire 162 (44.0), Berkshire 165-2 (46.3). Berkshire won by 8 wickets.

Today I returned to my *alma mater* for the first time since I left in 1982. Inevitably, it was a strange, slightly surreal experience. Much has changed, most of it for the better, and there is now not only a splendid new cricket pavilion but also an indoor practice facility. The pavilion has an honours board listing centuries and outstanding bowling analyses. It starts in 2003, so my name is not on it! Actually, even if it had started in 1976 then it still wouldn't have been!

Some of my memories have disappeared into the annals of time. I remember both footballs and cricket balls running away down the slope to the main hall/dining hall/gym/changing rooms, and sometimes even further down the road which curved round the side to the right – you never wanted to be fielding on the lower side of the ground because, if the ball beat you, it was an awfully long way to go and retrieve it. However, there is now an astroturf pitch (with fencing all round) where the old playground used to be, so this doesn't happen any more.

The cricket was interesting. The Buckinghamshire captain looked an outstanding batsman and, opening the innings, scored 30 or so very quickly before giving his wicket away, and this set the tone for the rest of the innings. The Berkshire opening batsmen, by contrast, played steadily and knocked off the runs with ease.

There was one item of umpiring interest. There was a double overthrow and the second one crossed the boundary. I consulted with my colleague and we decided that two runs had been scored at the time the second throw was made – we did not think that the batsmen had yet crossed for a third run. So I awarded six runs. I cannot be certain that I got this right – there was so much going on with yes/no/wait calls from the batsmen as well as the misdirected throws – and sometimes you just have to make an educated guess.

Overall it was a nice day. The tea was excellent, and the weather was glorious. A shower and a beer after the match would have made it perfect, but these are unrealistic expectations for a school ground and match, so I went for a swim afterwards instead.

Great Kingshill C.C., Tuesday, 2nd July, 2013

BCB Under 17 (20/20). Great Kingshill 147-5 (18.0), Chalfont St. Peter 91-9 (18.0). Great Kingshill won by 58 runs.

This was another trip down memory lane for me. Like Bledlow Ridge a couple of weeks ago, I returned to one of my favourite grounds, this time after maybe twenty years. It has a nice open playing area surrounded by trees and houses, and with a couple of decent pubs to socialise in after the match. I remembered playing one of my best innings on this ground for Chalfont Saints in a Mid Bucks League match, but had to look up the details in my records. 60 in 1988.

I also remember being done like a kipper here by a wise old fox. He was an ageing fast bowler in his late 40s, early 50s, still good enough to put it on a spot but now only a medium pacer. I opened the batting and played out the first two balls. Pitched up, fairly gentle, all very comfortable. The next ball was the same run up, same action, a tad shorter, much faster. I pushed forward. Glove. Wicketkeeper. Out. I had been outwitted, lulled into a false sense of security. This was not a man to be playing forward to on the third ball of the innings with a new ball in his hand.

The match itself was uneventful, and actually slightly dull in the way that win/lose matches sometimes can be when the team batting first has made a match-winning total and the opposition have no chance of chasing it down. I had a part-time colleague, who was wearing tracksuit bottoms and a football shirt. I doff my cap to him for volunteering but, as the old saying goes, 'even if you can't play, always look as if you can ...'

High Wycombe C.C., Thursday, 4th July, 2013

Buckinghamshire Under 15 Knockout Cup Final (20/20). High Wycombe 201-6 (20.0), Chesham 97 (18.4). High Wycombe won by 104 runs.

I came across the Buckinghamshire Under 15s captain and opening batsman from last Sunday again this evening, and he gave a repeat performance. Two sumptuous boundary fours, then a top edge caught at mid-off. Three balls, 8–1. He is obviously a very good player – he is currently batting 7 or 8 and bowling slow left arm for High Wycombe 1st XI in the HCPCL, no mean achievement for one so young. But he bats like a millionaire! Hopefully, he will learn. It is funny how some players think you have to score off every ball in a twenty overs aside match; they seem to forget that there are 120 balls in the innings, and having your best batsmen face the majority of them will give the best chance of victory.

I made a really embarrassing error today. I am not a great mobile phone user and normally leave it in the glove box of my car for emergencies. However, today I had made a call just before the match and then inadvertently left the phone switched on in my lapel pocket. Sod's law then dictated that it started ringing with me at the bowler's end and the bowler running in; and, double sod's law, it did not turn out to be a regulation dot ball or casually run single. The batsman hit the ball straight back down the ground, it clipped the non-striker's foot, ricocheted up and broke the wicket with the non-striker well out of his ground. The fielders appealed and, flustered and with my phone still ringing, I gave the batsman out. I realised immediately that I had made the wrong decision and reversed it – the batsman can only be run out if one of the fielding team touches the ball before it breaks the wicket! It was embarrassing. The problem here was one of routine. I do not normally keep my mobile phone on my person on the cricket field, so putting it on silent is not part of my routine.

There was also a fairly extraordinary GWL incident in today's match.[37] The pitch at the High Wycombe ground runs east to west, and during the second innings today the sun setting at the western end of the ground was blinding the batsman on strike, which worried my colleague and me with regard to both fairness and safety. During the second innings we therefore decided to bowl eight overs in succession from the eastern end – until the sun had fallen so low that it was no longer a problem at the western end. I think that this was a sensible and practical use of Law 43.

The High Wycombe ground is attractive. Non-cricketers are often surprised when I say this, because they only know

---

[37] Laws 3.8, 'Fitness of ground, weather and light'; 3.9, 'Suspension of play for adverse conditions of ground, weather or light'; and 7.2, 'Fitness of the pitch for play'.

the ground from the perspective of the busy A40 London Road. However, the clubhouse is the best facility in local cricket; the view from the first floor is glorious, looking out on to the Rye with the Chiltern Hills in the background; and there are always people milling around, watching, chatting and having a beer, which gives the ground a real 'cricket' atmosphere.

Reading C.C., Saturday, 6th July, 2013

TVCL Division 2B. Chiswick & Latymer 218-7 dec. (50.0) Reading II 175 (50.0). Chiswick & Latymer won by 43 runs.

Imagine a hypothetical match situation. It is an important match, bottom against next to bottom, and the last ball is about to be bowled. The batting team are nine wickets down and are playing for a draw. The batsman on strike has successfully negotiated the last ten or twelve overs. He has lost a couple of tail end partners along the way, but he has managed to keep most of the strike for himself with judiciously taken singles. The last ball is bowled. Most of the fielders are crowded around the bat. The batsman clips the ball through midwicket and it runs off towards the boundary, although it is clearly not going to make it all the way. Job done, thinks the batsman, who turns round, taps his bat on the crease and starts to walk off. Except that he has forgotten or misunderstood one crucial thing. The ball is still in play. The pavilion is at mid-on and the batsman strides off, now accompanied by his colleague, bat under arm. The fielding team urge one of their number to chase the ball, which he does. The batsmen hear this but carry on walking off, turning just momentarily to watch what is happening out in the middle. The throw comes in to the wicketkeeper, who takes it, removes the bails and appeals. What is the decision of the square leg umpire?

It is the sort of hypothetical scenario that might be envisaged on an umpire training course. An imaginary 'what if' to make you think about when the ball becomes dead. Of course, it would never actually happen in a match. Except that it did. Today. In my match. And I was the square leg umpire. I gave the batsman out. What else could I have done? My colleague had (quite rightly) not called time, the ball was still in play[38] and the batsman was out of his ground.

Of course, the fact that the pavilion was at the bowler's end was significant – if it had been at the batsman's end then the striking batsman would not have been out of his ground. However, the key thing then would have been what the non-striker would have done? I think he would probably have followed his colleague and walked off, which would have meant different batsman run out, same result!

All hell broke loose when I raised my finger. Chiswick celebrated like they had just won the World Cup. The Reading batsmen, and the Reading scorer, were both indignant and vented their fury at my colleague. They apparently thought that the ball was dead, and that my colleague should have called time. A couple of the other Reading players were more magnanimous, and accepted that their batsman should have waited for time to be called before leaving his crease. The atmosphere in the bar afterwards was not pleasant. Chiswick of course were happy enough but,

---

[38] Law 23.1, 'Ball is dead'.

probably wisely, decided to beat a hasty retreat. The Reading players were angry, some irrationally with my colleague (they blamed him rather than me), others with their batsman for his ignorance of the laws, and they too dissipated rapidly. And my colleague and I had to fill out a disciplinary report – some of the language used after the match was foul and abusive – rather than enjoy a post-match pint and chat.

At least the Lions won, although I did not get to see it.

Dr. Challoner's Grammar School, Monday, 8th July, 2013

BSCA Under 13 Semi Final (20/20). Aylesbury Grammar School 63 (14.2), Royal Grammar School, High Wycombe, 65-8 (18.1). RGS won by 2 wickets.

BSCA Under 13 Final (20/20). Dr. Challoner's Grammar School 103-9 (20.0), Royal Grammar School, High Wycombe, 57 (18.0). Dr. Challoner's won by 46 runs.

It's like buses! I wait thirty years to return to my old school and then within eight days I am back again! Today was slightly different as it was a school day and all the boys were wearing their uniforms and ties. Cue more nostalgia. It was a finals day with four schools competing, semi-finals in the morning and final/third place play-off in the afternoon. It was a pleasant day all round, with a nice tea and more glorious sunny weather, but rather uneventful from an umpiring perspective.

One of my fellow umpires today is the chairman of the Buckinghamshire ACO and we had an interesting conversation about umpire progression, a bugbear of mine. I am not ambitious personally, although I would like to get some TVCL Level 1 appointments. My concern is more altruistic. Talented new umpires, especially if they are young or have played the game to a high standard, are fast-tracked, and this is fine. But the majority of new umpires hit a ceiling beyond which it is hard to progress, with more experienced umpires above them blocking their progress. It is a classic 'dead men's shoes' situation. I think that the ACOs and leagues are going to have to find a way of moving umpires *down* the hierarchy as well as *up* in the future. It has to be a meritocracy with equal opportunity for all.

Thursday, 11th July, 2013

I am an enthusiastic supporter of the DRS because I believe that getting the right decision trumps any other consideration. However, its costs are subsidised by television and this unfortunately creates a conflict of interest. Today, in the first Ashes Test Match at Trent Bridge, when Jonathan Trott came to the wicket after Joe Root was out, the latter's dismissal was still being replayed before and after the former faced his first ball. There was a huge LBW appeal but Trott got a faint inside edge. Aleem Dar gave him not out – an excellent decision. However, Michael Clarke, the Australian captain, referred it to the DRS. The action replay showing Trott's inside edge was not available to the third umpire (because Root's dismissal was being replayed at the time), so Dar was obliged by a flaw in the DRS procedures to overturn his original not out decision – even though he himself *knew* that there had been an inside edge. Clearly, the ICC needs to sort out this procedural flaw *post haste*, and also to discuss with the television company why the replay of Trott's dismissal was not available.

Friday, 12th July, 2013

It went from bad to worse for the DRS today. Stuart Broad nicked the ball. It hit the wicketkeeper's gloves and was then caught at first slip. He was clearly out but chose to stand his ground. Aleem Dar gave him not out. Michael Clarke had used up his reviews, so Broad remained at the crease and went on to play a (match-winning, as it turned out) innings of 65. I empathised with Dar on two counts. Firstly, he had clearly lost concentration at the end of a long, hot day, and there but for the grace of god ... Secondly, in the space of two days he has now made a good decision and been undermined by the DRS, and then made a bad mistake and not been saved by it!

To walk or not to walk, that is the question. Do professional sportsmen have a wider responsibility to set the right example of sportsmanship and fair play? Will Broad's action make life harder for recreational umpires, with players following his lead? Yes and yes, in my opinion.

Marlow C.C., Saturday, 13th July, 2013

TVCL Division 2A. North Maidenhead 163 (48.4), Marlow 165-2 (22.3). Marlow won by 8 wickets.

This match was a no contest. Marlow are top of the league; North Maidenhead are mid-table and most of their players, all Muslims, were fasting on a baking hot day. I spoke to some of them about the difficulty of playing sport while fasting, and the gist of their response was that it is not a problem. I have to say that the evidence from today's match would suggest otherwise. Marlow's Australian overseas player scored 80 odd not out and was especially pleasing on the eye. But the match lacked a competitive edge and was all over just after 6.00pm.

I live in Marlow so I had the rare pleasure today of being able to walk to the ground. There are two cricket clubs in Marlow. Both have attractive grounds but they mirror the 'Bushy Park juxtaposition'.[39] Marlow has a private ground with better facilities; Marlow Park is located in a public park by the river and therefore attracts lots of passers by and has a great atmosphere. Put them together and you would have the perfect cricket club. You get a decent local pint at both, Brakspear or Rebellion.

Beaconsfield C.C., Sunday, 14th July, 2013

BCB Under 12 Final (20/20). Chesham 130-4 (20.0), Cublington 101-8 (20.0). Chesham won by 29 runs.

BCB Under 13 Final (20/20). Ballinger Waggoners 125-9 (20.0), Buckingham Town 58 (19.1). Ballinger Waggoners won by 67 runs.

During the 1980s Beaconsfield was *the* club in the local area – the best team, the best junior set-up and the best ground and facilities. Sadly, for them, this is no longer the case – in any of these respects. It is, however, still the ideal

---

[39] See entry for NPL Teddington C.C., Saturday, 2nd July, 2011.

venue for staging finals – today, the Buckinghamshire junior finals, six twenty overs a-side matches played on three grounds, morning and afternoon, Under 10 through Under 15, and I was one of six umpires on duty.

The Under 13 final was rather one-sided. Buckingham needed a major contribution from at least one, and probably two, of their top four, but all of them threw their wickets away within the first couple of overs. When I was a boy all the wizened old pros used to tell me that, "you can't score runs from the pavilion". Well, I am on the other side now and much has changed in the game, but you still can't score runs from the pavilion.

The final moments of the First Ashes Test Match at Trent Bridge were played out during the first matches. Overnight, Australia were 174 for 6 chasing a highly improbable 311 to win. Nobody gave them much chance. As the day progressed they got closer and closer – 100 to win, then 80, then 60, 40, 20. It is difficult to concentrate on your own match when everyone else is at very least mildly distracted by events elsewhere. Then, all of a sudden, there was a huge cheer and the tension lifted – the final Australian wicket had fallen and England had won by 14 runs!

Amersham C.C., Tuesday, 16th July, 2013

ECB Over 60 (45/45). Buckinghamshire 275-3 (45.0), Berkshire 278-5 (43.5). Berkshire won by 5 wickets.

This was my first Over 60s match and it was an interesting experience. The overall standard of play was high: the batsmen still have good hand-eye co-ordination, the seam bowlers do a bit with it and the slower bowlers are canny. There is no fast bowling, of course, and the rather pedestrian fielding is matched by leisurely running (often walking) between wickets. Well, it usually is. One eminent player noted for his competitiveness in his prime was exhorting his captain and batting partner to run quick singles and to turn ones into twos, and I was beginning to fear that I might have a coronary on my hands at any moment. But all was well and Berkshire won a high-scoring and very close match. And, as one would expect, it was very sociable afterwards; these players are from a generation when *après-cricket* was *de rigueur*.

It was unusual for me today to be, aged 49, by some distance the youngest person on the field of play. The last time this happened, I think, was in about 1978!

High Wycombe C.C., Saturday, 20th July, 2013

TVCL Division 1. High Wycombe II 277-5 (52.0), Kew 278-5 (47.3). Kew won by 5 wickets.

As a panel umpire in the TVCL you get sent your list of match appointments at the beginning of the season. However, you are put on standby two or three times rather than being given a match so that the appointments officer can fill late dropouts and special requests. Today, I was on standby and it worked out well for me – I was appointed to my first Division 1 match (if you exclude my late and ultimately fruitless diversion to Cove in 2011).

This was the highest standard of club cricket that I have ever been involved in – a few months short of my fiftieth birthday. Neither I nor the club I played for were ever good enough to play at this exalted level. I suppose this confirms something that I already knew – that I am a better umpire than I ever was a player. I was struck by the fact that all the fielders seemed to know roughly what positions to take up for each bowler, and that the match moved on more quickly as a result. The other notable aspect was the depth of batting in both teams.

Before the match my colleague and I were told that one of the bowlers has a suspect action. I was able to observe him from square leg and his action did indeed seem a little suspicious. However, it was not possible, with the naked eye, to say whether or not his elbow extension was greater than 15 degrees (the latest ICC guidance), and there was no way that I was going to no ball him.[40] Realistically, suspicious bowling actions – as opposed to the occasional illegal 'effort' or faster ball – have to be handled by reporting them to the appropriate authorities.

My colleague today is a Berkshire ACO Training Officer and he made an on-field assessment of me during the match. I have been asking my own association, Buckinghamshire, to assess me for some time. An on-field colleague cannot properly assess you because he has more than enough on his plate with his own umpiring duties. However, he did give me some useful advice, which was gratefully received. We talked about 'handing over the pitch', a (to me, anyway) new idea whereby the bowler's end umpire does not leave his position

---

[40] Law 24.3, 'Definition of fair delivery – the arm'.

at the end of the over until his colleague has reached the bowler's end position at the other end. The rationale for this is that one umpire is then always 'in control of' the pitch.

He also reproached me after the game for trying to keep the score. There is a division of opinion here between the Berkshire and Buckinghamshire associations, with the former advocating that umpires should not try to keep the score and the latter of the view that they should. I belong to the Buckinghamshire association but have now come to the view that Berkshire are right on this one. My first and foremost responsibility is to umpire to the best of my ability, and for me trying to keep the score detracts from this.

Chalfont St. Peter C.C., Friday, 2nd August, 2013

ECB Girls Under 17 (45/45). Surrey 164 (44.5), Buckinghamshire 39 (18.0). Surrey won by 125 runs.

Times change. Girls did not play cricket when I was sixteen. Mind you, that was 33 years ago! The standard of play today was a little mixed. One of the Surrey batsmen played well for her fifty and the bowling was generally good on both sides. But some of the Buckinghamshire batting was, it has to be said, nothing to write home about.

Ever the pedant, I am now wondering how one should describe a female batsman? Batswoman does not sound right – more comic book hero than cricket? It is a minefield. What about other common cricketing phrases such as third man, twelfth man, fieldsman? Elsewhere in the English language 'man' is deemed to be gender neutral, for instance, manslaughter, manned space flights etc. So batsman it is.

My colleague today was an elderly gentleman who is a familiar figure in local cricket circles. He usually arrives for matches on his bicycle, wearing a grey suit with clips on his trousers, as if he has just been transported from the set of a *Miss Marple* drama.

Like in the professional game, most umpires in recreational cricket are retired players. However, whereas most professional cricketers nowadays hang up their boots in their thirties, their recreational counterparts still tend to continue playing into their middle years before swapping willow and leather for the white coat. As a result, I would estimate that the average age of recreational umpires in local cricket is sixty plus.

Boyne Hill C.C., Saturday, 3rd August, 2013

TVCL Division 2B. Boyne Hill 230 (50.0), Sonning 170 (41.0). Boyne Hill won by 60 runs.

The previous week one of the Sonning batsmen had been timed out, and this was, unsurprisingly, the topic of much conversation today. My initial reaction was to feel great sympathy for the umpires involved. The consensus of opinion amongst the Sonning players was that the umpires had acted correctly: firstly, the batsman was tardy making his way onto the field and certainly took longer than the three minutes allowed by the laws to do so; and, secondly, he also showed himself to be ignorant of the timed out law – he completed putting his kit on after crossing the boundary rope in the mistaken belief that entering the field of play, as opposed to being ready to take guard or his place at the non-striker's end, was the point at which the clock stops.[41] Their ire was directed primarily at the opposition, and especially the captain, for making the appeal in the first place – they did not think that such an action was within the Spirit of Cricket! I think that I will hear more about this one in the next few weeks. Who were the umpires, I wonder? Stories are always that little bit more titillating if one knows the people involved!

There was a story doing the rounds recently about a timed out incident in an ECB Premier League match in Leicestershire. Apparently, there was a rain break and one of the batsmen, 50 odd not out at the time, decided to take advantage of the situation and go and do some shopping. However, although he saved himself a post-match chore he paid a heavy price – his wicket, because when he returned, he found that the match had restarted and he had been timed out! I rather imagine that Geoffrey Boycott never made that particular mistake!

My club, Chalfont St. Peter, also has an infamous timed out story, which has passed into legend. It was a Sunday match many years ago, and we were eight wickets down and playing for a draw at Maidenhead & Bray. With just a few balls left our ninth wicket fell. However, our number 11 batsman was suddenly nowhere to be seen. A search party was hastily arranged and he was found in one of the cubicles in the Gents. However, by the time that he had finished his

---

[41] Law 31.1, 'Out timed out'.

ablutions and readied himself for battle he had been timed out and the match lost! I do not think that he played many more games for the club!

I stood again today with the colleague who assessed me at High Wycombe two weeks ago, so we were able to hand over the pitch. I thought that it worked well, and I found it easy to incorporate it into my routine. And for the first time I did not keep the score today!

Kidmore End C.C., Thursday, 8th August, 2013

Friendly (40/40). TVCL Representative XI 157 (36.4), Kidmore End 158-4 (30.3). Kidmore End won by 6 wickets.

This was an odd match. The Rep XI was strong on paper but batted like millionaires, as such teams sometimes do. Kidmore had a few ringers playing, and on paper they needed them. But, as it turned out, the Rep XI was at least fifty runs short and the match was disappointingly one-sided.

I made two mistakes in one today. The bowler clipped the stumps in his delivery action and I called no ball. I would have been right next year, because this is the new law coming into effect in October, but today I was wrong – the present law requires me to either call dead ball, or not, as I see fit. Then, having consulted and been put right by my colleague, I compounded my error by failing to reverse my original call. This has rather spoilt my day. Such is life for an umpire. I always sulked when I was out as a batsman but only for ten or fifteen minutes; as an umpire, mistakes haunt me for considerably longer than that!

I think that I also got an LBW wrong today as well. A right arm seamer was bowling round the wicket; he brought one up the slope to a left-handed batsman, who played all round it and was rapped on the pads. I thought that he had got outside the line and gave him the benefit of the doubt, but I could easily have given him out – it was a 'judgement call'. After the match in the bar, the bowler, the batsman and the non-striker all said that they thought it was out. This is fair enough, I like to discuss my decisions if the opportunity arises, and I took on board their comments. After all, it is not often that a batsman volunteers that he thinks he was out! The bowler said that his only doubt was whether the ball might have been missing leg stump; I think (hope!) that he was just exaggerating to make his point! However, unlike my error when the bowler broke the stumps, I will not be losing any sleep over this one. 'Judgement calls' have to be answered one way or another – and you just have to call them how you see them, for better or for worse!

My colleague today, by coincidence, was another Berkshire ACO Training Officer, and he too asserted his county's position on (not) scoring. He also had a mobile communication device (which looked like something out of *Starsky and Hutch*) to enable him to communicate with the scorers. Although a staunch traditionalist, I am also a great enthusiast of technological advance and have never really understood the technophobe or Luddite position. Being able to clear up misunderstandings and discrepancies with the scorer real time, rather than having to wait for a scheduled interval, would seem to me to be a progressive development. It did feel a little bit like umpiring with an undercover policeman, though, or someone who was buying and selling on the London Stock Exchange!

In the bar afterwards I heard the 'timed out' story[42] from the perspective of the other team involved, Kidmore End. The umpires gave the fielding (Kidmore) captain every opportunity to withdraw his appeal but he chose not to do so. It is an interesting one. The captain was within his rights to uphold the appeal, and the umpires were correct to give him out. I think it would have been better all round if he (the captain) had withdrawn his appeal, but then I am on old romantic.

Chesham C.C., Saturday, 10th August, 2013

TVCL Division 4A. Chesham II 262-4 dec. (44.0), High Wycombe III 237-7 (56.0). Match drawn.

This was my first visit to Chesham for a number of years. Since then their pavilion has burnt down in a fire and a very grand new one is taking shaping in its place. It is interesting to compare it to the other new pavilions at Kidmore End and Wokingham. Kidmore and Chesham have remained at the same ground and their designs were therefore constrained by existing space (or lack of), whereas Wokingham had a blank piece of paper at their new ground. And while neither Kidmore's nor Wokingham's appear to have been built with the ongoing commercial imperative in mind, a third of Chesham's new pavilion has been set aside for external hire, including on match days. Wokingham have a second ground on site, which will be a great advantage, but Chesham have

---

[42] See entry for Boyne Hill C.C., Saturday, 3rd August, 2013.

kept their in-town location and this will greatly help their community profile. Anyway, good luck to them all, each has a magnificent new facility.

Chesham's ground is attractive, with the River Chess on one side and grassy tree-lined banks on the other. There are usually passers by on their way to the football ground next door, and they often stop to watch a few overs. However, the proximity of the football ground means that, on an August afternoon, the cricketers must endure ninety minutes of whistle blowing and loud 'football talk', a rather vulgar dialect which seemingly includes the f*** word in every sentence.

The main point of umpiring interest for me today was a big LBW shout near the end of the match when Chesham were pushing hard for victory. It was a good shout. I think it was probably hitting the stumps, but I was concerned about both height and whether it might have been going down, so not out was the correct call. I had dinner after the match with the Chesham chairman, an old friend of mine, and a few other people, all of whom had a connection in one way or another to the Chesham club. My friend made repeated jocular references throughout the evening to "a ball that was hitting half way up middle". I told him to look in the book. It was good banter.

Burnham C.C., Sunday, 11th August, 2013

ECB Under 11 (40/40). Buckinghamshire 163-7 (40.0), Surrey 81 (29.2). Buckinghamshire won by 82 runs

Surrey are a first-class county with a long and distinguished cricket history, and their junior teams usually have their Buckinghamshire counterparts for breakfast. Usually but not always, and that is the beauty of sport.

One of the lower order Surrey batsmen today had an annoying routine at the crease. It involved getting into position, as if he was ready, then partially withdrawing, re-marking his guard, and then finally readying himself to receive. It confused the Buckinghamshire bowlers, who several times aborted their run-up in response. It was very annoying, and the over rate started to plummet. When I conferred with my colleague during a natural break we concurred – woe betide him if the ball strikes his pads! However, soon afterwards he put us out of our misery by spooning one up in the air and getting caught.

An earlier Surrey batsman had been playing with his pads, i.e. thrusting his left foot forward (he was a right-hander) on the line of the ball and then placing the bat outside it. This technique is a good one to avoid 'nicking off', but simultaneously increases the chances of being given out LBW. I played for many years with a batsman who did this, and we used to have a running annual pre-season joke about whether he had 'knocked in his pads'.

Wormsley, Wednesday, 14th August, 2013

Today, I went to watch the last day of the Women's Ashes Test Match at Wormsley. The match petered out into a tame draw, which was a shame. It was, of course, a professional match with professional umpires, but doing a multi-day match at a venue like this could be a possible step up for me in the future. Multi-day matches offer several new challenges to recreational umpires; for instance, they are responsible for the pitch and outfield overnight while the match remains in progress, and must supervise the preparation of the pitch and the cutting of the outfield on the second and subsequent mornings.

Wokingham C.C., Saturday, 17th August, 2013

TVCL Division 2A. Wokingham II 82 (29.4), Windsor 83-3 (24.3). Windsor won by 7 wickets.

When the Windsor players arrived I told the bowler who had used my towel earlier in the season that he might do well to bowl from the other end if he wanted any LBW decisions to be upheld! This led to some amusing banter involving players from both teams, which I think is always nice to see. As it transpired, Windsor won easily and said player, a spinner, did not even get a bowl!

The scorers' room at Wokingham is square on to the popping crease at the top end of the ground – the end at which I was standing today. After the match, one of the scorers told me that I had missed a no ball. I am sure that she was right, partly because I remembered the ball in question and partly because she was in the perfect place to see, high up and square on. I gave five LBWs and a caught behind today – it's unusual for me to fire out six batsmen in one day! - but am confident that they were all out.

After the match, I heard a story about the use of an illegal substitute in a recent league match. Apparently a player (a top order batsman) represented his club's 1st XI in an away match, which was lost in quick time, and then returned to his home ground where he batted again for his club's 2nd XI – instead of one of the players who had fielded. Neither the umpires nor the opposition captain had been informed – of course, they would have objected! The illegal substitute nearly won the match for his 2nd XI. The skulduggery came to light because said player went in to bat at No. 9 and showed such a high level of prowess that the opposition began to question why a player of this calibre would be batting so low when he had not bowled. Amusingly, the captain had not covered his tracks very well – the substituted player had taken a catch but had not batted, and this was reflected in the scorebook!

The Oval, Monday, 19th August, 2013

My umpiring career has not undertaken a sudden rapid rise – this was a seminar with the Ashes umpires which was open to all current ACO members. It was an evening that would have been enjoyed by any cricketing enthusiast, but for a recreational umpire like myself it was fascinating to hear the perspectives and opinions of professional counterparts.

Tony Hill confirmed what I had long suspected. When there is no DRS (as in his previous appointment, which was in Zimbabwe), he does what any recreational umpire should do and gives the benefit of doubt to the batsman; when there is DRS, that goes out of the window and it becomes a percentage game. He knows that every decision he makes when the DRS is in use is going to be played back and analysed, regardless of whether or not it is appealed, so if he is 60/40 that a batsman is out, then his finger goes up.

Aleem Dar gave what was, for me, the most pertinent and interesting bit of advice. I have struggled with the (rapid) transfer of vision from the bowler's feet to the batsman, and the related problem of keeping my head still and only moving my eyes. Dar's advice was 'to not get hung up' on the no ball, and to get into the rhythm of transferring your focus quickly to the batsman. His rationale was that if you concentrate too hard on the no ball then you will inevitably lose focus on the batsman, and the latter is more important than the former. In effect, he was saying that something has to give, and rather miss a no ball than something at the business end. Of course, he was not saying ignore the no ball – you can still call the obvious ones and get a feel for how close to overstepping the bowler is getting and anticipate. I suspect that before too long, in international cricket, no balls (and run outs) will be called automatically by the line technology currently being used in tennis and football and that the umpires will have no say in the matter.

Farnham Royal C.C., Tuesday, 20th August, 2013

ECB Over 60 (45/45). Norfolk 177-6 (45.0), Buckinghamshire 178-1 (34.3). Buckinghamshire won by 9 wickets.

The ground at Farnham Royal is now completely surrounded by trees and houses but there is an interesting old aerial photograph in the clubhouse that shows it completely surrounded by fields. It is a nice ground and the clubhouse always has a good atmosphere. As a club Farnham have done very well to reach the dizzy heights of the HCPCL, but I hear that not many of their 1st XI players live locally and this may become an issue for them at some point. Their 2nd XI plays in Level 5 of the TVCL, so that is a gap between them of six levels and I cannot imagine that they have much movement of players between 1st and 2nd XIs.

It was a very hot day, and the match was even more leisurely than the one I umpired at Amersham last month. Norfolk never got going properly with the bat and Buckinghamshire chased down their total easily. The main item of umpiring interest was the left-arm opening bowler for Buckinghamshire at my end. He was bowling late inswingers and had several good LBW shouts. The problem with these types of decision is trying to predict the line of the ball between the interception and the stumps. I gave him one and turned down three or four. It would have been fascinating to see these deliveries played back on the DRS.

The Oval, Thursday, 22nd August, 2013

I had a frustrating day as a spectator at the Ashes Test Match at The Oval today, watching the rain fall all morning and well into the early afternoon before play finally started. After Australia had declared, Mitchell Starc, the Australian opening bowler, came out and bowled a dozen practice deliveries during the innings break. He was technically on the square, which at The Oval stretches across almost the entire outfield, and was thus in breach of the practice on the field laws, which preclude practice on the square during the match.[43] However, I presume that there is an ICC regulation to cater for professional grounds with huge squares – he was a very long way away from the wicket!

Hayes C.C., Saturday, 24th August, 2013

TVCL Division 3A. Hayes v. Purley-on-Thames. Match cancelled.

Today was one of those frustrating days that are part and parcel of one's involvement in the game of the cricket. I live in Marlow, and my match today was twenty odd miles to the east in Hayes. The weather forecast was awful. When I woke up this morning it was already raining and I felt that the prospects for play were bleak. The *TMS* commentators at the Ashes Test at The Oval, a further twenty miles east, were saying that there was no chance of any play today. The BBC weather forecast was of the same view – rain all day in the London area. So I was hoping to get a call from Hayes this morning saying that the match was off and to thus avoid a wasted journey. The call did not come. I was not especially surprised. I knew that Hayes were top of the league with two teams breathing down their necks, and understood that they would be desperate to play if at all possible. So, at the last minute, I called Hayes, introduced myself as today's umpire and asked if the match was still on? The young lady who answered the phone was obviously not versed in the finer points of the Laws of Cricket.

"Isn't that your decision?" she said.

---

[43] Law 17.1, 'Practice on the field'.

"I live in Marlow, twenty miles away. It's the decision of the home club until I arrive at the ground."

"Oh."

"I'm trying to avoid a wasted journey. Please could you ask the groundsman or captain to come to the phone?"

The groundsman and captain turned out to be one and the same person. The match was still on. I set off in rain, and it rained all the way there. To be fair, once I had arrived at the ground it did stop for about twenty minutes, but then it started again. After another hour or so the two captains had a private chat in a marquee by the side of the clubhouse and agreed to call the match off. I stayed for a quick chat. Then I set off for home and got stuck in a traffic jam on the Uxbridge Road. I eventually got home about four hours after setting off from Marlow in the morning. It was still raining. It was not the best day of my cricketing life. However, I must say that I am not cross with Hayes. They wanted to play, and did everything they could to get the game on, and I cannot knock them for that. And the Purley players had a considerably longer wasted journey than me!

The way that the match was called off replicated what had happened earlier in the season at Sonning, with the captains taking the initiative.[44] My colleague and I were doing our calculations, working out the latest time that play could start according to the TVCL match rules and discussing conditions. We were confident that, if it stopped raining, the pitch would be playable because it was very well covered, but thought that the bowlers' run-ups and the adjoining pitches were unlikely to be fit for play. There was still another 30-45

---

[44] See entry for Sonning C.C., Saturday, 15th June, 2013.

minutes to go before the cut-off time would be reached, and I was expecting that we would have to sit it out. But then the captains walked over and said that they had shaken hands and agreed to abandon. As at Sonning, my colleague and I went with the flow. This time, unlike at Sonning, I did not think that the captains' decision to throw in the towel early was contentious.

Hayes have spent a lot of money on a new practice facility at the top end of the ground, and it is now apparently completed. If it had not been such a miserable day then I would have walked over and had a look. The umpires' changing room has, however, not got any bigger since my last visit!

Sunday, 25th August, 2013

I felt sorry for the umpires at the conclusion of the final Ashes Test Match at The Oval today when they were booed off by (a minority of) the crowd. I was driving home from a social event as England's innings began, having been set a target of 227 runs to win the match from a nominal 44 overs. I normally defer to the expertise of the *TMS* commentators and expert analysts, but today I could not believe that nobody seemed to understand that time and not overs was going to be the key factor. The match was going to finish at the same time as play had stopped (for bad light) on the previous days of the match, not when the specified number of overs had been bowled. The umpires interpreted the ICC match rules correctly, and then got booed off. Poor them!

However, I cannot defend Aleem Dar for not having his light meter on the field when matters came to a head. I thought that I had had a bad day when I forgot my kit at British Airways!

Bagshot C.C., Saturday, 31st August, 2013

TVCL Division 2B. Boyne Hill 129 (33.4), Bagshot 134-6 (28.0). Bagshot won by 4 wickets.

Bagshot's young opening bowler took a 'nine for' today at my end (including the first seven, I think) and deserved it, bowling fast and straight. He was a rather studious looking chap and removed his spectacles at the start of each over. He reminded me of Paul Allot, the Lancashire and England bowler of the early 1980s.

His performance also reminded me, after a fashion, of a friend of mine who likewise took nine wickets, for Chalfont St. Peter II *against* Bagshot II in 1999. My friend did not bowl fast and straight, he just tossed them up and the Bagshot batsmen committed *hara-kiri*, most of them caught between long-off and deep cow. But it says nine for in the book just the same! In fact, this incident was a classic example of how statistics do not always tell the full story. Another friend of mine bowled a superlative spell of accurate medium pace at the other end, and it was this that created the (scoreboard) pressure on the Bagshot batsmen and led to their poor shot selections at the other end.

When a wicket fell during the Bagshot innings today I walked to the other end to consult with my colleague. He was busy trying to remake the wicket and was struggling with what appeared to be a stone below one of the stumps. When he had sorted it out he asked me to check that it was straight. Rather than walk all the way back to my end, I just walked half way and then stepped onto the wicket to make the check. At this point one of the Boyne Hill players called out to me, "excuse me, umps, please could you remind yourself to keep off the pitch at all times ..." Cue much laughter at my expense.

Henley C.C., Sunday, 1st September, 2013

Today I had declined a social event to umpire a match, and was not terribly pleased when the latter was called off late in the day, just before I was about to leave. So, at a loose end, I ended up going for a late evening walk by the Thames, and sat down for a while to watch a few overs of a Sunday game at Henley. It is a pretty ground with its old (but now refurbished) colonial-style pavilion, steep wooded slopes on one side and the river with its pubs and restaurants on the other. They have just won the HCPCL again and, along with High Wycombe, are the dominant force in local cricket. This venue is, however, blighted by the Heathrow flight path, and there is not much tranquillity when the aeroplanes are landing at Heathrow from the west – they make their turn into their final approach at Henley. I wonder whether I am obsessed by aeroplane noise? Do other people not notice it? Or do they just blank it out? Today the aeroplanes were taking off to the west (and were thus long out of earshot before getting anywhere near to Henley), so it was an idyllic English rural scene.

While watching, I observed a run out incident from the midwicket boundary. A player umpire upheld an appeal and it did indeed look like the batsman had failed to make his ground. However, the wicketkeeper did not take the ball cleanly and I was not convinced that he had effected a legitimate breaking of the wicket.[45] I would have given the benefit of the doubt to the batsman and said not out if I had been standing. But nobody else seemed to notice.

This incident reminded me of a match at Chartridge, Chesham's second ground, in 2010. On the last ball of the match, Chesham needed three runs to win, Chalfont St. Peter one wicket. The ball was struck out to deep midwicket and the batsmen ran one and turned for a second. However, as the throw came in it looked like there would be a run out and that Chalfont would get their tenth wicket and win the match. However, in his excitement, the Chalfont wicketkeeper dislodged the bails before the ball arrived. Fortunately, the player umpire at square leg spotted this and correctly said not out, so match drawn with scores level.

I think that (close) run outs are the hardest decisions for an umpire to get right: they look easy when they are slowed down on television replays but, in real time, they are anything but – not least because the umpire has to check the legitimate breaking of the wicket at the *same time* as he is trying to judge whether or not the batsman has made his ground. I open my stance so that I can keep one eye on the ball as it is coming in, because otherwise everything happens in a flash and it is harder to make a good call.

---

[45] Law 28.1, 'Wicket put down'.

Finchampstead C.C., Saturday, 7th September, 2013

TVCL Division 2A. Finchampstead II 259-4 (52.0), Tring Park II 201–6 (48.0). Match drawn.

It is always a pleasure to get an appointment at Finchampstead: one of my favourite grounds, a great tea and a good social atmosphere afterwards. But today's match was a tad anti-climactic; neither team had anything to play for, and the Finch players seemed more interested in how their 1st XI was faring in the Division 1 decider at Amersham. News eventually filtered through that they had missed out on the league title by the narrowest of margins.

The bright spot of the day was the tea, which was superb: a wide choice of sandwiches, fresh strawberries and pineapple, and an unbelievable selection of homemade cakes. The tea at Finch is always superb, but apparently on the last day of the season the tea ladies compete in their own local version of *Bake Off*. The players and officials are the beneficiaries of this parochial rivalry, although perhaps not the opening bowlers and batsmen in the second innings?

I think I made a mistake on a caught behind today. The batsman flicked at a ball of half-volley length on leg stump. There were two noises and the second was definitely ball on pad. The key question was whether the first one was bat on pad or bat on ball. I was not sure at the time and said not out. Thinking about it later, as I am wont to do, I think that the bat was in front of the pad, so it was probably bat on ball. Ho hum.

There was a fancy dress party after the match and I felt somewhat underdressed. In view of this, I thought that I would just have a quick pint and then get off, but the US Open tennis semi-final was being shown on the big screen so I stayed and watched Rafael Nadal crush Richard Gasquet. And the American Werewolf in London, aka the Finch captain, bought me another one for the road.

Beaconsfield C.C., Saturday, 14th September, 2013

BCB Challenge Cup Final (45/45). Cublington 126 (36.5), Chalfont St. Giles 127-0 (24.2). Chalfont St. Giles won by 10 wickets.

The two senior Buckinghamshire Cup Finals were played at Beaconsfield today. High Wycombe defeated Burnham in the primary competition on the main ground; I officiated in what is known as the Challenge Cup Final on the second ground. The latter has an excellent square and outfield, but the facilities by modern standards are primitive. There is what the French would call a *pissoir* behind the changing rooms, and if that does not serve purpose then a long walk to the main clubhouse is required.

On a good day the Beaconsfield groundsman is convivial and chatty. Today he had two damp wickets to get playable, and the changing rooms on the second ground had been vandalised overnight. In short, it was not a good day, and convivial and chatty he was not. He was driving around on his tractor like a man possessed, and woe betide anyone who got in his way. But he got two games on in miserable wet conditions, so I doff my cap to him. One might guess from the scorecard that the pitch was damp at the beginning and then dried out, making batting easier, but this was not the case – it played well throughout.

I did hear one or two of the Cublington players having a grumble but I think that was just cricketers being cricketers. I have noticed over the years that players and groundsmen each tend to blame the other for their own shortcomings.

Fast bowler: "There's no bounce or carry ..."
Spinner: "There's nothing in it for me ..."
Batsman: "The ball's not coming on ..."
Groundsman: "He'd have been okay if he was on the front foot ..."

I thought that rain delays would come into play today because the forecast was not good. However, as it turned out, the only time lost was at the start of the match. D/L is not, at present, widely used in recreational win/lose games, because a) there is not yet a widely available app (as far as I am aware) to perform the complex calculations and b) scoreboards at club grounds are not set up to display it. However, I think it is only a matter of time. Each club competition has rules and regulations to cater for rain delays but they usually favour the team batting second. In a 50 overs per side match, if the team batting first is, say, 100–2 after 30 overs, then they are probably well-placed to post a good total; however, if it then rains and when the match resumes it has become, say, 40 overs per side, then they are not. Today, despite the poor weather forecast, the Cublington skipper chose to bat first when he won the toss. This surprised me, but maybe his team do not chase well? Unfortunately, they did not post a target very well today either!

There was an interesting incident today, which was similar to one I was involved in at Wooburn Narkovians earlier in the season. The bowler at my end delivered a short-pitched ball that may have bounced above shoulder height, which according to the competition rules is a no ball. I was not sure whether or not to call it, but just as I looked across to my colleague for a second opinion he called no ball. He should not have done this as it was my call, and he later apologised. However, I think I must take some of the blame here because I do not think I was decisive enough.

I had a boundary assessment today by the Buckinghamshire ACO Education Officer. He was broadly positive about my performance, which was pleasing. He did however give me some very useful tips. Firstly, he suggested that I should stand the same difference from the stumps at square leg as one does at the striker's end, so roughly 24 yards. Secondly, we discussed positioning when one is at the striker's end and there is a run out possibility. He advocated going to same side as the ball if it goes outside the V (imaginary lines from the batsman to mid on and mid off respectively) but to the opposite side if the ball is inside the V; this seemed sensible to me. Thirdly, he recommended walking backwards to square leg, which means that you can continue to observe the pitch while moving into position at square leg. Finally, he suggested that I should move into position more quickly. This advice was the exact opposite to what one of his Berkshire counterparts told me earlier in the season – he said that I was moving too quickly into position and that a slower, more deliberate movement would help me to keep focus on the fielders and the ball. I will ponder both pieces of advice and decide which suits me best.

There is a slightly amusing disharmony between the Buckinghamshire and Berkshire ACOs. They behave like divorced parents trying to put on a brave face for the kids: publicly polite and reasonable, privately sniping at the other and each adamant that their own procedures and ways are the best. Buckinghamshire think umpires should keep the score, Berkshire do not; Berkshire champion training courses and qualifications, Buckinghamshire respect grandfather rights; Berkshire have their own county league and seem to be somewhat disengaged with the TVCL, Buckinghamshire are active in TVCL committee work.

Postscript to the 2013 season

I must say that the 2013 cricket season was a memorable one for me – I umpired 43 matches and watched countless others. Being out of work and living off my savings was not really what I had planned for my fiftieth year, but being out in the fresh air in a long, hot summer was preferable to being stuck behind a desk in a stuffy office, diminishing savings or not!

The 2014 season

I have been allocated six TVCL Division 1 matches this season, which is good for my personal development as an umpire. Apart from anything else, it means that my ACO grade should move up from C3 to C2 at the end of the season. An umpire's ACO grade reflects the highest standard of cricket to which (s)he was appointed on a minimum of six occasions in the preceding season. I have also picked up some additional social appointments from a new source, so alongside a few Buckinghamshire junior and senior fixtures I should see a wide spectrum of cricket this summer.

MCC has introduced some new laws for the 2014 season. There is a general view that a good opportunity to bring the laws for the professional and amateur games closer together has been missed. Most disappointingly, there will not be a new edition of *Tom Smith* to reflect the changes. *Tom Smith* is 'the cricket umpire's bible' – the definitive guide to the interpretation and application of the Laws of Cricket, first published in 1980 and revised and updated many times since, most recently in 2011. I carry it around with me at all times; it is invaluable.

Ilkley C.C. and Olicanian C.C., Saturday, 19th April, 2014

This weekend I am in Ilkley, Yorkshire, for the Easter holiday. The A&WCL season started today – three weeks before the TVCL begins down south. Today I sat and watched the game at Ilkley for a while. Another spectator was friendly. "How do?" he said. Then one of the fielders came within speaking distance. "Ayup, Fred", he said, to my new friend. I am definitely in Yorkshire – this is not how one is greeted in the Home Counties!

The A&WCL is similar in standard to the TVCL but the cricket up here is very different to down south. Firstly, it is village based. There are no 3rd or 4th XIs but every village has a club. Driving north out of Leeds on the A65 one passes Horsforth, then Rawdon, Guiseley, Green Lanes, Menston, Burley and Ben Rhydding, before reaching Ilkley – and each has its own A&WCL club. In the TVCL, big clubs dominate – they field four or even five XIs each Saturday and their lower XIs play against and beat many other clubs' 1st XIs. In the A&WCL, the clubs are of more evenly matched strength, there is no promotion to an ECB Premier League and 2nd XIs play in their own separate competition.

Secondly, my impression is that the cricket up north is tougher. Not necessarily better, just harder, more attritional and less Corinthian. I remember stopping to watch the end of a match up here a few years ago, with the batting team 150–5 chasing 200 to win with ten overs to go. Well, this should be a good finish, I thought. Not a bit of it. They dobbed out for a draw.

Ilkley has two cricket clubs, Ilkley and Olicanian, both in attractive settings close to the Wharfe and underneath the moor, which dominates the town. It was quite useful today to just sit and watch for an hour or two, firstly at Ilkley and then at Olicanian. Batsmen can use pre-season nets to get their eye in, and bowlers can likewise find their rhythm before the first match. However, there are no such opportunities for umpires (although I have heard extreme examples of umpires attending indoor net sessions and standing at the bowler's end!), so it was helpful to sit and watch the umpires today and re-attune myself in preparation for my first matches of the season next week. I have also been revising my knowledge of the laws by re-reading (bits of) *Tom Smith* and going through my notes.

There was one incident of umpiring interest today. A bowler lost his run-up and overstepped the popping crease. The umpire duly called no ball but the bowler did not release the ball. So he (the umpire) then had to revoke his signal.[46] He was completely blameless – an umpire cannot wait to see if the ball has been released before opening his vocal chords! – and acted correctly, but nonetheless looked rather foolish. This is one of the curiosities of the Laws of Cricket, and as an umpire one has to take it on the chin. I did once, however, see a disgruntled bowler, angry that an LBW appeal had been turned down, do this on purpose in a rather pathetic attempt to humiliate the umpire!

Burnham C.C., Saturday, 26th April, 2014

BCB Senior Cup Group C (45/45). Burnham v. Chalfont St. Peter. Match cancelled.

Today was going to be a rare opportunity for me to stand in a match for my own club, because panel umpires are not appointed to the round robin matches of the Buckinghamshire Cup. However, it was too wet and we were unable to get the match started. Aside from the fitness of the

---

[46] Law 24.9, 'Revoking a call of no ball'.

ground for play, at this stage of the season one has to respect the wider picture for the home club and the groundsman; there is no point risking damage to the square and putting one or more strips out of use for the whole season just for the sake of playing one early season match!

Gerrards Cross C.C., Saturday, 3rd May, 2014

BCB Senior Cup Group C (45/45). Gerrards Cross 290–7 (45.0), Chalfont St. Peter 122 (34.0). Gerrards Cross won by 168 runs.

It was great to get a game in today after last week's washout. The match itself was one-sided – Gerrards Cross play five divisions above Chalfont St. Peter, and they were far too strong today. Win/lose matches are rather dull when the team batting first gets a lot of runs and then knocks over a few early wickets. The Chalfont innings went on for 34 overs but there was never the remotest chance that they were going to chase down 290.

I made one significant mistake today. Late in the evening I was standing at square leg looking directly into the sun and there was an appeal for a stumping. The batsman made no attempt to move his back foot and the wicketkeeper appealed with confidence, clearly of the view that he (the batsman) did not have any part of his foot behind the popping crease. In all probability the batsman was out, but I could not see clearly so I said not out. In my defence, the creases had not been re-marked during the tea interval and it was difficult to see exactly where the popping crease was. However, I should have anticipated this problem and gone to stand on the off side instead!

The tea today comprised a baked potato with a choice of tuna, cheese or baked beans. A hot meal is not what I want in the middle of a cricket match. After the match, fine. During it, no thank you very much.

I was standing today with my colleague who competes on affirmative decisions. I won easily this time, 3–0, an LBW, a caught behind and a stumping, so the first round was on him!

Edmonton C.C., Sunday, 4th May, 2014

Friendly (45/45). Guy's, King's and St Thomas' 50 (19.5), University College Medics 51-2 (11.3). University College Medics won by 8 wickets.

This was the first of my new social appointments, University College Medics against Guy's, King's and St Thomas' (GKT) – doctors against doctors and pharmacists, was how one player described it to me – and it was all done and dusted in two and a half hours. The University College opening bowler had a memorable day, taking 10-8 (yes, ten wickets for eight runs!) from 9.5 overs at my end, including two hat-tricks! The GKT batting was poor, but I must say that it was also very good bowling!

GKT had a weak team and the captain knew it before the toss. If a captain goes into a league match with a weakened team and expecting to be beaten then his main priority will normally be to accrue as many bonus points as possible.

However, in a friendly, he would traditionally be expected to 'make a game of it' (i.e. prolong the day) by inviting the opposition to bat. (When I went on a tour of Kennington Oval, Barbados, a few years ago, the guide's opening gambit was to envisage an imaginary cricket match, Barbados against All-Comers. The Barbados XI would be Greenidge, Haynes, the 'Three Ws', Sobers, Marshall, Garner and Hall. "That's nine", he said, "and it's probably enough, but we'll drag a number seven and an offie off the streets to make up the numbers!" "Okay," the chap next to me said, "you can have a bat ...") Sadly, however, it would appear that this tradition of making a game of it is disappearing, maybe because younger players play so little non-competitive cricket these days? The GKT captain won the toss and batted, the three batsmen capable of making a score all failed, and that was that. Nobody even suggested a beer match. Later, when half the players had left, I heard one or two of those still there saying that they could have played another match. "Well, that ship's sailed", I thought to myself.

Today I knew absolutely nobody. I had never been to Edmonton before, and did not know any of the players or my colleague. I think this is the first time that I have been in this position as an umpire. This did not *per se* detract from my enjoyment of the day, but it did strike me as I was driving home that I might quite possibly never meet any of today's protagonists again, so reminiscing about today's game in the years to come will be unlikely.

Sunbury C.C., Wednesday, 7th May, 2014

ECB Over 60 (45/45 reduced to 40/40). Buckinghamshire II 168-6 (40.0), Surrey II 169-0 (30.2). Surrey II won by 10 wickets.

I have once or twice stopped off and watched a few overs at the Sunbury ground but had never played or umpired here before today. It is magnificent, with two huge squares (you could easily play two junior matches at a time on each square), an immaculate flat outfield and a secluded location enclosed by mature trees and houses. The club was founded in 1937, so it's a bit of a whippersnapper compared to East Molesey[47] a couple of miles away on the other side of the river, but it is nonetheless one of the top clubs in the Surrey Championship.

Some threatening rain clouds nearly denied me the chance to umpire here, but fortunately after a delayed start we got a whole game in. In fact, there turned out to be an even greater threat to our day than the weather: a few miles away a notorious armed criminal on the run from the police, known as the 'Skull Cracker' in the tabloid press, had just robbed a local post office and then gone on the run. When I saw the groundsman coming out on to the field to speak to me, I thought that he was upset about us continuing to play on his square during light drizzle, but it was actually to warn us that the Skull Cracker was on the loose and not be approached.

The match itself was fairly uneventful. Buckinghamshire did not get enough runs and Surrey knocked them off easily. My colleague gave what can only be described as a very brave LBW decision. The bowler made the quietest and most polite

---

[47] See entry for East Molesey C.C., Friday, 14th May, 2014.

of appeals, which was not supported by any of his teammates. My colleague however thought that it was out and so raised his finger. I could not say whether it was a good decision or not from square leg, but it was certainly brave!

I made a mistake today. I was at the bowler's end and, in his delivery stride, the bowler's hand flicked the stumps and removed one of the bails. I did notice it but did not react quickly enough, and only called no ball after the ball became dead and when I had collected my thoughts. This is a shortcoming in my umpiring, which I must address. I sometimes hesitate on wides and then it is too late to call them. I must act more quickly and decisively.

Beaconsfield C.C., Saturday, 10th May, 2014

TVCL Division 1. Henley II 31-1 (9.4). Match abandoned.

When to apply Law 43? It was wet overnight and we did well to start on time. We played for about 40 minutes and then it rained. It stopped raining, started again, then stopped again. We took an early tea. It rained again during tea, then the sun came out. By 4.15pm my colleague and I had a decision to make. The pitch was covered and fine. The square was a bit squelchy but playable. However, the bowlers' run-ups had not been re-covered during one of the (very heavy and rather sudden) downpours and were muddy and slippery. The umpires are the sole judges of the fitness of conditions for play[48] and we thought that they were unsuitable. However, it was a very marginal call, and we were aware that both captains wanted to play. So, we decided to invoke Law

---

[48] Law 7.2, 'Fitness of the pitch for play'.

43 and allow play to start – provided that both captains still wanted to do so. However, by the time we consulted them, one had changed his mind (a couple of his senior bowlers had not been so keen to play), so we called the match off. I fear that, unfortunately, this made us look indecisive and weak. The easy option would have been to call the match off without consultation, but I think we did the right thing. If both captains had wanted to play then to do so would have been the right decision!

The Beaconsfield groundsman has many fine qualities, but enthusiasm to get a game on in wet conditions is not one of them. He was constantly in our ear, telling us that he thought it was dangerous underfoot and that there were more dark clouds rolling in. My colleague and I told him that we would give him a signal from the square if the match was off. "Yes, give me the thumbs up", he said. "No", I replied, "I'll give you the thumbs *down*." He accepted my rebuke in good spirit with a smile, but there was no doubt which outcome he was hoping for.

The sacking of Kevin Pietersen during the winter came up in the bar after the match. Which is more important, individual skill or team morale? It is a more complicated debate in cricket than, say, football or rugby, because cricket is, essentially, a team game comprising a series of individual contests. The debate was getting quite interesting. Then one player interjected: "we don't want him any more because he's a c***!" Cue much laughter and end of debate.

Wellington College, Sunday, 11th May, 2014

Friendly (40/40). Sherborne Pilgrims 183-5 (40.0), Old Wellingtonians 186-9 (38.2). Old Wellingtonians won by 1 wicket.

I am a middle-class grammar school boy. I am more comfortable in this refined public (aka fee-paying) school environment than I am in a baying crowd at a football match, but I still felt a little bit like a fish out of water today. A bit like Ronnie Barker in the 'I look up to him' sketch!

The Wellington College ground is absolutely stunning. Mature trees, elegant buildings, gardens and lakes. The cricket facilities are superb, too: an immaculate (although sloping and slightly open) outfield, a huge well-maintained square, and magnificent practice facilities. Funnily enough, though, given that they are a relatively inexpensive item of cricketing hardware, they only had one sightscreen at each end, and quite a lot of time was wasted moving them back and forth. I could have happily spent more time looking round the elegant Victorian pavilion, which was full of fascinating old photographs and cricketing memorabilia. The standard of play was mixed, some good, some less so, but it was a good match with a tight finish.

Today I was standing with my 'unconventional' colleague. So handing over the pitch, maintaining eye contact, working as a team etc. was all out. I did my end, he did his. And when we did confer he kept calling me Richard. I corrected him a couple of times, but then gave up. "Great to stand with you again, Richard", he said, as we parted. It was like Trigger and Rodney in *Only Fools and Horses*. He said he was doing a match at Ascott Park next week. So am I. Ho hum!

Hampton Wick Royal C.C., Wednesday, 14th May, 2014

The Hampton Wick Royal ground is located in the eastern corner of Bushy Park, i.e. on the Kingston side. Today I was working in Hampton and it was a pleasant early summer evening, so after I left the office I walked across the park, had a sandwich and a pint, watched a few overs of a 20 overs per side evening match and then walked back to the Hampton side where my car was parked.

The batting fundamentals of this type of cricket – T20 in the modern parlance – are actually the same as any other form of the game. In other words, rotate the strike, keep the scoreboard ticking over and lay a platform. This evening, the team batting first had 80 off 10 overs – but were six down, mostly as far as I witnessed either caught on the boundary, bowled having an almighty heave or run out. I did not stay to the end, but I bet that they ended up 'under par'.

TVCL Level 2 was the highest standard of cricket that I played, and I only managed one fifty at this level. It was against Hampton Wick Royal in 1993. I wonder whether they know how unlucky they were?

East Molesey C.C., Friday, 16th May, 2014

Today turned out to be my last day working in Hampton, so I decided to make a post-work visit to East Molesey while I still had a good opportunity to do so. I knew that it was one of the oldest cricket clubs in England, and there is a board near the entrance that explains that cricket was first played at

Moulsey Hurst, some 500 metres from the site of the present ground, on Saturday, 7th June, 1735. The first recorded LBW decision was given there (on the old ground), in 1795, after the laws had been modified to remove batsman intent (previously, a batsman could only be given out LBW if he *deliberately* intercepted the ball with his leg!) I wonder what the Georgians would have made of Jimmy Adams hiding his bat behind his front pad?

The present ground dates to 1871 and is attractively enclosed by a picket fence and some Poplar trees. Today there was a junior match in progress so I sat down briefly and watched a few overs.

High Wycombe C.C., Saturday, 17th May, 2014

TVCL Division 1. Eversley 244 (52.0), High Wycombe II 239-9 (48.0). Match drawn.

This was a really good match, intense, competitive and interesting to the last. High Wycombe II were 59–5 at one point but nearly pulled off an unlikely victory.

However, the real drama came after the match. On the last ball High Wycombe had two wickets in hand and needed six runs to bring the scores level, so barring a no ball the match was effectively over, because neither side could win. As it transpired, the batsman went for a big hit and was caught at deep mid-wicket, earning Eversley an extra bonus point. Everyone shook hands and walked off. My colleague and I checked that everything was okay with the scorers, had a shower and then went into the bar for a pint. At this point we realised that the scorers were still in their hut and that something was wrong. They were not happy with the final score, and eventually settled on 239 rather than 238. This did not matter now – but it would have done if the last ball had gone for six, as it very nearly did! I no longer keep score but my colleague did and he had 238. If that last ball had gone for six then I think that my colleague and I, as the final arbiters of the correctness of the score and the result, would have had to go through the scorebooks with a fine toothcomb.[49]

Interestingly, today, I, a Buckinghamshire umpire who does *not* score, was standing with a Berkshire colleague who *does*. Our bickering parents (our respective ACOs!) would have been at sixes and sevens! Although I am now settled in my mind that an umpire should not try to keep the score, today's events show that there is a strong argument for the alternative point of view.[50]

I must also give myself a black mark today, because I lost concentration badly towards the end of the match. I was hot and tired, but that cannot be used as an excuse. The ball had run away to fine leg, the batsman had run two comfortably but had then verbally declined a third – and so I assumed that the ball was dead and looked away. The next thing I knew the wicketkeeper had whipped off the bails and was appealing for a run out. I had to apologise and admit that I had not been paying attention. I had not actually seen what had happened. If the batsman had watched the ball into the wicketkeeper's gloves and waited for a moment or two, and

---

[49] Laws 3.15, 'Correctness of score'; 4.2, 'Correctness of score'; and 21.8, 'Correctness of result'.
[50] See entry for High Wycombe C.C., Saturday, 20th July, 2013.

only then moved out of his ground, then the ball probably was dead, but if he had moved out before the ball had become finally settled in the wicketkeeper's gloves then it was not, and he could have been run out.[51] The wicketkeeper was cross with me (reasonably) and niggled away at me for the rest of the match (unreasonably).

Ascott Park, Sunday, 18th May, 2014

Friendly. Stragglers of Asia 228-7 dec. (47.3), Grannies 230-3 (30.5). Grannies won by 7 wickets.

This was a 'Jeeves and Wooster' match at the magnificent Ascott Park ground, involving two wandering clubs, the Stragglers of Asia and the Grannies. Tea, coffee and biscuits on arrival, 11.30am start, the morning session, a cold buffet for lunch, the afternoon session including a declaration, a conventional cricket tea of sandwiches and cakes, then the evening session with 20 overs from 5.30pm. The Ascott Park ground is stunning, with an elegant pavilion, magnificent mature trees all around and a perfectly flat outfield and square; the cricket was friendly and gentle, competitive but not intense, occasionally of good standard but mostly not; and the spreads were superb – I skipped my evening meal when I got home, I just wasn't hungry! It was a world away from the intensity of my TVCL match at High Wycombe yesterday – but just as enjoyable in a completely different way.

It was really nice to be involved in a time match with a declaration and twenty overs in the last hour. This is the

---

[51] Law 23.2, 'Ball finally settled'.

type of cricket I grew up with as a boy and I like it; there is more to it than win/lose contests.

Some of the not so good cricket was memorable. One batsman hit a full toss straight to cover point. "Good cricket", said one of the fielders. Well, it was a good catch. Another played inside his first ball and then heard the dreaded death rattle (he was not so much on the wrong line as the wrong platform!) A new bowler at my end then purveyed two overs of slow left arm 'buffet'[52]. The old pro who faced (most of) the first over of slow long hops resisted gorging himself in the hope of a second helping, which he (or at least his team) got. His younger colleague faced the next over and succumbed to gluttony, so the buffet was withdrawn.

As expected, I was standing today with my unconventional colleague. I have now got used to him and enjoyed his company today. He is eighty years old and a former Minor Counties umpire, and as sharp as a needle both on and off the field.

The Stragglers of Asia are a wandering club originally set up by a group of expats and army officers living in India, and you used to have to have lived for two years 'east of Suez' to be eligible to play. Cricket clubs cannot afford to be so choosy these days so they have reduced the qualification to anyone committed to playing cricket in the Corinthian spirit. Amen to that.

---

[52] This is cricketing parlance for bowling which allows the batsman to 'help himself'.

Amersham Hill C.C., Wednesday, 21st May, 2014

ECB Over 50 (45/45). Buckinghamshire 253-8 (45.0), Essex 254-9 (44.3). Essex won by 1 wicket.

Who would be an umpire? There are five balls to go. The batting team needs two runs, the fielding team one wicket. The number eleven batsman has had a few swishes, connected with a couple, missed a couple. He has another hoick across the line and misses. There is a huge LBW appeal. And it is down to me to call it. The match has been nip and tuck for six hours but now it is all down to me. And it is a fiendishly difficult call. It could be clipping leg stump or it could be missing. Benefit of doubt to the batsman. Not out. The batting team win. The fielding team are disappointed.

Mostly, professional umpires are under far more pressure and scrutiny than their recreational colleagues, but my call today was an exception to that rule. If the teams had been able to refer my decision to the DRS then the pressure would have been off me. Of course, I would have liked to see my decision proved correct, but if it was not then at least the 'correct' decision would have been reached. Anyway, it was a cracking game of cricket.

Amersham Hill is a curate's egg of a cricket ground. It has an attractive location surrounded by mature trees and houses, and a good square, but the straight boundaries are too short, especially with modern bats, and it is not uncommon here for a leading edge to go for six. They have an attractive albeit small new clubhouse, but there are no changing rooms for umpires. The noise from the trains running along one side of the ground becomes somewhat tiresome, although for me much less so than cars or aeroplanes, and parking is difficult. But for all that it is a nice club and not one that I was at all disappointed to see on my list of appointments.

My colleague today was telling me stories from the many overseas cricket tours he has been on to non-cricketing countries, mostly on the European mainland. (He should be writing this diary!) The most amusing one was about a match at a football ground in Bulgaria. The groundsman had apparently followed his unfamiliar instructions carefully and to the letter – and had produced a reasonable turf wicket. The only problem was that he had sited it on the side of the pitch as if it was a baseball match!

Cookham Dean C.C., Saturday, 24th May, 2014

TVCL Division 2A. Cookham Dean 200-7 (52.0), Finchampstead II 160-9 (48.0). Match drawn.

Most matches in the TVCL today were rained off but mine at Cookham Dean survived. Indeed, Cookham seemed to be caught in its own little weather micro system, with menacing dark clouds swirling around the ground but miraculously missing it all day! It was cold and damp, and the Heathrow flight path was changed to annoy us all (or maybe just me?) at about 6.00pm, but it was nonetheless a good match with an exciting finish.

That said, the most memorable incident of the day had nothing to do with cricket. Late in the day, a red kite swooped in dramatically behind the fielder at mid-off to capture some prey, and it was a breathtaking sight! Most people saw it but the fielder himself, who was facing in the opposite direction and only yards away, was completely oblivious.

There was one item of interest today with regard to the laws. My colleague and I should have given one of the Cookham batsmen (and his team) a first and final warning for running on the pitch[53], but neither of us was decisive enough and the moment passed. I have mentioned my lack of assertiveness before – it is my biggest weakness as an umpire and I need to address it!

An impressive new electronic scoreboard housed in a solid brick building, separate to the main clubhouse, has been erected since my last visit here two years ago. There is also a new umpires' changing room in this building which is very comfortable but alas without access to running water or toilets. This does not preclude a post-match shower *per se*, but it does not make it easy.

Hampstead C.C., Sunday, 25th May, 2014

Friendly (40/40). Hampstead 256-6 (40.0), UCS Old Boys 202-9 (40.0). Hampstead won by 54 runs.

This was my first visit to Hampstead. It is one of the top Middlesex clubs and has an attractive setting surrounded by mature trees, tennis courts and elegant residential properties. And, like another cricket ground a couple of miles down the

---

53 Law 42.14, 'Batsman damaging pitch'.

Finchley Road, it slopes from left to right as you look out from the pavilion.

There are some fascinating old photographs, scorecards and averages on display in the clubhouse. It is sometimes hard to relate the modern game to the so-called Golden Age of Cricket (the two decades before the outbreak of World War One). There was an article about the exploits of Andrew Stoddart, a stalwart of the club, which included a description of how he once scored 485 in one day, against Stoics, on 4th August, 1886. What was even more extraordinary than the score was the fact that there were no declarations in club matches in those days, so Hampstead just batted all day and the players then shook hands for a draw! Extraordinary! The Stoics were at least appropriately named! The other one that caught my eye was an article about Fred Spofforth, 'The Demon Bowler'. Apparently, he played some games for Hampstead in 1904, at the age of 51, and took 65 wickets at an average of 5.24 each. Obviously, as Trevor Bailey might have said, "he could bowl".

The match today was not as close as the score suggests. UCS (University College School) Old Boys were not strong enough to compete, which is always a shame in a friendly fixture, and it was only some fine hitting from one of their lower order batsmen, who made 84 in a lost cause, which added some respectability to the scorecard.

My colleague today was inexperienced – I think this was only his second or third game as an umpire. He reminded me of myself when I first started umpiring, both good points and bad. On the plus side, he has played the game, he knows the laws and was composed and on the ball throughout; on the down side he was far too passive. It was interesting for me to observe this following my reproachful comments about myself yesterday, and actually reassured me that I have learnt a lot in the past few years. At one point there was a loud and concerted appeal for LBW at my colleague's end and he just stood there impassively, finally quietly and almost apologetically saying not out. I told him later that I now say not out loud and clear – more Mr Mackay than Mr Barrowclough, to use a *Porridge* analogy – and usually accompany it with a little hand signal indicating too high, missing off, going down etc. It is essential that an umpire is decisive and exudes authority. Even if you cannot umpire, always look as though you can!

Sonning C.C., Saturday, 31st May, 2014

TVCL Division 2B. Stoke Green 141 (50.1), Sonning 102 (43.0). Stoke Green won by 39 runs.

This was a slow, attritional game of cricket and a really tough one to umpire. During Stoke Green's innings there was an extended period when there was a batsman with a runner and, just to complicate matters further, a left/right hand batting combination! Then, during Sonning's innings, two left-arm spinners bowled throughout with close catchers, and there were any number of appeals, LBWs, bat/pad catches, sometimes both! I gave three LBWs today, and had two particularly difficult calls to make. On reflection I think that I got one wrong and one right.

Re the former, the Stoke Green left-arm spinner had a very good well-disguised arm ball, and Sonning's right-hand batsman was thrusting his pad at every delivery in an effort to get outside the line. He was wrapped on the pad and I gave him out. My judgement was that it hit him on the line of off stump and would have hit middle and leg. I think I was probably right on this but, concentrating so hard on these two factors, I think that I forgot about height – and there was probably enough doubt to say not out.

Re the latter, the left-arm spinner pitched a delivery on leg stump, which straightened and then struck the batsman on the pad as he played a rather ungainly slog sweep. My instinct was that he was out: the ball had pitched in line and I had seen it straighten on the line of leg stump. However, with the naked eye it was just too close to call, and I gave the batsman the benefit of the doubt. The bowler was disappointed, and asked me about it at the end of the over. I said to him that if this was a Test Match with DRS then I would have given the batsman out, because I think 70/30 he was. But 70/30 in a match without the DRS is not good enough. He accepted my reasoning with good grace. I am not going to lose any sleep over either of these decisions because you cannot get everything right, and they were both 'judgement calls'; but I do think it is important to be self-critical in order to learn and improve.

My colleague and I also got another important decision right today but I must say that it was more through luck than judgement. A bowler injured the fingernail on the second finger of his bowling hand while trying to take a difficult caught and bowled. He went off for a while and then returned with said finger plastered up. Should he be allowed to bowl again? We decided he should because he was neither seeking nor gaining an advantage. Gratifyingly, a quick check of the laws later confirmed that, 'protection for the hand or fingers may be worn ... with the consent of the umpires.'[54] (That said, this law relates to fielding not bowling; so I may need to seek further clarification on this one.)

Dr. Challoner's Grammar School, Sunday, 1st June, 2014

ECB Under 15 (50/50). Buckinghamshire 181-7 (50.0), Staffordshire 80 (33.3). Buckinghamshire won by 101 runs.

The ECB, one understands, is short of money. So they keep things simple by having one standard set of match rules for all their junior competitions with just a few variations to cover the needs of different age groups. Not. They have separate match rules for everything, and compound this by changing them at the last minute. I downloaded the match rules for today's contest from the ECB website this morning and then spent fifteen minutes reading and digesting them. When I arrived at the ground the coaches told me that the goalposts (if I am allowed to mix my sporting metaphors?) had already moved – and that my match rules (and the ECB website) were out of date. Ye gods!

I do not understand why an Under 15 cricket match has to have powerplays, free hits, fielding restrictions and so forth. The Laws of Cricket have facilitated perfectly good matches for many years, so why change 'what ain't broke?' And, furthermore, these are 14/15-year-old boys. Just let them play

---

[54] Law 41.1, 'Protective equipment'.

cricket! Does it really matter how many fielders are on the leg side, or within circles? I suppose that the counter argument is that they will encounter these sorts of things as they rise up the cricketing ladder so they need experience of them now.

I made a bad mistake today. I called a no ball incorrectly – I thought that the fielding team did not have enough players within the fielding circle – and had to reverse my decision. It was embarrassing – not least because it was my colleague's call at square leg and not mine!

Today's match followed a similar pattern to yesterday's. The captain who won the toss inserted the opposition in the hope of exploiting dampness in the pitch, but it backfired badly as the opposition posted a score and then defended it with ease. Anyway, it was a pleasant day back at my *alma mater* with an especially nice tea. I stood at the pavilion end today and the view from square leg (to the right hander) is pleasant, with an attractive tree line all the way round.

I have noticed a new addition to the cricketing dictionary this year: 'good *set*, Fred', or a variation on this theme of 'come on Fred, complete the *set*!' I presume that it is a tennis metaphor and it seems to mean, interchangeably, either over or spell.

Tuesday, 3rd June, 2014

There was a controversial incident in the ODI between England and Sri Lanka at Edgbaston today when the England batsman, Jos Buttler, was 'mankaded' by the Sri Lankan bowler, Sachithra Senanayake. To mankad (named after the Indian cricketer, Vinoo Mankad) means to run out a batsman who has backed up too far at the non-striker's end. I have heard many former players on the radio this evening criticising Senanayake for his action, and also his captain, Angelo Matthews, for upholding the appeal, but I do not understand their outrage. England were trying to pinch quick singles and Sri Lanka were trying to stop them. Buttler was out of his ground and Senanayake ran him out; Buttler was careless, Senanayake's action was reasonable. Why should a batsman be allowed to seek unfair advantage without risking dismissal?

What really intrigued me about this incident, however, was not so much the morality as the letter of the law. When I saw it on television I immediately thought that the umpire, Michael Gough, had made a mistake, because Senanayake effected the run out *after* entering his delivery stride. The Laws of Cricket state that 'the bowler is permitted, *before* entering his delivery stride, to attempt to run out the non-striker'.[55] However, there is apparently an ICC playing regulation that permits the bowler to effect the run out *after* entering his delivery stride. The differences between ICC playing regulations and the Laws of Cricket cause unhelpful confusion in the recreational game.

Ascott Park, Sunday, 8th June, 2014

Friendly Bedouins 211-7 dec. (59.0), Lord Gnome's XI 212-5 (49.2). Lord Gnome's XI won by 5 wickets.

---

[55] Law 42.15, 'Bowler attempting to run out non-striker before delivery'.

This was another social match between two wandering clubs; similar to the previous one I umpired at Ascott Park three weeks ago. My colleague today was one of those irrepressibly cheerful upper crust military types – think the regimental dinner scene in *Carry On Up the Khyber*. He told me about being stationed with the British Army in Germany and playing cricket out there. "We even got some of the *Jerries* to join in, and they turned out to be quite decent chaps, actually, yes, I'd have to say, good eggs, you really wouldn't have thought ..." Later, at lunch, he mistook one of the players, a Sri Lankan gentleman, immaculately dressed in whites and a blazer, for a waiter. And after the match he told me about umpiring a women's match recently. "You see quite a lot of leg, you know!"

There was some good banter on the field as well. One of the fielding team was a Chelsea fan and he discovered during the lunch interval that my colleague supported Arsenal. When we got out onto the field after lunch, he kept asking him, "Can you count to six, umps?" He was making reference to the Premier League match the previous season between the two teams, which had ended in a 6–0 win for Chelsea. "If you're struggling then you could give each ball a name. The first one would be Eto'o, the second Hazard ...", he continued. "If you come out to bat later on then I wouldn't get hit on the pads", replied my colleague.

We had two difficult incidents to deal with today. The first one involved a run out. I was standing at square leg and the wicketkeeper was covering the stumps (i.e. blocking my view) when a direct hit ran out the batsman by some distance. I thought that the wicketkeeper had dislodged the bails with his pad prior to the ball hitting the stumps and was therefore about to say not out, but one of the fielders was adamant that he (the wicketkeeper) had only knocked off one bail and the ball had then knocked off the other. If this was the case then the wicket would have been fairly put down.[56] My colleague agreed with the fielder so I gave the batsman out. It reminded me of an incident many years ago, when I was still playing, when a fielder, ignorant of the laws, removed a stump (the wicket having previously been put down) with one hand while holding the ball in his other. He learnt the law the hard way!

The second one was a possible obstructing the field incident. The batsman top-edged the ball and it went a long way up into the air directly above the pitch. The bowler and the wicketkeeper both converged on the ball to take the catch but the bowler collided with the non-striking batsman. In the confusion, nobody even put a hand on the ball and it thudded into the ground. The bowler politely appealed for obstructing the field and I said not out, because I did not think that the non-striking batsman's action had been wilful.[57] Gratifyingly, having made a few mistakes last weekend, I think I got both these decisions right.

Chalfont St. Peter C.C., Thursday, 12th June, 2014

BCB Under 14 (20/20). Beaconsfield II 100-8 (20.0), Chalfont St. Peter 64-9 (20.0). Beaconsfield II won by 36 runs.

---

[56] Law 28.2, 'One bail off'.
[57] Law 37.1, 'Out obstructing the field'.

173

The power of television became very apparent to me one Sunday morning at Chalfont St. Peter in 1993. I was helping out with junior practice and, instead of all wanting to run in and bowl as fast as they could, many of the youngsters were trying to bowl leg-breaks off a couple of paces. Three days earlier Shane Warne had bowled 'the ball of the century'.

This evening one of the Under 14s copied Senanayake's action last week and 'mankaded' a batsman. I discarded my umpiring hat in favour of a schoolmasterly one and said that, "we don't want that sort of thing going on in our cricket". The batsman was not actually trying to gain an unfair advantage, he was either not concentrating or blissfully unaware of the laws. From an umpiring perspective, I should have asked the fielding captain if he wanted to uphold the appeal and, if he should have answered in the affirmative, have then given the batsman out, but I am content this evening that I used Law 43 to good effect.

Lord's, Friday, 13th June, 2014

I went to Lord's today for the second day of the Test Match between England and Sri Lanka. There was one controversial umpiring incident. The Sri Lankan batsman, Kaushal Silva, was seemingly caught behind off Liam Plunkett but stood his ground and was then spared by the television replays. Zoomed-in cameras tend to introduce an element of doubt to catches taken low to the ground and so it was this time. This is unsatisfactory, but if the technology cannot prove that the catch has been fairly taken then the batsman must be given not out. I am a technophile, so I think the best remedy would be to improve camera technology.

It was nice to see the two umpires walking out at the start of play unaccompanied by television cameras – nice not just for them but also for the spectators. It contrasts with the opening (and subsequent incoming) batsmen who must walk out to the middle preceded by a cameraman walking backwards two paces in front of them – and pointing his camera into their faces. It is the same when the captains go out to toss before the start of play. It may be great for the television viewer, but there is something special about the isolation of a batsmen as he strides out to the middle, or walks disconsolately back; and, for the paying spectator watching at the ground, the sense of watching this unfold is, to a degree, lost.

High Wycombe C.C., Saturday, 14th June, 2014

TVCL Division 2A. High Wycombe II 184 (46.3), Marlow 186-4 (32.0). Marlow won by 6 wickets.

I wrote the previous entry yesterday evening. Honestly. Today a batsman edged a ball to first slip, where the catch was apparently cleanly taken, but did not walk. I say apparently because I was at square leg and the wicketkeeper was blocking my view. My colleague consulted with me but I was not able to help him; he was not sure that the ball had carried, so he correctly said not out. Cue an almighty kerfuffle and fractious exchanges. I think it is a sad state of affairs when a batsman does not accept the word of a fielder, but that I am afraid is the way that the game is going. Coaches and captains tell batsmen not to walk and to let the umpire make the decision. That would be fine if they also told their charges that all decisions, good or bad, should be accepted unquestioningly and with good grace, but of course they do not do this.

My colleague had a difficult day because one of the bowlers at his end, an experienced and very good cricketer, inexplicably bowled two beamers above waist height. He consulted with me and we agreed that neither was deliberate.[58] My colleague issued a first warning and then a second and final warning, making clear on the latter occasion to both captain and bowler that if it happened again then the bowler would be disqualified from bowling with immediate effect.[59] It is funny how, in some matches, one umpire gets all the difficult calls!

Ascott Park, Sunday, 15th June, 2014

Friendly. Stragglers of Asia 239-6 dec. (46.2), Butterflies 116 (29.4). Stragglers of Asia won by 123 runs.

Most weather forecasters use the terms good and hot interchangeably, as if they are one and the same thing. For me and, I think, a significant minority, they are not. I had a nice day at Lord's on Friday but I roasted. Yesterday at High Wycombe it was hot again. Today, it was overcast with a cool breeze, and it was bliss. Unfortunately, the cricket matched neither the improved weather nor the magnificent setting of Ascott Park. The Butterflies Cricket Club is a famous wandering club made up of the former pupils of Rugby, Charterhouse, Eton, Harrow, Winchester and

---

[58] Law 42.8, 'Deliberate bowling of high full-pitched balls'.
[59] Law 42.7, 'Dangerous and unfair bowling – action by the umpire'.

Westminster; it includes Douglas Jardine, Gubby Allen and Peter May amongst its alumni. Unfortunately, they were under strength today, both numerically and in terms of quality, and the match was rather disappointingly one-sided as a result.

There are two current laws which, given a free hand, I would change. I have already discussed the first one, when overthrows result from a throw hitting the wicket and the ball running away.[60] The second one concerns an aspect of the LBW law, which I do not like.[61] When the batsman is struck on the pad by a full toss, *Tom Smith* states that, even if the umpire thinks that the ball would have pitched before hitting the stumps, (s)he must disregard any possible deviation in the line of the ball due to either spin or the roughness of the ground. In other words, (s)he should only consider 'the path of the ball before it was intercepted'.[62] This is fine re swing bowling, because if the umpire observes, say, late in-swing, which would have taken the ball past leg stump, then he can say not out. However, it is to me problematic with regard to spin bowling. Today, the off-spinner at my end was extracting sharp turn. He over-pitched one, and the batsman missed it and was struck on the full on the toe. Unless it was an arm ball, I think it would have turned past leg stump, and I would therefore have preferred to say not out. However, the current laws preclude me from doing that, so I raised my finger. It was unsatisfactory to two of the parties involved, namely myself and the batsman, but not, of course, to the bowler!

---

[60] See entry for Wormsley, Sunday, 18th September, 2011.
[61] Law 36.1, 'Out LBW'.
[62] *Tom Smith* (2004), p.235.

On a more amusing note, one of the players today was wearing an old, rather scruffy sweater, which was too small to cope with his middle age spread. It turned out that it was a lucky charm and, despite the fact that he looked ridiculous, he could not bring himself not to wear it. Superstitions are as rife in recreational cricket as they apparently are in the professional game. One of my friends always used to sleep with his bat if he made a century – he began this tradition as a teenager and continued it even after he was married! He was worried that if he did not he might never make another one! Another friend of mine once happened to take two wickets while wearing two jockstraps. The following week he wore a pair of boxers over the two jockstraps and took three wickets. So the following week, you guessed it ... but this time it did not work and all he got was a new nickname, "four pants".

Chenies & Latimer C.C., Monday, 16th June, 2014

BCB Under 14 (20/20). Chalfont St. Peter 93-8 (20.0), Chenies & Latimer 78 (19.1). Chalfont St. Peter won by 15 runs.

Chenies is not the best ground to visit if you suffer from hay fever and the pollen count is high. I do and it was, so I soon began to regret taking this match on! It was actually my first visit here for several years. It is a good village club with a nice pavilion, an attractive rural setting and short, inviting square boundaries. One of their stalwarts was a right arm slow bowler. He was not a great spinner of the ball but flighted it nicely with a bit of away drift. He used to float it up just short of driving length outside off-stump. He was a tease, basically. I always really fancied getting after him, but never quite managed it. Essentially, I was not quite good enough. I once hit him for four boundaries in quick succession, all through the offside, two good shots and two streaky ones – and then just when I had him riled I nicked off. Another year one of my colleagues hit him out of the attack with some lovely clean off-driving, on the ground through the covers, high over mid off. It was nice to watch but I really wish I could have done it myself, just once. But no, sadly, that was not to be.

The dramatic conclusion to the Lord's Test Match unfolded while this game was in progress. Reading about it afterwards, there were two major umpiring incidents in the final over bowled by Stuart Broad, which began with Sri Lanka eight wickets down. On the first ball the batsman, Rangana Herath, gloved a ball down the leg side and walked. If he had stood his ground then he would have been given not out because his hand was not holding the bat when it was struck by the ball.[63] (As I have said before, the players, even professional ones, often do not know the laws!) Then, with two balls to go and now only one wicket needed, the last man, Nuwan Pradeep, was given out LBW. It looked plumb, but he appealed the decision, and the DRS identified a slight inside edge, so not out; and Pradeep then successfully negotiated the final ball (by the skin of his teeth). So, a draw – and a great triumph for the DRS!

Kentish Lane Farm, Thursday, 19th June, 2014

---

[63] Law 6.3, 'Hand or glove to count as part of the bat'.

Friendly (15/15 8-ball overs). Gussets 114 (13.7), Arbib 115-6 (14.6). Arbib won by 4 wickets.

I got this appointment along with a few others at the beginning of the season and it immediately stood out. An evening midweek match, a fair way to travel and an odd location – my internet searches for Kentish Lane Farm cricket drew a blank. I was not too sure about it, to be honest, but I knew my colleague and consulted him. He had been before and said, "Oh, you must take it, the hospitality will be wonderful." I was not really sure what he meant by hospitality but it sounded promising.

It transpired that, like John Paul Getty at Wormsley, the owner of the farm had decided to build his own cricket ground on site, and he now stages four or five 'cricket evenings' every summer, with the Gussets taking on other wandering or nomadic XIs. I travelled with my colleague and we gained access by knocking on the front door. Our changing room was a bedroom with en suite facilities – it felt like we were checking into a B&B. We then went out to inspect the ground. It has two strips, so more a rectangle than a square, and three trees inside the playing area, each one creating blind spots for the batsmen, fielders and umpires alike. (The local rule is two runs and dead ball if the ball touches any of them.)

The standard of play was quite high at times – a couple of the players were Cambridge Blues – but it was gentle and social rather than overtly competitive. As an umpire you have to fit in with the match you are standing in. This evening two players were practising on the adjoining pitch before the match started, which is not permitted[64] and three batsmen came to the crease wearing thigh pads outside their flannels, which is illegal.[65] If it had been a TVCL or ECB match then I would have intervened, but it wasn't so I didn't.

There was also an interesting incident when a delivery bounced more than twice before it reached the batsman. I called no ball[66] and the batsman swiped it away uppishly towards the cover boundary for four. It reminded me of a match I played in many years ago when I was batting at the non-striker's end. A delivery slipped out of the bowler's hand and ran along the ground. My colleague took a wild swipe and – to his horror – spooned it up and got caught at cover point! Nowadays, this too should be called no ball[67] but this law was not in effect then so my colleague, distraught, had to go. The rest of the team organised a suicide watch in the dressing room.

There was an amusing moment during the match. One of the fielders shouted out, "Telegraph",[68] to the scorers. As quick as a flash, one of the batting team shouted back, "Losing 1-0 – Suarez" (England were playing Uruguay in the football World Cup at the time!)

However, by far the most memorable aspect of the evening was the hospitality. I did not really know what to expect. Maybe a few sandwiches before and a beer or two

---

[64] Law 17.1, 'Practice on the field'.
[65] Appendix D.
[66] Law 24.7, 'Ball coming to rest in front of striker's wicket'.
[67] Law 24.7, 'Ball coming to rest in front of striker's wicket'.
[68] In cricketing parlance this is a request for the scoreboard to be updated.

after, I thought. On arrival there were sandwiches and cakes. And real ale on tap, red wine, white wine. I settled for a few cheese and tomato sandwiches with a glass of red wine. However, this was only the aperitif. After the match there was a magnificent spread, with a choice of various main dishes and desserts. I had a fillet steak and roast potatoes, washed down with fresh strawberries, raspberries and blueberries with ice cream. "Would you come again?" asked the owner as we left. I think that I could probably be persuaded.

Henley C.C., Saturday, 21st June, 2014

TVCL Division 1. Henley II 148 (44.4), Yateley 152-2 (30.2). Yateley won by 8 wickets.

I have played at Henley many times over the years but today was my first visit as an umpire. The clubhouse has been refurbished since the last time I played here, maybe ten or more years ago? It now has a superb umpires' changing room with a rare window view of the playing area, and the bar/kitchen area is very comfortable with a magnificent collection of old photographs dating back to the 1920s. The cricket today was a little disappointing (from a neutral perspective!) because Yateley won very easily, but it was a pleasant day with an excellent tea – a great selection of sandwiches with fresh strawberries and pineapple to follow.

My colleague today was ambivalent (as most are) about which end he wanted to stand at, so I chose the far or southern end, primarily so that I could enjoy the view of the magnificent Poplar trees which run along the eastern side of the ground from square leg (to the right-handed batsman). I have written previously about how much I like Poplar trees.[69]

The most memorable moment of the day was incidental to the match. In the early evening some middle-aged spectators, dressed up formally for a night out on the town, were walking round the boundary. When the ball was struck out to the boundary near them, one gentleman of comfortable build suddenly imagined that he was Derek Randall in his prime and decided to try to field the ball. It was a big mistake. He swooped down, lost his footing and ended up on his backside with both legs up in the air – to the considerable amusement of players, umpires and his friends alike.

Marston Sports Ground, Sunday, 22nd June, 2014

Friendly (50/50). Oxford University Authentics 216-6 (50.0), Frogs 189 (49.1). Oxford University Authentics won by 27 runs.

Most of the college grounds in Oxford are magnificent and it was a great pleasure to stand at one of them today. The old St. Catherine's College ground is now the Marston Sports Ground and has a huge, immaculately flat playing area surrounded by mature trees and tidy hedgerows, and for the second consecutive day I was able to enjoy a view of Poplar trees from square leg. The Authentics are Oxford University's 2nd XI and the Frogs are a wandering club who today fielded some useful players, including a couple of

---

[69] See entry for NPL Teddington C.C., Saturday, 2nd July, 2011.

Oxford Blues. So the standard of play was, at times, both high and competitive.

I had two difficult caught behind decisions to make today. On the first one I neither saw nor heard a nick so I said not out, to the consternation of the fielding team! You need a really thick skin on these occasions! The second one involved a batsman digging out a yorker and hitting the ground at the same time. There was no doubt that he hit it, but I had to decide whether or not it was a bump ball; I decided that it was not and gave him out.

The students had the run of the pavilion after the match – the captain had the key and there were no other staff present. They took advantage by putting on some loud music and partying. They kindly invited me to join them but I felt about 30 years too old and so politely made my apologies, preferring a quiet drive home through the lanes and some Mozart. They had amused me during the day with their nicknames for each other, which were both cryptic and esoteric. However, they had clearly run out of inspiration at some point because the player who was explaining all to me at square leg was simply called, "Chemistry".

Amersham C.C., Friday, 27th June, 2014

Is there, I wonder, a collective noun for umpires? There were certainly enough for two XIs at a Buckinghamshire ACO barbecue this evening. One chap was talking about having to retire due to his diminished oral capabilities. "My eyes are fine", he lamented, "I just can't hear the nicks any more!" Time stands still for no man.

It did remind me of an umpiring story from my Chalfont Saints days. Our umpire was a charming man, now long since dead, a raconteur and *bon viveur* who had never actually played the game but had a passion for its traditional values. I wouldn't say that he was a bad umpire *per se*, but his eyesight was not the best! We were on tour in the Malverns in about 1980 and he was umpiring and I was scoring. He had turned to me and was signalling four byes, and was getting agitated because I was not acknowledging his signal. However, I had good reason. The batsman had been bowled! (N.b. to be fair to said umpire, the ball had just clipped one of the bails and then shot off to the boundary – it was not as if stumps were cartwheeling!)

North Maidenhead C.C., Saturday, 28th June, 2014

TVCL Division 2A. North Maidenhead 134 (34.5), Fleet 107-7 (41.0). Match drawn.

In the TVCL match rules, if there is a stoppage due to GWL during the first innings then an adjustment is made to the total number of overs permitted in the match, thus ensuring that it should still finish at 7.30pm. However, there are no such provisions in the second innings, because a traditional format match cannot be reduced in the second innings without making it hard for at least one team (almost always the fielding team and often the batting one, too) to still have a reasonable chance of victory. Thus, the only way that the umpires can abandon the match is if they either a) think there is no prospect of play due to the condition of the pitch or outfield or b) calculate that there will not be enough daylight to complete the match.

Today, at about 7.15pm, it began to rain, so my colleague and I suspended play. At this point there were six overs left and Fleet were 83-7. North Maidenhead thought that they had a chance of winning; Fleet would have preferred to shake hands and call it a day. My colleague and I were caught between the proverbial rock and a hard place. We had no reason to abandon the match, so we waited for the rain to stop. Eventually, at about 8.25pm, it did. We then got the covers taken off and went out to inspect the pitch. It was wet, because quite a lot of water had got onto it before the covers had been put on, but after much deliberation we decided that it was playable. So the match resumed at 8.40pm. The North Maidenhead skipper then pushed his luck by bringing back himself (medium-fast) and then, when that did not work, his main strike bowler (fast). At this point my colleague and I intervened and told him that if he did this we would abandon the match due to the fading light and risk of injury to the batsmen; so he saw sense and reverted to his slow bowlers. Fleet held on for the draw. It was a really difficult situation to manage but I think that my colleague and I made a decent fist of it on this occasion.

One of my favourite cricket trivia scenarios occurred this evening. When we resumed, North Maidenhead needed three wickets to win, but one of the Fleet batsmen had earlier retired hurt and left the ground, so effectively North Maidenhead only needed two wickets to win. Or did they? If they had taken the ninth wicket any time up to and including the penultimate delivery then, yes, they would have won the match. But what if the ninth wicket was to fall on the last ball of the match? What then would be the result of the match? Would it be a draw or would the fielding have team won? The answer is that it would have been the former, a draw. The players were all, of course, blissfully unaware of the laws. With two balls to go, one of the fielders called out, "come on boys, keep going, we can still win this one." I chuckled quietly to myself. "I don't think so, my friend." (Notwithstanding a run out on a no ball, or a stumping on a wide, of course.)

I mentioned the injury to one of the Fleet batsman. He was struck on the helmet by a short-pitched fast ball, and somehow or other the ball either got through his visor or jammed the helmet itself onto his eyebrow? He suffered a nasty cut and there was a considerable amount of blood. He was helped off the field by his teammates and taken to A&E, although fortunately reports later said that his injuries were superficial only with just a couple of stitches required. I think the debate about wearing, or not, helmets has now passed; junior batsmen wear them at all times and very few senior batsmen do not wear them against anything but the most gentle slow bowling. One almost assumes that they work, i.e. that they safeguard a batsman (or wicketkeeper/fielder) from serious injury. It could be argued that today the helmet failed, but it probably did actually still do a large part of its job in reducing, if not stopping, the impact of the ball on the batsman's head.

Away from GWL issues I also had two difficult caught behind decisions today. They both involved the same protagonists, bowler, batsman and fielder (aka the wicketkeeper). What made them difficult is that the batsman was getting his left elbow forward pointing at mid-off and turning even further towards extra cover as he shouldered arms; and the bowler was getting both bounce and in-swing. The first one probably clipped the batsman's glove as he shouldered arms at the last minute. I say probably because, although I could not see the ball striking his glove and also did not hear anything, and therefore said not out, the fielders were visibly distraught. The next over the same thing happened. Again, I could not see any contact, but this time I heard the faint sound of ball on glove, so gave the batsman out. After the match had finished, my colleague told me that he had heard the sound of ball on glove both times. I appreciated his candour. I have been in this position with roles reversed many times, and there is no doubt in my mind that it is easier to hear thin nicks and double noises from square leg than at the bowler's end. Why this should be I do not know?

There was a topical comedic moment when we took an early tea. One of the players announced to his teammates that we were having 'an early Suarez' (a reference to the Uruguayan footballer with a predilection for biting people!)

Ascott Park, Sunday, 29th June, 2014

Friendly. Stragglers of Asia v. Kenya Kongonis. Match cancelled.

In the 'olden days' there were always, of course, c***-ups with fixtures. I remember several times when the opposition failed to show up during my playing career, and one memorable occasion when *two* visiting teams turned up to play my club, Chalfont Saints, in the 1980s. Three is definitely a crowd when it comes to cricket matches, so the Saints players did the honourable thing and stood down, allowing the two visiting XIs to play each other. However, I do think that these c***-ups have become more commonplace since the advent of, firstly, telephone answer machines, and then more recently email and mobile phones. I think that some (irresponsible) people think that leaving an unanswered message is adequate. It is not. The wrong number can be dialled, computers break down, mobile phones get lost. Today, I turned up at Ascott Park to umpire a match, which had apparently been cancelled several days ago. The club that had appointed me apologised profusely when I called them.

Hampton School, Wednesday, 2nd July, 2014

Friendly (40/40). Hampton School 176-6 (40.0), Elizabeth College, Guernsey 178-6 (40.0). Elizabeth College won by 4 wickets.

I was supposed to be standing at RMA Sandhurst today but that match was cancelled yesterday. There was then a possibility that I might be appointed to a match against an Australian touring XI at Tring Park, but this came to nothing. Then I was offered this match at Hampton School, which I accepted. Then I was offered the Tring Park match after all, which I had to decline.

Pangloss would have said, *'Tout est au mieux'* – and on this occasion, at least, he would have been right: another new ground to visit, and an absolutely cracking game as well. Three to win off the last ball. Thumping cover drive, despairing dive from the fielder, four runs! The two batsmen and their teammates in the pavilion were elated; the fielding team distraught. This is team sport at its best; the winning team will have a great evening, the losing team will share the pain together. Tennis players, golfers and athletes win and lose on their own, and have nobody to share their triumphs and failures with. The batsman who struck the winning runs today, and all his teammates, have a wonderful memory to share for the rest of their lives! I must admit that I felt a slight tinge of envy for the winning team today in their moment of triumph. I love umpiring but it can never be quite the same as playing! You are part of the event but alone, detached, neither elated nor distraught at the end, just an interested but impartial observer.

I had an interesting situation re wides today. It is now common to see '(profile) wide lines' marked out on the crease and, at a tense moment in today's match, a batsman was disappointed when I declined to call a wide to a ball which passed outside the aforementioned. The problem was that I had been informed at the toss that I should apply the Laws of Cricket re wides[70]. The batsman in question was tall, and he could easily have struck the ball playing a normal cricket shot.[71] I informed him why I had not called the wide and he accepted my explanation. I actually think that profile wides unfairly favour tall batsmen: they get wides which they would not get according to the Laws of Cricket, while their

---

[70] Laws 25.1, 'Judging a wide' and 25.2, 'Delivery not a wide'.
[71] Law 25.1, 'Judging a wide'.

'vertically challenged' peers would have got the wide under both interpretations anyway.

Wembley C.C., Thursday, 3rd July, 2014

ECB Over 60 (45/45). Middlesex 188-6 (45.0), Buckinghamshire 189-2 (38.0). Buckinghamshire won by 8 wickets.

The entrance to the ground at Wembley is inauspicious, but this is misleading because it is actually quite pleasant. It is encircled by hedgerows and has a magnificent row of Poplar trees along one side of the ground. They are more elegant, actually, than the ones at Henley, because they are more spaced out, and today, on a warm sunny day with a cooling breeze, they swayed gently in the wind. The clubhouse was clean, modern and comfortable, with interesting photographs to browse through, and the tea was also superb. So a good day all round.

During the afternoon some distant passers-by amused themselves by shouting, "How's that?" Do these people really think that they are cracking an original joke? One of the players shouted back at them: "Thanks lads, that's very amusing, I've never heard that one before ..."

Shiplake College, Saturday, 5th July, 2014

TVCL Division 1. Eversley 132 (47.2), Henley II 98 (38.3). Eversley won by 34 runs.

Henley's ground was unavailable today because of the regatta, so this match was instead played down the road at Shiplake College. I have driven past this ground many times but today was my first visit. The playing area is much bigger than it looks from the road, and it has a pleasant setting. It is surrounded by mature trees, has a comfortable, purpose-built pavilion, which is part of the wider school building, and the outfield and square are excellent. The only disappointing aspect is that there is nowhere to socialise after the game. I did quietly suggest the pub along the road but nobody seemed keen and everyone just drifted off home. This was rather anti-climactic, and a shame, especially after a really good, hard-fought game.

I made a silly, embarrassing mistake today, although fortunately it had no impact on the match. What happened was that silly point threw the ball back at the stumps in an attempt to run out the striking batsman, and the ball went for an overthrow. When the ball was dead I signalled leg bye – to the general astonishment of the striking batsman, who was by now at my (the non-striking) end. I immediately realised my mistake. He had hit this ball – it had been the previous one that had struck his pad (and had also been fielded by silly point). So I reversed my signal, to the general amusement of everyone and my blushes.

Some umpires and governing bodies prefer umpires to wear exactly the same attire. While I agree that this does look better, I do not think it should be observed at the expense of one umpire wearing or not wearing a garment of choice. My colleague today feels the cold but I generally do not; so, while he wore a long-sleeved shirt, a jumper and a blouson, I sported a short-sleeved shirt. We both felt comfortable and I am sure umpired the better for it.

High Wycombe C.C., Tuesday, 8th July, 2014

ECB Under 17 Championship (first day of two). Buckinghamshire 240 (82.0), Bedfordshire 40-1 (17.0).

Today represented a new challenge in my umpiring career, in fact a new challenge in my cricket career period: a multi-day match. The format of this ECB competition is similar to a first class or Test match: two days; three two-hour sessions with forty minutes for lunch and twenty minutes for tea; minimum 102 overs per day. Outright wins are rare, and the teams play mainly for 'first innings' victories and to gain experience of a longer match.

Lunch was a hot meal with a dessert; tea two hours later was sandwiches and cakes – too much for me so soon! But it was nice to have two breaks in a 100 over day – extra rest, better concentration, less backache!

The panoramas and skyscapes today were magnificent: combinations of blue sky, and white, grey and black clouds; the greens of the grass and trees; and sporadic sunshine lighting it up. Most Britons moan about our weather but I love it: varied, changeable, temperate. Apart, of course, from rain on cricket days – and we had a bit of that late on which curtailed play for the day!

We went off at 5.18pm and the scheduled close of play was 6.00pm. My colleague and I re-read the ECB match rules on

GWL for this competition and, needless to say, they were unfathomably complicated. We scratched our heads, agreed for a moment, then disagreed. Then, to our great relief, at about 5.50pm, the two coaches came in to see us and suggested that we call it a day; we metaphorically bit their hands off.

High Wycombe C.C., Wednesday, 9th July, 2014

ECB Under 17 Championship (second day of two). Buckinghamshire 240 and 267-3 dec. (42.4), Bedfordshire 244 (71.3). Match drawn.

There were a few new things to think about this morning, relating to rolling, mowing and the repairing of foot holes[72], and covering the pitch[73]. It helped that the groundsman at High Wycombe knew exactly what he was required to do and when, so all my colleague and I had to do was check and observe.

Lunch today was toad-in-the-hole followed by ice cream. One of the Buckinghamshire fast bowlers was given the first over after lunch. I do not think he was expecting it, and he had apparently over-indulged at lunchtime. I am actually quite surprised that modern nutritional advice has not yet reached junior county cricket. They have multiple coaches; extensive batting, bowling and fielding drills; and non-match training days with discussions about tactics and preparation. Nutrition, it would seem, has thus far not been addressed.

---

[72] Law 10, "Preparation and maintenance of the playing area".
[73] Law 11, "Covering the pitch".

As predicted yesterday, the most interesting aspect of the match was the battle for the first innings victory; it was nip and tuck all the way, and Bedfordshire sneaked home with one wicket to spare. Buckinghamshire then batted well, scoring quickly, and I thought that they might just be thinking about a declaration; instead, they played for second innings batting points. Prior to the commencement of the Buckinghamshire innings I achieved a personal umpiring first: my colleague and I changed ends!

The match finished quietly at 6.00pm, once again in Turneresque light, with bright sunshine and black, threatening clouds. My colleague showered and then put on his shirt, tie and jacket, which I thought was rather odd (I was dressed casually). He then called his wife. "Hello, darling, how's your day been? ... I've just hit the M1. I should be home by 9ish, what's for supper? ... Okay, great, see you later." Then he rang off and said, "Right, let's go and have a beer." "Err, okay, right you are." None of my business!

St. Edward's School, Friday, 11th July, 2014

Friendly. Stragglers of Asia 213-7 dec. (54.2), St. Edward's Martyrs 214-4 (37.5). St. Edward's Martyrs won by 6 wickets.

I had driven past this ground on the Woodstock Road in Oxford many times so it was nice to get an appointment here. It is surrounded by mature trees but is also open and spacious; there are attractive views in all directions; and it has a well-appointed modern pavilion at mid-off/fine leg – the ideal position for a clubhouse. The latter is full of old photographs featuring notable alumni of the school; these include Douglas Bader and John Woodcock.

The cricket was slightly disappointing; the Stragglers were weak all round and, although they battled hard to make a decent game of it, the outcome was never really in doubt. However, on the plus side, the food was superb and the Martyrs opened a few bottles of wine at lunchtime. I partook – it would have been rude not to! I do not know what effect it had on my umpiring? Red wine tends to make me feel drowsy, and I must admit that my concentration was wavering a little bit later in the day. I was watching the buses go past as if I was an extra in *Last Bust to Woodstock* – and half expecting a red Jag to pull up any time and Inspector Morse to get out!

Sometimes as an umpire you really do not know what has happened and you just have to play the percentages game. Today, there was an incident when a batsman played forward, the ball bounced up, hit something and then ran away, and the batsmen ambled a single. I was not sure what it had hit, so I made no signal. The batsman, who was by now at my (the non-striker's) end, looked at me with surprise. In that moment, I knew that he had not hit it. "Take the run, my friend", I said, and he smiled. Later, he asked me if I would have given him out if the wicketkeeper had caught the ball. "No", I said, "when I don't know what has happened I play the percentages game. I assess the situation and choose the least contentious option."

Stoke Green C.C., Saturday, 12th July, 2014

TVCL Division 2B. Stoke Green 224-8 dec. (47.0), Aldershot 185 (45.2). Stoke Green won by 39 runs.

Cricket can be a cruel game – for players and umpires alike. Today, one of the Aldershot fielders dropped a dolly and the Stoke Green batsman whom he dropped went on to make a match-winning ton. Later, when the hapless Aldershot fielder came out to bat, he took a while to get going. "Don't let him get off the mark!" said one of the Stoke Green fielders. "Off the mark?" said another, "this guy's on minus 110!"

Earlier, I gave a Stoke Green batsman out LBW. There was no problem with my decision *per se*. The batsman was struck on the back foot, he did not hit it, he had not got outside the line and it was not missing leg. The problem was that it also bowled him! It is actually not uncommon for an umpire to not see a bail being dislodged – the batsman can often block one's view – and to be fair to me the ball jammed in the batsman's pads and then rolled slowly backwards before dislodging one of the bails. But everyone else could see the bail on the ground and I looked foolish. I noticed later that the scorer had recorded the dismissal as LBW. This was entirely reasonable, as he would have both seen me raise my finger and, quite possibly, not seen the dislodged bail either. I told him that technically it should be recorded as bowled[74] but left it to his discretion to make, or not, the change.

Chesham C.C., Tuesday, 15th July, 2014

---

[74] Law 30.2, 'Bowled to take precedence'.

Friendly (50/50). Chairman's XI 219-8 (50.0), Chesham 220-3 (34.4). Chesham won by 7 wickets.

This was a gentle social match during Chesham's cricket week but with some quite good play on both sides. In the 'olden days' this would have been a time match with declarations and match management if appropriate, but nowadays the trend is for overs matches, and I must say that the latter can become rather predictable when one team is clearly stronger than the other. So it was today – there was never the slightest doubt that the club XI would win. In a time match, the chairman's XI would have been fed some extra runs to make a game of it.

For the second time in four days I succumbed to the temptation of red wine at lunchtime, and once again regretted it during a very hot afternoon session. My concentration was fine at the bowler's end but it wavered a bit at square leg. This is one of the key differences between playing and umpiring – in the latter you have to concentrate for every ball of the match, there is no 'down' time.

My colleague today was a little eccentric. At one point he propped himself up against the advertising boards on the (short) square leg boundary and chatted to some spectators; to be fair to him, he never missed a ball counting signal or took his eye off play. Later, he went and stood almost at the boundary edge on the other (long) square leg boundary; I could see no rhyme or reason for this, although someone rather unkindly suggested that he (being a gentleman of comfortable build who presumably enjoys his food) had smelt the barbecue?

I made one mistake today. Well, I may have made lots of mistakes, but one that I am aware of is what I meant. A new batsman flicked his first ball off his pads down to fine leg for four, so I duly signalled boundary four. Mid-on then said to him, "you didn't hit that, did you?" "No", I heard the batsman reply. (They were both Chesham players and clearly friends.)

Chesham C.C., Wednesday, 16th July, 2014

I watched the end of Chesham's match against MCC this afternoon: a time game won splendidly by Chesham in the penultimate over by one wicket. Amen to that! It was nice to have a stroll round the boundary and a chat – this is one of cricket's great pleasures to me, but of course one does not get the opportunity to do it when umpiring.

Later there was a dinner in Chesham's recently opened and magnificent new clubhouse, during which I had a long chat with an umpiring colleague. He told me that, since being hit by a cricket ball while umpiring, he has stopped clasping his hands behind his back, as I prefer to do, and now keeps his hands by his side to increase his balance and flexibility. On a lighter note, I had not realised that it was his son who flicked – or did not – his first ball down to fine leg yesterday. Apparently, he thinks that I am the best umpire ever!

Yateley C.C., Saturday, 19th July, 2014

TVCL Division 1. Yateley 182 (45.0), Kidmore End 141 (52.5). Yateley won by 41 runs.

This was my first visit to Yateley. It is a successful, well-run club with a modern pavilion and a spacious ground in a large park area that also contains a golf course and a football club. I went through my usual process in deciding which end I would prefer to stand at[75], and chose the one with a good view of the scoreboard as well as an attractive row of Ash trees from square leg. My colleague, as is usually the case, was more than happy to indulge me, and I was quite happy with my choice until half way through the second innings, when the Red Arrows began their display at the Farnborough air show behind my back at square leg. You win some, you lose some!

It was a curate's egg of a match. Yateley were 40–4, then 120–4, then 130–9, then 182 all out. Kidmore were always behind in their run chase, but at 120–5 seemed to have the chance of an unlikely win, before collapsing meekly in the end. At the outset of the match it seemed likely that the weather would be a factor, but the forecast thunderstorms and heavy rain never materialised. It strikes me that weather forecasters and umpires have more than a little in common: they both have a fiendishly difficult job; and while neither get much credit for getting it right, they both get slaughtered by all and sundry if they get it wrong!

I had another 'spin bowler/batsman hit on the full on the toe' LBW decision to make today, with a scenario almost identical to the one I had a few weeks ago at Ascott Park.[76] The batsman was a youth and I could see that he was

---

[75] See entry for Burnham C.C., Sunday, 12th May, 2013.
[76] See entry for Ascott Park, Sunday, 15th June, 2014.

disappointed when I adjudged him LBW. I would have liked to discuss this with him and his captain after the match – but by the time I had showered and changed they had both already left.

The tea today was especially nice: a good selection of sandwiches and some tomatoes and lettuce to wash it down. Lettuce, I would say, is an underestimated component to a good cricket tea, especially on a baking hot day when one tends to be somewhat dehydrated after three hours on the field.

After the match my colleague and I had a chat with the Yateley chairman. My colleague, who is a member at Beaconsfield, was lamenting the fact that university students these days miss most of the season, firstly with exams and then they all seem to disappear on holiday – and by the time they get home the season is over. "We don't have that problem at Yateley", said the chairman, "all our youngsters are thick and didn't go to university!"

Beaconsfield C.C., Sunday, 20th July, 2014

BCB Under 12 Final (20/20). Great Kingshill 108-4 (20.0), Stony Stratford 112-6 (15.1). Stony Stratford won by 4 wickets.

BCB Under 13 Final (20/20). Chesham 93-6 (20.0), Cublington 74-8 (20.0). Chesham won by 19 runs.

Today was mercifully cooler after yesterday's oppressive heat. The format was the same as last year's event and, interestingly, the Under 13 Final was a repeat of last year's Under 12 match – the boys were a year older, and bigger and stronger, but the result was the same.

One thing that I have noticed in junior cricket is batsmen taking a guard and then completely disregarding it thereafter. To be fair, this happens in senior cricket too, but for some of the juniors it is a tick list item, something you must do when you first arrive at the crease. They have not yet understood its wider importance, both in terms of a batsman's position *vis-à-vis* his stumps and, crucially, in response to the type of bowling he is to face.

Captaincy in the game of cricket is crucial. Today, in the Under 12 match, the Great Kingshill captain held back part of his best bowler's allotment for the end of the innings even though two Stony Stratford batsmen were well set mid-innings and getting after the weaker bowlers. The situation cried out for the best bowler to be brought back *post haste* to try to break the partnership. It was analogous to Nick Faldo's error at the Ryder Cup in 2008 when, behind going into the singles on the last day, he put his strongest players out last – only for the match to be already lost by the time they entered the fray.

Marlow C.C., Tuesday, 22nd July, 2014

ECB Women's T20 (20/20). Suffolk 140-7 (20.0), Buckinghamshire 142-1 (18.2). Buckinghamshire won by 9 wickets.

ECB Women's T20 (20/20). Shropshire 134-5 (20.0), Suffolk 136-2 (18.1). Suffolk won by 8 wickets.

I was appointed to stand in two of three Women's T20 matches today, my ones due to start at 10.00am and 1.00pm, and the third one at 4.00pm. However, some of the Suffolk team were late. They travelled in a convoy of five cars but two of them became detached and then unfortunately went the wrong way round the M25. Apparently they did not realise until they reached the Dartford Crossing! Cue some politically incorrect jokes about women drivers.

Their lateness put my colleague and me on the spot. It became clear that we would not be able to start the first match until 11.00am earliest, but neither team wanted to reduce the length of the match, and both promised to hurry through their overs. The match regulations were clear that we should reduce to prevent the last match running late, but we went with the flow – it is the players' game – and agreed not to reduce. Then, predictably, the over rate started to slip, and then there was an injury break, and I soon began to regret our decision. It did not affect me greatly as my second match finished at 5.15pm and I showered and set off for a meeting elsewhere, but my colleagues doing the last match may well have been *in situ* until 8.15pm or later. Lesson learnt – always follow the match regulations!

There was an amusing moment on the field of play today when, on the same ball, a catch was dropped and then a run out chance missed. There ensued some distinctly unladylike language from the bowler, quickly followed, when the red mist had evaporated, by profuse apologies.

There was also a relatively unusual dismissal today: a batsman was given out stumped off a wide. I was the bowler's end umpire at the time and, as I repeated my wide signal to the scorer, I saw the departing batsman look wistfully towards me, perhaps hoping for a reprieve? But I think she knew deep down that she had to go.[77] The dismissal came on the first ball of the over, so when the new batsman had taken guard I said to her, "Right arm over the wicket, *six* balls to come!" This too was an unusual pronouncement, and she looked up at me quizzically before settling down to take strike.

Hillingdon Manor C.C., Wednesday, 23rd July, 2014

Friendly: TVCL Representative XI 231–6 dec. (36.1), Hillingdon Manor 196 (47.2). TVCL Representative XI won by 35 runs.

The purpose of today's match was to celebrate Hillingdon's 180th anniversary. It is hard to imagine what cricket would have been like in 1834? This was a long time before over-arm bowling, six-ball overs, eleven-a-side, declarations etc! The earliest recorded matches played by my own club, Chalfont St. Peter, were in the 1850s against Beaconsfield and Amersham. In today's world these distances are small, but there were no cars in those days and railways (in the Chilterns at least) were still half a century away. How did the teams travel? Horse and cart? Back home before the light faded?

---

[77] Law 39.1, 'Out stumped'.

Today's match was played at Coney Green rather than at the RAF ground in Vine Road. This was disappointing in some respects, perhaps, but Coney Green is Hillingdon's real home, and therefore, I think, a more appropriate venue for this sort of match. It was a good day all round, social, friendly and (albeit slightly artificially) competitive.

Lord's, Thursday, 24th July, 2014

I went to Lord's this evening to see the T20 match between Middlesex and Surrey. As you will know by now, I am a traditionalist and not, in truth, a great fan of this format of the game. However, Lord's did look splendid under floodlights, especially the pavilion, and this is the format where T20 works. A 6.30pm start, all done and dusted in three hours, coloured clothing and white balls necessary in artificial light – and glorious weather and a tight finish to boot. It is when you get pyjamas in natural light, and then two or more T20s played back to back, when I start to feel that the format has moved away from what it was originally supposed to be, namely a short, fast-paced game which can be played on a single evening after people have left work.

"I don't know what's going off out there, it wasn't like this in my day!" I remember how I and my friends used to laugh at Fred Trueman on *TMS* in days of yore. Now I am middle-aged and I can empathise more easily with his view point. What has happened to the spine-tingling silence at the critical moments? Tonight we got a couple of bars of moronic pop music every time a boundary was struck or a wicket taken – and this seems to be the norm nowadays, it happens at Twickenham when a try is scored and at the ATP

Masters tennis at the O2. Test matches at Lord's and the championships at Wimbledon, it would seem, are the last bastions of resistance to the modern obsession with 'artificial noise'.

Finchampstead C.C., Saturday, 26th July, 2014

TVCL Division 2A. Finchampstead II 264-6 (52.0), Cookham Dean 268-7 (47.3). Cookham Dean won by 3 wickets.

When a fielder drops a catch he is tortured by every run that the batsman goes on to score. This happened today when one of the Cookham batsmen had a reprieve on his first ball and went on to make a match-winning century – except that his reprieve came not from a fielder but from one of the umpires. Me. I think I should have given him out LBW but did not. As I watched him play out the rest of his innings I was reminded every ball of my probable error. The key thing in cricket is always the next ball, but few players and umpires can truly blank out what has just happened, and I really struggled to do so today. The only credit I can take is that I stubbornly resisted subsequent opportunities to 'even it out', but I will not sleep well tonight.

In the bar afterwards I got talking to some of the Finchampstead players. They skirted round the subject for a while, and then one of them asked me why I had not given the Cookham batsman out. I just said that I thought that I had made a mistake, and they kindly accepted my admission. I think they appreciated my honesty. I have sometimes heard umpiring instructors advise their pupils not to admit mistakes. I think this is stupid. Umpires are human beings, and human beings make mistakes. I do not see any point in being in denial.

My experience today also reinforces my support for the DRS in the professional game. If Finchampstead today had been able to appeal my decision, then I think it would probably have been overturned. It is true to say that an umpire is, to a degree, humiliated by having his decision overturned in this way, but this passes. However, if his decision is not overturned then its consequences often continue to rankle, sometimes for the rest of the match and beyond.

Wellington College, Sunday, 27th July, 2014

Friendly. Old Wellingtonians 183 (47.1), Old Millfieldians 184-7 (37.5). Old Millfieldians won by 3 wickets.

Three years ago I absent-mindedly forgot to take my kitbag with me to a match at British Airways.[78] Today, I did it again. I arrived at the ground, parked my car, opened my boot and ... "Oh, no". Once is unfortunate but twice is careless! However, ever since the horrors of that day at BA, I have always travelled to grounds already changed, so today at least I only had to borrow a counter, pencil and paper, and a set of bails, and only my colleague and the scorers were aware of my unpreparedness.

I have noticed with these types of match that the captains usually take charge, often tossing up and agreeing the scheduled breaks and match rules between them and only

---

[78] See entry for British Airways C.C., Saturday, 3rd September, 2011.

then informing the umpires. This is irregular but, as far as I am concerned, fine – it is their game and I prefer to go with the flow. However, today, during the second innings, I noticed that, although the fielding team had eleven fielders, one of the batsmen who had scored fifty in the first innings was not amongst them. During the tea interval I checked the scorebook and discovered that one of the bowlers had not batted. Having ascertained my facts, I then politely asked the captain what was going on. "Oh, sorry, yes, I agreed this ... [with the other captain] ... at the toss. Should I have told you?" "Err, yes, I think you probably should!"

A batsman today was struck where it hurts most, which induced the usual *Schadenfreude* amongst everyone else while he writhed around on the ground in agony. I have never really understood why everyone other than the injured party seems to find this amusing? When he got to his feet he called out to my colleague, "One left, umps?" "Are you telling me or asking?" he replied.

During the tea interval my colleague told me an amusing story from a match he stood in recently. On the last ball of the match the batting team needed three runs to win and the fielding team one wicket. The batsman got an inside edge and the ball flew off towards fine leg. The wicketkeeper gave chase, having first thrown off his right glove to enable him to pick up and throw the ball in. His throw then struck the discarded glove, which was now lying on the ground, and the ball was then gathered in by one of the fielders who effected a run out. The fielding team then celebrated their win – until my colleague correctly awarded five penalty runs to the batting team for illegal fielding[79]. Whereupon the previously disconsolate batting team began to celebrate, leaving my colleague to reflect on one of the universal truths of cricket umpiring: the players do not know the laws!

Merchant Taylors' School, Monday, 28th July, 2014

Middlesex CCC Regional Cricket Week (Under 14, 40/40). All Stars 200-8 (40.0), Monarchs 172 (38.0). All Stars won by 28 runs.

I made myself available for this event (essentially a trial tournament for boys at Under 12 and Under 14 who are just outside the county XI) through a friend of a friend, but my availability got lost in translation. It is a five-day festival, Monday to Friday, and I said any two days Monday through Thursday. Some time later, however, I was appointed for all four days! As it was a new appointment contact I decided to accept the offer as it was, which has given me nine consecutive days of umpiring.

Too much of a good thing? When I found out on the Monday that there was no lunch or tea then I began to think so. I can honestly say that this is the first time I have ever played or umpired a full-length cricket match and not been fed and watered. My colleague, a regular Middlesex umpire – and thus forewarned and forearmed – kindly shared his banana and a biscuit with me between innings, and we managed to scrounge a cup of tea; it felt Dickensian. Needless to say, I will bring a packed lunch for the next three days.

---

[79] Laws 41.1, 'Protective equipment' and 41.2, 'Fielding the ball'.

The best view on the OMT ground is from the pavilion end. There is a row of mature trees, nicely spaced out, and today they formed an attractive foreground to some striking cloud formations in the distance. Like at High Wycombe a few weeks ago, the sun was shining on threatening black clouds, with patches of blue, white and grey as well. I also like the Metropolitan Line trains passing every now and again – they are far enough away to add atmosphere without being intrusive!

My colleague today was scoring. Watching him with his head buried in a notebook, and observing two of the coaches making an absolute dog's breakfast of both scorebook and scoreboard, offered a microcosm of the wider scoring debate. You could say that either my colleague or I needed to keep the score just in case; however, I would say that his performance as an umpire was being undermined by his attempts to keep score. He was unable to maintain regular eye contact with me and was certainly not observing events around him very well.

Merchant Taylors' School, Thursday, 31st July, 2014

Middlesex CCC Regional Cricket Week (Under 14, 40/40). Flyers 207-4 (40.0), Marauders 107-3 (31.2). Flyers won by 83 runs.

This was my fourth and final day at Merchant Taylors' School. If I am honest then I would have to say that I have not enjoyed it that much. The cricket has been good, and the venue is superb. But, for me, cricket is just not the same when there is neither a tea nor a beer and a chat afterwards. I did not expect the latter because the OMT clubhouse (which was being used rather than the school pavilion as the changing facility) is part of the school grounds and a bar would therefore be inappropriate, and anyway there is never any *après-cricket* after junior matches. However, everyone sitting apart between innings with their packed lunches did not feel right to me, almost the antithesis of the sociability that makes cricket the game it is. I did at least find a nice bench in the shade by the school ground, where I watched a little bit of the Middlesex v. Yorkshire Under 19 match.

There has been one odd thing that I have noticed this week. A lot of the boys asked for a middle and off guard against off-spinners, and even off stump. This is unusual (well, it certainly was to me!) and presumably reflects the latest coaching ideas about how best to play off-spin bowling.

I had to remove a bowler from the attack today for bowling three above waist-height beamers.[80] I do not think that the batsmen were in any danger, not least because they were wearing helmets and other protective equipment, and I felt sorry for the bowler in question – it was humiliating for him. However, the reasoning behind these laws is that a bowler who transgresses in this way is not in control, and thus *per se* a danger to others. Ultimately, I am an umpire, and it is my job to apply the laws rather than to analyse them – that is the responsibility of MCC!

Harefield C.C., Friday, 1st August, 2014

---

[80] Laws 42.6, 'Dangerous and unfair bowling' and 42.7, 'Dangerous and unfair bowling – action by the umpire'.

Friendly (40/40). TVCL Representative XI 186 (38.5), Harefield 118 (27.2). TVCL Representative XI won by 68 runs.

Today was my sixth of nine consecutive days of umpiring, and I must say that the hospitality and sociability of today's match made a pleasant contrast with the previous four days. Harefield has a well-deserved reputation as a friendly, sociable club and the teas are always superb. This was the first time I have umpired a match here and it is probably ten or fifteen years since I played here (although I have been back several times in the interim for meetings and other events) – and I had actually forgotten how steep the slope at the far end of the ground is. It is a small but attractive ground and the only thing I do not like about it are the tall and rather oppressive conifers at the far end.

I have stood with my colleague today several times and he has a rather amusing superstition. He does not like to cross once on the field of play, so we have to decide which end we are each going to stand at before crossing the boundary line for the first time. I know another chap who hops when the score reaches 'Nelson' (111), like the former international umpire, David Shepherd, used to do. I have tried to find out the exact origins of this latter superstition, but without success. It amuses me because you will often hear fielding teams shout out, "come on, boys, let's have one for the Admiral", when the score reaches 111. To be honest, as a rational and agnostic person, I find all these superstitions, like not walking under ladders or not looking at the full moon through glass, humorous but utterly ridiculous.

There was an odd incident today on the last ball of the first innings. I was at the bowler's end and a waist-high full toss was skied to mid-wicket where it was caught. I did not think it was *above* waist-height and was therefore not inclined to call no ball. Nonetheless, while the ball was in the air, I glanced across at my colleague for confirmation, and he was indeed *not* signalling that the ball was *above* waist-height, as the square-leg umpire would normally do to help his colleague. After the catch had been taken I looked at him again and he confirmed that he thought the delivery was fair. I therefore did not call no ball and the catch stood. A full toss is legal unless it passes *above* the waist height of the striker standing upright at the crease.[81] While walking back to the pavilion, my colleague and I agreed that we had made the correct decision, but later in the bar almost all the players, from both sides, disagreed. One said that he could not believe that, "the only two people on the ground who didn't think it was a no ball were the two umpires!" Cue laughter at our expense. *Plus ça change!*

Stoke Green C.C., Saturday, 2nd August, 2014

TVCL Division 2B. Stoke Green 171 (46.2), Sonning 66 (18.4). Stoke Green won by 105 runs.

I had two strange LBW incidents today, both during the Stoke Green innings. The first one was a strangled or half appeal. I thought that it was really close. I would not have given it because I think it was possibly sliding down the leg side, but I was surprised that there was not a much stronger appeal. Then later there was a massive appeal. This time I

---

[81] Law 42.6, 'Dangerous and unfair bowling'.

thought that, although the ball was hitting the stumps, it had struck the batsman outside the line and he was definitely playing a shot, so I said not out. The wicketkeeper (who was standing up) and bowler were apoplectic, and at this point I realised that they were appealing for caught behind. The batsman's body language suggested that he had nicked it onto his pad and then chosen not to walk. These 'double noise' decisions look easy on the DRS but they are much harder real time at a distance of 22 yards.

Stoke Green won the match easily. They have two very good slow left-arm spinners, and on a dusty pitch with variable bounce they were unplayable.

Gerrards Cross C.C., Sunday, 3rd August, 2014

ECB Under 10 (40/40). Buckinghamshire 113-6 (40.0), Surrey 114-3 (18.4). Surrey won by 7 wickets.

This was the last of my nine consecutive days of umpiring. Never again! Mercifully, it was a gentle and relatively short match, and a pleasantly cool, dry afternoon. But my back ached, really ached.

I was mentoring a new umpire today, which was a new experience for me. He was very good, and I limited myself to passing on a few general tips, relating mainly to positioning, signalling and body language.

The comments which you hear from the boys on the field in these matches can be quite amusing – for a while. Then they start to become repetitive and tiresome. The ones I heard today included the following: "dots balls are hot balls", "more blocks than Legoland" or "more leaves than a tree" (for dot balls); "more swings than a playground", "more misses than Henry VIII" or "bowl him a piano, see if he can play that" (for a play and miss); "his bat is like a polo – all edges and no middle" (for an edge); "all chips and no fish" (for a miscue that goes in the air); and "duck is on the menu today" (when a batsman is not yet off the mark). They have picked up these phrases from their coaches but have not yet learnt how to use them to telling effect. It reminds me of writing essays for my French 'O' Level, when you (apparently) got extra marks for including ludicrous memorised special phrases, such as *'les mains enfoncées dans les poches'* or *'le chapeau rabattu sur les yeux'*.

Sledging is actually an art form and timing is everything. I remember one classic example from my playing career. The opposition were about 130-0 chasing our total of about 200 but they were getting behind the clock. One of the batsmen was playing fluently and was about 80 or 90 not out, but his colleague was struggling a bit in comparison – not looking like he was going to get out any time soon, but not hitting boundaries or even rotating the strike very well. Then in two consecutive overs he took a single off the last ball. Finally, when the better batsman got on strike, one of my teammates shouted out, "Come on guys, new batsman!" Everyone, including the batsmen, laughed, but beneath the humour the sledge had cleverly got between the ears of both batsmen, reminding the better player that he was not getting enough strike and the weaker one that he was hogging it. Both got out soon afterwards, and they failed to chase down our total and the match ended in a draw. That was a brilliant sledge, both funny and effective.

Two local clubs (one from Buckinghamshire and one from Oxfordshire) were contesting the semi-final of the National Village Cup today. Those with only a casual interest in the recreational game might think that, from its name, this competition is for the lower echelons of recreational cricket, and features lusty blacksmiths smiting the vicar's long hops over cow corner! However, it is nothing of the sort. Granted, entry is restricted to 'villages' and the rules on player eligibility are strict, but both the teams involved today play in the HCPCL and the standard of play will have been very high. Nonetheless, what a thrill for the winners – a Lord's final!

Tring Park C.C., Saturday, 9th August, 2014

TVCL Division 2A. Gerrards Cross II 197-9 (52.0), Tring Park II 193-9 (48.0). Match drawn.

This was a great game of cricket. After the game, both teams were disappointed not to have won, and both had their chances. As an umpire, you miss out on the thrill of winning as a team – nothing can beat playing – but at least on occasions such as this you can enjoy the match as a purist or a neutral. And this was a great match. Tense and close throughout, but played in a good spirit.

Today we were on the top right of the square as you face the clubhouse, which meant that, as is sometimes also the case at Gerrards Cross, the sightscreens were directly in front of the clubhouse, something that I find aesthetically unattractive. There were actually two comedic sightscreen moments today. The first involved a jogger who, oblivious to the game of cricket, which he was circumnavigating, ran behind the double sightscreen at the bowler's end. We waited for him to emerge on the other side and pass out of the batsman's line of vision. But he did not appear. There was initially some concern that he might have collapsed in our blind spot, and a spectator moved round to investigate. However, it transpired that he was discreetly – or so he thought! – spending a penny. He re-emerged into view sheepishly and some of the players gave him a cheer. Poor chap! Then later a lady with a young child decided to wait politely for the end of the over before crossing. However, the bowling was at the other end, so a couple of fielders gestured to her to proceed. 'Funny old game, cricket!' she must have thought – one week they're shouting at me for passing without stopping, the next they're waving me across! Cricket is of course an esoteric game!

When I got home I picked up an email from a friend who plays for a team in Level 8 of the TVCL, where of course there are no panel umpires and usually no club umpires either. In his match today, a batsman played his shot, missed the ball, and then in frustration turned round and threw his bat to the ground – and in so doing put down his wicket. The fielding team appealed for hit wicket and the appeal was then upheld by a player umpire. After checking *Tom Smith*, I told my friend that this decision was incorrect. The batsman should have been given not out because the breaking of the wicket occurred 'after the batsman had completed any action in receiving the delivery'.[82]

Wormsley, Wednesday, 13th August, 2014

Today, I went to watch the first day of the Women's Test Match between England and India at Wormsley. Sixteen wickets fell, and ten of them were LBW decisions. Are more LBW decisions given in the higher standards of the game? I do think that, whereas a good, consistent 'not outer' is generally accepted by recreational players lower down the hierarchy, in the higher standards an umpire is 'expected' to give LBWs and thin nick catches, and to not hide behind 'giving the benefit of doubt to the batsman'.

Royal Ascot C.C., Thursday, 14th August, 2014

ECB Over 50 (45/45, reduced to 40/40). Berkshire II 150-8 (40.0), Buckinghamshire II 152-4 (32.5). Buckinghamshire II won by 6 wickets.

Royal Ascot Cricket Club is sited in the middle of the racecourse. I have never played here on a race day – I am told that the noise is deafening and that there's also lots of extra-curricular activity going on in the bushes and heathlands around the ground. Funnily enough, it has often been wet when I have played here in the past, and so it was again today. It is funny how you associate certain weather conditions with certain grounds that you perhaps only visit once every three or four years.

---

[82] Law 35.2, 'Not out hit wicket'.

We spent quite a lot of time sitting around in the pavilion waiting for the rain to stop. The conversation and banter was entertaining, much like *TMS* when rain has stopped play. One of the scorers, however, was in a rather grumpy mood – he had dropped his papers in transit from the scorebox to the pavilion and the rain had smudged his normally immaculate scoresheet. Then the tea ladies arrived with some homemade cakes. "Things are looking up", he said to me, his mood visibly lightening.

As a player I am ashamed to say that I did show dissent at umpiring decisions a couple of times. It was body language only and nothing verbal, but I should have known better. I am hardly in the poacher turned gamekeeper category, but remembering my indiscretions gives me now, perhaps, a more tolerant attitude to dissent than many of my fellow umpires. Today, however, a bowler showed real dissent at one of my decisions, and I was genuinely shocked by it – perhaps because, I think, I did not expect to encounter such behaviour in an Over 50s match. I had turned down an appeal for a stumping and the captain was disappointed. He bowled the next over at my end and I called him for a wide – and he reacted badly, saying that I had not called similar balls in the previous innings as wides and inferring that I was biased against his team. The stumping had been a close call, but the wide was beyond dispute. It all passed over fairly quickly after that, not least, I think, because he (the captain) then dropped a sitter and went into his shell. 'Maybe there is a god after all', I thought to myself.

There has been an amusing story doing the rounds recently about a roller getting stuck on the outfield during an

Over 50s match at Bledlow Village, and today I got a first-hand account. Apparently the roller's engine failed about an hour before the start of the match, and there was no way of moving it. So another pitch on the other side of the square was hastily prepared, and the match was played with a local rule – two runs and dead ball if the ball struck the roller. It was at silly point/short mid-wicket and was, by all accounts, the best fielder on show!

Maidenhead & Bray C.C., Saturday, 16th August, 2014

TVCL Division 2A. Harefield II 182 (42.5), Maidenhead & Bray 163 (55.4). Harefield II won by 19 runs.

This was a tense, exciting game, which went to the penultimate over. Bray is one of my favourite grounds and it was also a sunny but fresh, breezy day – not to everyone's taste, I know, but very much to mine. The only downside was a marquee, which blocked the view of the cricket from the pavilion, and *vice versa*. In a perfect world, cricket clubs would not stage weddings on match days, but because of the financial rewards it is a case, I think, of needs must.

I made an elementary error of preparation today. Reaching for my pencil to mark my card at the start of the second innings I was unable to locate it. No matter, I thought. I went to my box of tricks, aka the double-pocketed leather money belt, which I always wear when umpiring, to retrieve my spare pencil. It was there, but not sharpened – and I did not have a pencil sharpener. I made do as best I could. 'Be Prepared' is the boy scout motto! Sadly, I wasn't.

In the future, I will make sure that I also carry a pen as a reserve to eliminate the vagaries of sharpened or not pencils!

There was an amusing moment in today's match when one of the Bray batsmen, mid innings, suddenly asked for the sightscreen to be moved. On the next delivery he played and missed. "Do you want us to move it back?" chirped one of the Harefield fielders. The Bray batsman smiled and accepted the joke at his expense. I love this sort of banter. It is witty and amusing, and the antithesis of the inane and occasionally foul-mouthed comments that one sometimes hears on a cricket field.

I also overheard a father talking to his son today during the tea interval, and giving him some wicketkeeping advice. The Test Match between England and India was being shown on the television and he said, "Don't watch Dhoni, he never moves his feet and hands with the line of the ball, and he doesn't dive much either. He's too passive, he doesn't set the tone for the rest of the fielders." It was constructive criticism, and quite interesting to listen to. I presume that the father was either a coach or a former wicketkeeper himself?

Finchampstead C.C., Saturday, 23rd August, 2014

TVCL Division 2A. Tring Park II 230 (52.0), Finchampstead II 218 (47.1). Tring Park II won by 12 runs.

This was another tense and exciting match – and one of those strange days when all the difficult decisions came at my colleague's end. It is funny how this happens sometimes. When an umpire turns down an appeal, a lot of bowlers ask,

"What was wrong with that then, umps?" But the real question for the umpire to ask – before giving an affirmative decision – is, "Was everything right with that?" which is of course subtly different. In other words, the batsman should always get the benefit of the doubt.

There are two, more specific, variations on "What was wrong with that?" The first one is, "What was that missing then, umps?" following a rejected LBW appeal.[83] I usually give a brief explanation, such as "going down", "too high", "missing off", "pitched outside leg", "he hit it", "outside the line" etc. The second one is, "What did that hit then, umps?" following a rejected appeal for a catch.[84] On these occasions I say either "nothing" or "not the bat". I have formed the view that minimalistic answers following a rejected appeal are a good policy on the field. I am always available for a more detailed chat after the match if players want to discuss any of my decisions, but I have found that not many do.

Windsor C.C., Sunday, 24th August, 2014

Friendly (45/45). TVCL Representative XI 252 (44.1), Windsor 112 (34.2). TVCL Representative XI won by 140 runs.

I organised today's match and had to make a speech before the game. As a result I was not in my usual focussed state of mind as I walked out to umpire. I skippered Chalfont St. Peter Sunday 1st XI for four years and my batting form dipped during this period. Some players perform better when

---

[83] Law 36, 'Leg before wicket'.
[84] Law 32, 'Caught'.

captain and some worse, and there are many different dynamics that cause this. As an opening batsman I liked to prepare mentally before going out to bat. This did not mean cutting myself off from dressing room banter or isolating myself, but just uncluttering my mind and not thinking about anything else. When I was captain I was always worrying about batting orders, balls, umpires, scorers, teas, the bar etc. and then, before I had cleared my mind, I was batting – and it definitely affected my form. I tried dropping down the order but that did not work either. And then, in my first season back in the ranks, 1998, I recovered my batting form and had arguably my best ever season. Today, walking out to umpire, I was reminded of how I felt when I used to open the batting as captain.

It is such a shame about the aeroplanes at Windsor. During the afternoon they were relentlessly noisy but then in the early evening there were several periods of four or five minutes without one passing overhead. It showed how pleasant the venue must have been in days of pre-aviation yore. The view of the castle was less attractive today than usual because there was some scaffolding up; so I chose to stand at the castle end and face the opposite way for a change.

Wednesday, 27th August, 2014

Today I was listening to the *TMS* radio commentary on the ODI between England and India at Cardiff when Alastair Cook was given out LBW. Charles Dagnall and Ebony Rainford-Brent were commentating at the time, and both immediately asserted that it was absolutely plumb. Then they saw the replay on television and realised that the ball had pitched outside leg stump – and immediately started backtracking. "Well, it looked out from here, so I can't blame the umpire for giving it, but actually he shouldn't have done ..." It just goes to show what a hard job umpiring is! The DRS is not in use in this series because India are involved, so Cook was not reprieved.

High Wycombe C.C., Saturday, 30th August, 2014

TVCL Division 1. Wokingham 240-5 dec. (50.0), High Wycombe II 244-4 (46.1). High Wycombe II won by 6 wickets.

Thin nicks are the bane of an umpire's life. Today I missed one to the wicketkeeper late in the High Wycombe innings, when Wokingham still had an outside chance of winning. I was technically right to say not out, because I did not see or hear it, but I almost certainly got the decision wrong. My colleague later told me that he had heard the nick, and I also heard a comment from the High Wycombe batsman in the bar afterwards which implied that he had indeed hit the ball.

There was an odd moment at the toss today. The High Wycombe captain flicked the coin but the Wokingham captain failed to call. We all looked at him aghast and wondered what on earth was going on. He immediately apologised and said that he had been distracted by something else going on nearby. So I picked up the coin, gave it back to the home captain, and we duly restarted the process.

Ascott Park, Sunday, 31st August, 2014

Friendly. Old Seagullians 250-8 dec. (50.3), Butterflies 211 (41.1). Old Seagullians won by 39 runs.

"Nice view", said the fielder next to me at square leg just after lunch. For a moment I thought he was a fellow tree lover, admiring the magnificent view at Ascott Park (the autumn colours are early this year), or a fellow enthusiast of cloud formations (also splendid today as well). However, it transpired that he was being sarcastic about the new batsman's 'builder's bum', which was right in our eyeline. Attractive it was not. Then the chap ran himself out by half the length of the pitch. "Back to the cake trolley, then", said my new friend. In fact, plan A for one of these Ascott Park fixtures is be a batsman, bat first, make some runs, get out just before lunch, enjoy the hospitality and then sit back in a deckchair and await the afternoon mid-session declaration. What you really do not want to be doing is batting or – even worse – bowling just after lunch!

Old Seagullians are a wandering XI made up exclusively from the alumni of the University of St. Andrews. The Scottish independence referendum popped up briefly in conversation, but soon descended into Pythonesque 'what have they ever done for us' humour. Contrary to popular perception south of the border, a lot of cricket is played in Scotland.

Tuesday, 2nd September, 2014

I watched some of the ODI between England and India at Edgbaston on television today. India trounced England again, a dramatic reversal of fortunes from the recent Test series. In the professional game the two formats of the game are chalk and cheese but, interestingly, this is not yet the case in recreational cricket.

The other thing that struck me today is that both teams were playing in blue. As a traditionalist I do not much care for pyjamas whether they are blue, red or any other colour. But, surely, if you are going to have them, then the two teams ought to be in different colours? Have cricket's marketing men not heard of away strips? It is rare for them to miss an extra opportunity to rip off the fans!

Cookham Dean C.C., Saturday, 6th September, 2014

TVCL Division 2A. Cookham Dean 288-7 dec. (39.0), Fleet 198 (48.3). Cookham Dean won by 90 runs.

I seem to have had a lot of difficult caught behind decisions this season. I had another really tough one today. The conditions were ideal for seam bowling and a left-handed batsman pushed across a ball from a right-arm fast bowler. I was fairly sure that his bat clipped his front pad. The key question I had to answer was whether or not he had also hit the ball? The batsman stood his ground; the bowler, wicketkeeper and slip fielders appealed loudly. I was not sure so I said not out. The bowler and fielders were disappointed, but I did hear second slip subsequently say to the bowler that he was not sure. This was gratifying. It was at very least a tacit acknowledgement of just how hard a job umpiring sometimes can be.

Amersham C.C., Sunday, 7th September, 2014

Friendly. Amersham 243-5 dec. (46.0), Frogs 210-9 (47.0). Match drawn.

This was a gentle and sociable end-of-season match. It was a perfect September day, sunny with a gentle breeze. Why does the English cricket season now peter out gently in early September? It is such a lovely time to play cricket, usually (in my anecdotal experience) drier and warmer than the start of the season in April and May.

I stood at the southern end of the ground today and, from the bowler's end, the new Field of Remembrance at Shardeloes was visible. During one of the intervals I went and had a look. Each four-foot high cross commemorates 50,000 lives lost in World War One. It was quite sobering to stand there for a moment and contemplate the scale of this human catastrophe.

It was an all-day match. Lunch was minced beef with chillies and rice. It was very nice but, as I have said before, I am not especially keen on hot meals in the middle of a cricket match. Tea was more conventional cricketing fare with sandwiches and cakes – much more to my taste!

There was an amusing exchange amongst some of the Frogs fielders today. One of the aforementioned had arrived late in a flashy sports car and had then parked it in the sort of spot that an experienced cricketer should have known not to. Deep square leg, basically. Cue Frogs opening bowler drops one short, and Amersham opening batsman pulls the ball hard and high behind square for six – narrowly missing the expensive metal. The owner of the car then took some stick about stupid parking spots. "Well, where would you have parked?" he replied. "If you were bowling, probably at first slip", came the reply.

Gerrards Cross C.C., Sunday, 14th September, 2014

BCB Senior Cup Semi-Final (45/45). Bledlow Village 246 (44.4), Gerrards Cross 187 (41.1). Bledlow Village won by 59 runs.

I find these competitive win/lose matches the hardest to umpire because of the additional fielding restrictions that one has to monitor from square leg. This means that the slight relaxation of one's concentration, which can normally be afforded when away from the bowler's end, is not possible. Today's restrictions were maximum five fielders on the leg side and minimum four fielders inside the fielding circles, both throughout the innings; mercifully, there were no powerplays to complicate matters further.

The match was surprisingly one-sided with the underdogs outperforming their opponents in all three aspects of the game, batting, bowling and fielding. There were two odd incidents during the match. One of the Gerrards Cross out fielders periodically took it upon himself to make loud animal noises, like a wild cat in the Maasai Mara. It was beyond explanation; his teammates seemed to accept it as the norm and largely ignored it, and the Bledlow batsmen were perplexed rather than distracted. Then, later on during the Gerrards Cross innings, a batsman came to the crease wearing earphones. I have no idea what he was listening to but it did not do him much good – he only lasted three balls before he was bowled neck and crop! "Play it again, Sam", said one of the Bledlow fielders as he departed.

After the match the showers were cold, so I went straight home rather than socialising. It is unusual for me to do this. I can sometimes tolerate a cold shower – but not when I have sun cream oil to wash off my skin, because this requires hot water and soap. Another factor in my decision was that my colleague, a non-drinker, had already departed. It feels odd going straight home after a cricket match, a bit like leaving the theatre before the final act.

My colleague and I made one mistake each today, in reasonably close succession. He called wide ball (a one day wide) when the batsman maybe got a faint nick down to fine leg; then I did not call wide ball because I thought the batsman had got bat on ball – but everyone seemed to think he had missed it! Both incidents occurred towards the end of the game but I think the players lost a little bit of confidence in us as a result. I found this irritating – we had stood there for six or seven hours previously and, I think, got everything else right! You need a thick skin to do this job!

Postscript to the 2014 season

I umpired 63 matches during the 2014 season. Too many? Perhaps. It did not make any difference in the 'most important' matches (TVCL, ECB etc.), but I think I did come up a little short a few times re concentration and intensity in some of the 'less important' matches (social, lower age group junior, etc.) that I did. I have not been working for most of the last two years and enjoy umpiring, so it seems silly not to accept appointments as and when they are offered to me. However, one can have 'too much of a good thing' and I plan to manage my schedule more carefully next season.

The 2015 season

The close season always seems to go on forever and then all of a sudden the new season starts and the game takes over my life: from famine to feast.

There was an interesting discussion at the pre-season TVCL panel umpires meeting last week re the movement of fielders after the ball has come into play.[85] The background to this was the Steve Smith catch in an ODI during the winter when he ran round from first slip to leg slip, before the batsman had played his shot, and then took a catch. The ICC has subsequently ruled that this is acceptable, but the Laws of Cricket have not been changed and TVCL Match Rule 1 states that all matches shall be played according to the Laws of Cricket. So: 'Any significant movement by any fielder after the ball comes into play and before the ball reaches the striker is unfair' and any transgression of this law will result in a) a call of dead ball and b) possible further action.[86] What odds that this discrepancy between the Laws of Cricket and what players have seen on television will cause confusion and misunderstanding in the recreational game somewhere this season?

Harrow School, Monday, 13th April, 2015

Under 15 Friendly. Harrow School v. Middlesex Academy. Match cancelled.

---

[85] Law 41.7, 'Movement by Fielders'.
[86] Law 42.4, 'Deliberate Attempt to Distract Striker'.

Many things in the game of cricket have changed and evolved over the years, and will no doubt continue to do so in the future. However, some things remain constant: arriving at the ground on a nice sunny, spring day; meeting and greeting old friends; the sound of willow on leather as the players practise before the match; and that sickening feeling when you realise that the opposition are not going to turn up and that there has been a fixture "c***-up".

Once it had been established that the Middlesex Academy XI would not be coming it was decided that the Harrow boys would play an inter-school double-wicket competition. It was moderately enjoyable and at least helped me to blow away my umpiring cobwebs after the winter break. But I always find inter-school or club matches rather anaemic. Of course, there are always rivalries between batsmen and bowlers who otherwise never get to face each other in a 'match' situation, but these games always lack something that I cannot quite put my finger on. I think that the essential problem is one of artificiality: the individual contest is real, but the team aspect – and cricket *is* a team game – is not.

After the double wicket competition was over I sat and watched some of the match on the 1st XI ground, which is attractive from all vantage points. I then got talking to one of the school coaches. He was a typical cricket enthusiast, making signs with his right hand to indicate seam-up, off-break or leg-break, and clicking his tongue as he demonstrated a few shots. The season is underway and it is good to be back in the swing.

University College School, Saturday, 18th April, 2015

Friendly (40/40). Queen Elizabeth's School 212-6 (40.0), University College School 183-9 (40.0). Queen Elizabeth's School won by 29 runs.

The UCS sports ground in Hampstead has three cricket squares, two traditional pavilions and a pleasant outlook surrounded by some splendid oak trees, a few poplars and some very elegant houses. However, it is rather open and today there was no escape from a bitterly cold wind. I do not mind the latter when walking the fells in the Lake District but *vis-à-vis* cricket the only thing worse is rain!

The tea today was, metaphorically, a sandwich short of a picnic: a hot meal with a glass of orange squash. A cup of tea or coffee, or even a glass of red wine would have been perfect, as the chicken in tomato pasta was rather good. But the orange squash did not work for me at all.

The match itself flattered to deceive. UCS looked like they might make a fist of the run chase every now and again, but I always felt that they would fall short, and the margin of victory for Queen Elizabeth's was actually more comfortable than 29 runs suggests.

My colleague today was quite an interesting character. He was very 'old school', and reprimanded some of the boys for crossing the boundary line – and thus entering the field of play – before the umpires. "Who goes out first onto the field at Lord's in a Test Match?" he asked them, reproachfully. "The cameraman," replied one of the boys, quick as a flash. During the first innings, when one of the fielders got injured, he told me that there was a new law this season that runners were no longer allowed. I knew that he was wrong[87] but decided not to argue, and fortunately the boy had recovered by the time it was his turn to bat, so the matter did not arise. Later, I noticed that he was counting the balls with six marbles, and he told me that the phrase, 'to lose one's marbles', originated from an umpire who could not count. I thought that this story was rather doubtful, too, and so looked it up this evening. My guess was that it probably related to the Greeks 'losing' the Elgin Marbles, but there is no evidence for this and apparently the phrase originates from an American game in the late nineteenth century. 'Never let the truth get in the way of a good story', a late friend of mine was wont to say.

There were two interesting run out incidents today. On the first one the batsman hit a straight drive which knocked his partner off his feet, leaving him stranded in mid-pitch, and then ricocheted onto the wicket at the bowler's end. The bowler had his wits about him and quickly grabbed the ball in both hands and then pulled a stump out of the ground, thus legitimately breaking the wicket, and my colleague gave the (unlucky) non-striker out.[88] Later, in a separate incident, I thought that the wicketkeeper had accidentally knocked the bails off before receiving the ball and effecting a run out, but my colleague at square leg did not see this and upheld the run out appeal. This created a dilemma for me: to intervene or not? I decided not to on the basis that a) I was not absolutely

---

[87] An ICC regulation was introduced in 2011 banning the use of runners in international matches but they are still permitted by the Laws of Cricket. Law 2.1, 'Substitutes and runners'.
[88] Law 28.1, 'Wicket put down'.

sure, and b) my colleague had had the opportunity to consult me but had chosen not to do so – and I did not want to undermine him. If he had consulted me then I would have advised that I thought the wicket was put down unfairly.[89]

The Haberdashers' Aske's School, Wednesday, 22nd April, 2015

Friendly (40/40). Queen Elizabeth's School 130 (31.5), The Haberdashers' Aske's School 131-3 (21.4). The Haberdashers' Aske's School won by 7 wickets.

The main ground at Haberdashers' is magnificent. It is both spacious and enclosed by mature trees and the school buildings, which is a rare combination. The only downside today was that the pavilion was closed for refurbishment, so there were no changing facilities. Ever since my disaster at British Airways in 2011[90] I have always arrived fully changed at the ground, and today I reaped the benefit of so doing.

The other main feature of the Haberdashers' ground is the proximity of the Elstree Aerodrome. The light aircraft provide the same difficulty for umpires re faint nicks as the jumbo jets, albeit the noise comes and goes more quickly and they are considerably more interesting and aesthetically pleasing to watch as they pass by.

The match was one-sided. Queen Elizabeth's batted like millionaires and paid the price, and Haberdashers' knocked off the runs easily. There was, however, one item of

---

[89] Law 28.1, 'Wicket put down'.
[90] See entry for British Airways C.C., Saturday, 3rd September, 2011.

umpiring interest. Queen Elizabeth's opening batsman edged the ball into his pads and the ball popped up before landing on the pitch and starting to roll back towards his stumps. There were no fielders nearby, and he could have just stopped the ball with his foot, but instead chose to kick it away, quite violently and I thought 'wilfully'. The ball travelled some twenty or thirty yards – and one of the fielders had to go and retrieve it. The batsmen did not attempt to run and nobody appealed, although a couple of the fielders asked me, politely, whether he was allowed to do that? The incident passed and I took the next opportunity to quietly advise the batsman not to do that again! If there had been an appeal then I would of course have consulted with my colleague and agreed a course of action, but at the time I personally was minded to give him out for obstructing the field.[91] However, on reflection later, having consulted *Tom Smith* and taken advice from my umpiring mentor, I came to the view that this would have been the wrong decision. The batsman did not wilfully obstruct the fielding team because there was nobody close enough to him to have had an opportunity to field the ball. However, he may have caused damage to what was then a fairly new ball, so I could have cited him for a disciplinary transgression. It was a bizarre incident.

Queen Elizabeth's School, Saturday, 25th April, 2015

Friendly (40/40). Queen Elizabeth's School 107 (31.3), RGS High Wycombe 111-2 (17.2). RGS High Wycombe won by 8 wickets.

---

[91] Law 37.1, 'Out obstructing the field'.

This was the fourth school ground I have umpired at this season and the first state one. Its facilities are good but, unsurprisingly, not in the same class as those of the fee-paying schools. They have two cricket grounds but the outfields double up as rugby pitches in the winter and this year's dry spring has caused problems. The elegant school building dominates the main ground, and I made sure to choose the far end so that it was in my line of sight at the bowler's end.

I recognised some of the RGS High Wycombe boys – I live in Marlow so our paths have crossed a few times in recent seasons. They gave the impression of not recognising me, which is not uncommon. Umpires remember players but only rarely vice versa – unless of course you gave them out or turned down a 'stone dead' LBW.

I got lucky today when I made that classic mistake that all sportsmen and officials make from time to time: I took my eye off the ball! I was standing at square leg and there was a confident LBW appeal. While my colleague contemplated his decision, and I watched him in anticipation and thus took my eyes off what was happening at my end, the fielder at first slip threw down the wicket and promptly appealed. Fortunately, for me if not the batsman, my colleague was at this very moment raising his finger, which made first slip's appeal to me academic.

After the match I had an interesting discussion with one of the teachers about the expansive shot making of schoolboy batsmen these days compared to when I was their age. One top order batsman played a huge swipe to midwicket early in his innings and was nearly bowled. I did this once when batting with a very experienced cricketer who had played in the Bradford League in his prime – and I remember him walking half way down the wicket, doing a bit of 'gardening', and then saying to me, pithily, "think on, son, think on". Needless to say, I did not do it again.

Harrow School, Sunday, 26th April, 2015

Friendly (40/40). Harrow Wanderers 108 (37.2), Eton Ramblers 111-4. Eton Ramblers won by 6 wickets.

This was good quality cricket, with some especially fine seam bowling, played on a traditional English green top on a very cold early season day. Harrow had one outstanding left-arm seamer but no support at the other end – otherwise they might have won with just 108 on the board.

Lunch was rather odd: no catering arrangements had been made, so we were instead offered a very nice beefburger, chips and salad, washed down with a glass of red wine, in the nearby pub. I find that I can get away with a glass of red wine much better on a cold day like this. On a hot day it has a soporific effect on me in the afternoon, but today it made no difference at all.

After the match I had a look at the photographs and memorabilia in the pavilion, something which I always enjoy doing. I noted the many Old Harrovians who have played for England, from F.S. Jackson in the Golden Age of Cricket to Gary Ballance, who is currently putting in some stellar performances in the West Indies.

There was quite an interesting discussion on the recent 'Marlon Samuels salute'. It would be fair to say that opinion was divided, with some thinking it witty and others crude.

Maidenhead & Bray C.C., Tuesday, 28th April, 2015

ECB Over 60 (45/45). Berkshire 224-5 (45.0), Buckinghamshire 220-9 (45.0). Berkshire won by 4 runs.

The Bray ground looked stunning today in the spring sunshine, and it was a good day all round: an exciting match which was in the balance all the way through; a superb tea; and a beer and a chat afterwards. The latter has been missing during the school matches I have done so far this season, and there is nothing to beat a traditional cricket club bar after a good match.

There was a classic 'yes, wait, sorry' run out today. Apparently the culprit has some 'previous'– one of his teammates told me that, "he'd seen a few accidents over the years". Funnily enough, earlier on, a different batsman was calling "go" instead of "yes", which is a classic schoolboy error because it sounds so similar to "no". If he has not worked this out at 60 then he never will.

Imperial College, Wednesday, 29th April, 2015

BUCS South East 5B (35/35). Imperial College Medics 194 (32.5), School of Oriental and African Studies 152 (32.4). Imperial College Medics won by 42 runs.

This match was played at the Imperial College aka old British Airways ground. The name may have changed but nothing else has.[92] Today it was wet and cold when I arrived, and even more unlovely than usual, although the cloud cover was at least dulling the sound of the aeroplanes. This ground would pass any gradings and standards inspection with flying colours, because everything in isolation is very good. But isolation is the key word – everything is a long way apart and it has no cricketing ambience. And my mood was not improved during the tea interval when curry and cold drinks were on the menu rather than the traditional sandwich and a cup of tea. This is a worrying trend (for me) in recreational cricket. Perhaps I should start asking what type of tea is to be provided before accepting appointments in the future?

The cricket was fairly unremarkable and more one-sided than the score suggests. SOAS were a bit of a rabble – they had one very good player who, having bowled very well, looked briefly like he might win the match single-handedly with the bat – but not much else and a captain who was basically out of his depth. He had not planned his bowling changes or fielding positions, and it took his team an age to bowl their overs. Slow over rates are the bane of the recreational game.

I have noticed this season that ever more batsmen have started marking their guard with one of the bails. They use the bail as a makeshift drill, and bang it into the ground to make a hole some six to nine inches behind the popping crease. I wouldn't mind so much but they are *my* bails!

---

[92] See entry for British Airways C.C., Saturday, 3rd September, 2011.

Radlett C.C., Saturday, 2nd May, 2015

Friendly (50/50). Radlett 281-5 (50.0), Teddington 142 (40.1). Radlett won by 139 runs.

This has long been one of the grounds that I have wanted to visit so it was great to get an appointment here today – and it did not disappoint. The ground is visually attractive with mature trees and trimmed hedges, the playing area is immaculate and the pavilion probably the best I have seen in club cricket – it is ergonomically designed with large glass windows providing visibility of the playing area from anywhere in the main bar area. The only negative is the proximity of the main train line into King's Cross.

The standard of cricket today was very high but Teddington were under strength and, disappointingly from my neutral perspective, failed miserably in their run chase. It was also bitterly cold. This time last year all the grounds were waterlogged and little cricket was being played; this season the grounds are all bone dry but the temperatures are below average for the time of year.

Harrow School, Thursday, 7th May, 2015

Friendly (35/35). John Lyon School 152 (34.1), Harrow School II 153-4 (30.1). Harrow School II won by 6 wickets.

April was ridiculously warm and dry but normal service has now been resumed. First it got colder with a biting wind, and now the rain has arrived – and my last two matches, on Sunday and yesterday, have fallen victim to it. Mercifully, today was dry again. My match today was not especially interesting, and I found my concentration wavering a little. I counted nine squares in the school grounds, and was pleased to note that eight of them were in use, which meant circa 176 boys getting a game.

During the tea interval I overheard an amusing discussion between two or three boys who were trying to define a 'swivel-eyed loon'. They were talking about the supporters of one of the political parties taking part in today's General Election.

I have encountered a few odd superstitions amongst colleagues over the last few years[93] but came across a new one today. My colleague explained that he likes to always stand at the far end from the pavilion. I largely share this view but for aesthetic rather than superstitious reasons.[94] I sometimes wonder how superstitious people can be capable of the logical thought required by an umpire.

There were two bizarre incidents today. The first one involved a photographer walking onto the field, while play was in progress, and lining up a picture. There was a brief silence while everyone looked at him in stunned disbelief, and then we asked him to return to the boundary, which he duly did. As we were at Harrow School, and playing the gentleman's game of cricket, polite and courteous language was used. I can think of other situations when a little more Anglo-Saxon may have been included.

---

[93] See entry for Harefield C.C., Friday, 1st August, 2014.
[94] See entry for Burnham C.C., Sunday, 12th May, 2013.

The second one was more interesting re the Laws of Cricket. After the second over of Harrow's innings one of the batsman walked off the pitch without speaking to my colleague and me. His colleague then informed us that he was retiring because he had to sit an exam. We therefore informed the John Lyon captain and the Harrow batsman still at the crease that the exiting batsman was thus retired out – and it seemed that this was the end of the matter. However, about forty minutes later we saw him return with his kit bag and pad up to bat, presumably next wicket down. At this point I consulted with my colleague and we decided to invoke Law 43: we asked the John Lyon captain if he was prepared, in the interests of The Spirit of Cricket, to allow the retired batsman to resume his innings. He said that he was not. So we walked to the pavilion and explained the situation to the returned Harrow batsman and his captain. I think that we acted correctly and I would do exactly the same again; I am also pleased that I acted decisively and did not let the situation drift. I regret that the John Lyon captain took the attitude that he did – but accept that he was entirely within his rights to do so. I have a Corinthian attitude to recreational sport, but most young people nowadays take their lead from the ruthless professionalism they see on television.[95]

Merchant Taylors' School, Saturday, 9th May, 2015

TVCL Division 2A. Finchampstead II 142 (48.3), Old Merchant Taylors' 143-4 (40.0). Old Merchant Taylors' won by 6 wickets.

---

[95] See entries for Boyne Hill C.C., Saturday, 3rd August, 2013 and Kidmore End C.C., Thursday, 8th August, 2013.

Today it was back to league cricket after the good manners and serenity of school and social matches. If I had any doubt about this, OMT's cover point fielder soon removed them by joining in on an LBW appeal. That said I enjoyed the standard of play, the intensity and the fact that it really mattered – the teams were competing for points and my and my colleague's performances will be assessed by the captains.

I had one major although not controversial incident to deal with. Finch took the new ball after 16 overs of the OMT innings and the new ball bowler decided not to waste any energy on 'warm up' deliveries with the old ball. This proved a mistake as 'the new cherry' slipped out of his hand on three of the first four deliveries, causing him to bowl above waist-height beamers. So for the second time in my umpiring career I had to remove a bowler from the attack.[96] Coincidentally, both occurrences have been on the same ground – John Motson would have been thrilled. In the aftermath of the incident, his teammates were very supportive but the usual cricketing humour soon kicked in. "Unlucky, Fred, don't worry about it, we're all right behind you ... But it's a huge, huge fine!"

'Fred' has a double-barrelled surname, and there was some amusement in the bar after the match when my colleague, himself a well-spoken Old Wellingtonian, asked if he was one of "*the* Fotherington-Thomases". "Of course, he f****** well

---

[96] Laws 42.6, 'Dangerous and unfair bowling' and 42.7, 'Dangerous and unfair bowling – action by the umpire'.

is, that's his name", interjected one of the, dare I say it, 'less sophisticated' Finch players. Everyone laughed.

There was also an interesting discussion about Kevin Pietersen, with views evenly split re whether or not he should be recalled to the England team. I observed that many of the players were in favour, whereas the ex- or non-players, the umpires, scorers and administrators, the selfless volunteers who keep the grassroots game alive, were broadly against. Personally, I cannot quite see how a man who sent treacherous text messages to the opposition during a Test Match, wanted to miss England matches so that he could play in the IPL and then trashed his employers and teammates in a book, can realistically expect to be accepted back into the fold as if nothing has happened? During the discussion I remembered a similar debate this time last year at Beaconsfield.[97]

Ascott Park, Sunday, 10th May, 2015

Friendly. Cryptics 244-6 dec. (53.0), Stragglers of Asia 160 (40.5). Cryptics won by 84 runs.

Ever since I forgot to take my kit bag to British Airways in 2011[98] I have always turned up at grounds already changed, and today was no different. So I was somewhat taken aback when one of the players came up to me on arrival, introduced himself and then asked whether I was playing for the Stragglers or the Cryptics. I was gobsmacked and just looked down at my white blouson, with the ECB ACO

---

[97] See entry for Beaconsfield C.C., Saturday, 10th May, 2014.
[98] See entry for British Airways C.C., Saturday, 3rd September, 2011.

mnemonic and logo clearly displayed, and my navy trousers and white cricket shoes. "Oh, right, yes, you're the umpire, of course," said Tim Nice But Dim.

Anyway, it was great to be back again at the magnificent Ascott Park ground. The Cryptics are another of the famous wandering clubs with a particular tradition for overseas tours. The one great regret of my own cricket career is that I never went on an overseas tour. It has always struck me that travelling abroad, seeing new places *and* playing cricket would be, as Pangloss might have said, the best of all possible worlds. Speaking of touring, one of the Cryptics players was telling me about a fixture they played last year at Valley of the Rocks C.C. on the Exmoor coast in North Devon. I remember this ground coming into view as I headed west out of Lynton one day on the coastal path – it was a breathtaking sight!

There was a 'Richie Benaud' moment during the Stragglers innings. The Cryptics bowler moved a boundary fielder and the batsman promptly holed out to him next ball. I heard the television commentary in my head as it happened. "I think I'd have a man out at deep midwicket ... [long pause] ... [wicket falls] ... [another long pause] ... Yes, just about there!"

Little Marlow C.C., Wednesday, 13th May, 2015

BUCS South East 4A (45/45). Imperial College II 260 (45.0), Buckinghamshire University 165 (33.5). Imperial College II won by 95 runs.

Today was a glorious warm spring day and I discarded my blouson for the first time this season. I have mixed feelings about this. On the plus side it is great to wear a short-sleeved shirt on a warm spring afternoon; on the minus I do not like sun cream lotion. It is sticky, and if I sweat then it gets in my eyes and stains my white shirts.

The cricket was uneventful. Imperial got too many runs (from the neutral perspective) and there was never any doubt during Buckinghamshire's innings that they (Imperial) were going to win. The reader will by now be aware of my views on the shortcomings of win/lose cricket!

Kidmore End C.C., Saturday, 16th May, 2015

TVCL Division 2A. British Airways 74 (28.0), Kidmore End 78-3 (15.4). Kidmore End won by 7 wickets.

My day began with a glorious drive through a corner of England's green and pleasant land, along the Thames to Henley and then through the lanes to Kidmore. The cricket was something of an anti-climax and finished early at 4.15pm. We ate the tea after the match, which always feels odd, although a decent pint of bitter goes well with sandwiches. The countryside was still glorious as I drove home, but it always feels odd when the cricket has ended prematurely. I think I feel this more acutely as an umpire. As a player, you have either won well or lost badly, and you have to deal with the twin imposters accordingly, but as a neutral observer you just have an overwhelming feeling of anti-climax.

My colleague today was the wicketkeeper for Stragglers of Asia in last Sunday's match at Ascott Park. "Poacher turned gamekeeper this week," he said. When the captain gave us our fee before the match, he said, "Ah, bribes, this is my language!" He is an Italian.

Stowe School, Sunday, 17th May, 2015

Friendly (45/45). Flashmen 226 (45.0), Stowe Templars 106 (29.5). Flashmen won by 120 runs.

The main cricket ground at Stowe School is located directly in front of the magnificent neo-classical house, with rows of mature tress on the eastern and western sides and magnificent panoramic views of the countryside to the north. I chose to stand facing the house at the northern end but the views in all directions were equally attractive.

The cricket was of a reasonably good standard. The Flashmen are a wandering club with military connections run out of a pub in Chelsea, and they were too strong for the Templars today. In fact, I think the Templars may have been struggling a little bit for an XI. One chap was playing his first match of the season and had apparently put on a bit of weight over the winter. He was having a bit of a nightmare in the field and to everyone's amusement, and despite the best efforts of his captain to find new hiding places for him, the ball kept following him. "Just save as many as you can," said one of his teammates.

I noticed a batsman in the nets using a bowling machine on his own, i.e. without anyone feeding the balls into the machine. It did strike me that if he had got hurt, or someone distracted his attention, or there was a stray ball on a length, then he would have no way of stopping the next delivery, and the next one … Or maybe he had some sort of remote control over the feeder?

There was also an interesting moment when a bowler released a ball behind my back.[99] *Tom Smith* is really good on this subject. The first consideration is whether or not the bowler's back foot was within the return crease. *Tom Smith* advises that, if the umpire is happy that the flight of the ball is travelling in a straight line down the pitch, wicket to wicket, then he can reasonably assume that the bowler's feet were legally placed. The second consideration is whether or not the ball might have been thrown. In this case you are reliant on your colleague at square leg.[100]

Lord's, Thursday, 21st May, 2015

I am working at Lord's as a Match Day Steward during the Test match against New Zealand so have a two-week break from umpiring. But it is hard to get out of old habits: every time a ball was bowled today I felt myself reaching down for my counter!

I find as an umpire that I have a different perspective on the DRS to other spectators. To me it invariably proves just how good the professional umpires are. If it is umpire's call because he (the umpire) has said not out and the ball has just clipped the side or top of the stumps, then this to me –

---

[99] Law 24.5, 'Fair delivery – the feet'.
[100] *Tom Smith* (2004), pp.178–9.

factoring in the margin of error in the technology – shows what a *good* call he has made. Sadly, I do not think that the cricketing public really understands this. Who would be an umpire?

Lord's, Monday, 25th May, 2015

Today there was free entry for children under 16 and adults only paid £20 – and the ground was full. Has it never occurred to the ECB that many cricket fans are priced out of the modern game, with tickets for a Lord's Test match starting at £60 per day for New Zealand and £100 for Australia later in the summer? Today, thousands of the next generation of cricket fans saw a thrilling final day's play. But the ECB will not learn. If they can get away with selling tickets in advance for the last day they will do so. It is the same argument as the lack of cricket on terrestrial television. The ECB may make a lot of money from television deals with pay-per-view providers, but how much is it losing in the longer term by not reaching millions of young/less affluent viewers?

I was asked about my availability for upcoming matches today. One of my colleagues recommended the Eton v. Harrow match as a good one to put one's name down for. "It's like a posh football match. Each team's spectators chant songs at each other – but with better grammar and no swearing!"

Taplow C.C., Wednesday, 27th May, 2015

I scored a match today for the first time in some 40 years. It was quite an interesting experience. As an umpire, one is sometimes frustrated by scorers either not acknowledging your signals or, especially when you have multiple signals to make, waving but not looking at you. As a scorer today, I felt the reverse frustration – wanting the umpire to go ahead and make his signals so I could start updating the scorebook, and feeling irritated when berated for not acknowledging a no ball or wide signal when the aforementioned had not been called loudly enough.

I played at Taplow many times but this was my first visit to the ground for at least ten years. It is attractive with a traditional pavilion at one end, complete with three mature trees growing through the patio roof. I wanted to have a walk round the ground and explore, but this is the major downside of scoring, as with umpiring – you are in the game for every ball of the match and you do not have the downtime afforded to batsmen not currently in the fray.

North Maidenhead C.C., Saturday, 30th May, 2015

TVCL Division 2A. British Airways 93 (21.1), North Maidenhead 95-2 (15.5). North Maidenhead won by 8 wickets.

The BA captain is not a fan of my abilities as an umpire, and he was unimpressed with my performance again today. His main criticism was a run out decision I gave against one of his batsmen. In my opinion he was clearly out because he failed to ground his bat, but without the DRS we will never be able to prove it one way or another. One thing I must say, though, is that although I have found his criticisms of my performance in the last two matches I have done for BA a little unpalatable, I do welcome it when players challenge my decisions after the game. I think it is always good to discuss and part on friendly terms, even if you have to agree to differ, and you cannot improve as an umpire if your (perceived) mistakes are not challenged.

Today's match was so one-sided that it finished before the F.A. Cup Final had even kicked off, and the pattern of the cricket proved an auspicious omen for the football, with Arsenal's attacking play cutting through the Aston Villa defence as decisively as North Maidenhead's bowling attack had the BA batting.

Amersham C.C., Sunday, 31st May, 2015

Friendly. Amersham v. Jesters. Match cancelled.

Most teams and captains make genuine efforts to look after the peripheral people who are so vital to the game – umpires, scorers, groundsman, tea ladies etc. But every now and again they forget us and this happened today. I arrived at the ground 45 minutes before the start and was surprised to see nobody else there. Not good, I thought. Then I spotted the Jesters' scorer, who was thinking the same. A quick phone call confirmed that the match had been called off earlier that morning but we had not been informed.

The Jesters' captain apologised profusely, and of course I accepted his apology. Nobody makes these sorts of mistakes on purpose – he had probably spent all week sorting out his

XI and then all morning trying to find out if the game was still on. However, the annoying thing about his forgetfulness is that my day has been wasted. If I had known at 10.00am this morning that the game was off then I could have done something else. As it was, it was 2.30pm by the time I got home and any opportunity to do something worthwhile had passed.

Beaconsfield C.C., Saturday, 6th June, 2015

TVCL Division 1. Beaconsfield 141 (49.4), Kew 121 (42.0). Beaconsfield won by 20 runs.

This was a hard match to umpire: low-scoring on a poor pitch. I gave six decisions; four LBWs and two caught behinds, and turned down at least six more very good appeals. I think that I got all the appeals that I upheld right but perhaps should have given two other LBWs that I turned down. But the batsman should get the benefit of the doubt so overall I am happy with my decision-making today.

One of the appeals I turned down was because the batsman was struck outside the line of off-stump. This is the easiest 'not out' decision for an umpire because you are in the perfect position to see where the batsman has been struck, albeit, of course, that it is much harder to judge if he is hit on the move. Today, when the bowler asked me why I had turned down one of his appeals, and I said, "outside the line", he was surprised, and said that he thought the only possible reason could have been that the ball was going down the leg side. This amused me. It was proof if ever it is needed that a bowler, falling away to the off side after his delivery stride, is not in a good position to see the line of either the ball or the batsman's feet. "Oh, umps", he said, "that just felt so out, I'm 90% certain it was hitting!" "90% is not out in my book", I replied. He smiled ruefully. I do not mind these exchanges between bowler and umpire, they are usually informative for both parties.

I did have an embarrassing moment today when a ball leapt from a length and struck the batsman on the hand. I thought that it had hit him on the arm and then run off to fine leg for four. So I signalled four leg-byes. By this time the batsman was wringing his knuckles in agony, and everyone was laughing at my leg-bye signal. Sometimes you just want the ground to swallow you up. In the circumstances, as there could have been no doubt whatsoever that the ball had struck the batsman on the glove while he was still holding the bat, I decided to reverse my signal. Unfortunately, the scorers did not seem to be on my wavelength, and when they failed to acknowledge my reversal signal, I had to walk over to them and verbally clarify – all of which only further heightened my embarrassment.

When I sat down with my colleague after the match to do our paperwork, the discussion turned to our man of the match nomination. "I'd give it to the groundsman", said my colleague, flippantly.

Radley College, Sunday, 7th June, 2015

Friendly (50/50). Radley Rangers 216-9 (50.0), Sherborne Pilgrims 217-3 (34.5). Sherborne Pilgrims won by 7 wickets.

This was my first visit to Radley College. The setting is magnificent, with an immaculately flat pitch and an elegant raised pavilion dating back to 1900. I counted seven squares, a comparable number to the other public schools which I have visited in recent years, not to mention multiple practice wickets, sightscreens on every ground and full covers for the two main ones. The second square was split in two with pitches on the second half running in the opposite direction – I have not seen this before!

The pavilion has team pictures and memorabilia dating back to 1859 and I spotted Ted Dexter and Andrew Strauss amongst the alumni. I imagined Lord Ted's cover drives racing across the immaculate outfield – what a sight he must have been in full flow. The historical analogies continued when I received the Rangers team sheet – their opening batsman was listed as W.G. Grace! I thought that this must be a joke but apparently not. His parents must be cricket fans with a sense of humour. When my colleague gave him out LBW, I half expected him to stand his ground and say, "Nonsense, man, the crowd haven't come to watch you umpire ..."

Yesterday's league match was tense and challenging, and I felt under pressure throughout, but today's was gentle and easy. In fact, so gentle that I only had three or four appeals to answer, and turned them all down. The standard of play was, of course, lower, but the spreads were in a different league. Yesterday we had stale sandwiches and bought cakes, and the only bright spot was a nice cup of tea. Today there was a carvery with potatoes and vegetables for lunch, followed by sandwiches and homemade lemon drizzle cake at teatime. As

Mrs Merton might have said, "What was it that first attracted you to this sort of cricket?"

Little Marlow C.C., Wednesday, 10th June, 2015

BUCS South East 4A (45/45). Buckinghamshire University v. St. George's, University of London. Match cancelled.

The weather was warmer and the venue different, but aside from that this was similar to events at Harrow School in April[101]. At first we thought that St. George's were late. Then, when their captain did not answer his phone we were worried. Then the Buckinghamshire captain mentioned that it was a "re-arranged" fixture. "Oh, dear!" I thought, and soon afterwards we all agreed that St. George's were not coming and decided to go home.

Finchampstead C.C., Saturday, 13th June, 2015

TVCL Division 2A. Finchampstead II 223-6 (52.0), Kidmore End 225-6 (47.5). Kidmore End won by 4 wickets.

There are two basic principles when it comes to wides. Firstly, apply the match rules (i.e. Laws of Cricket, 'profile' wides, 'leg side' wides, guidelines agreed with the captains beforehand in friendlies etc.) and secondly, be consistent. In the TVCL the Laws of Cricket apply, so that bit at least is straightforward. I tend, broadly, to be lenient, and I think this is what the players want.

---

[101] See entry for Harrow School, Monday, 13th April, 2015.

However, today, I ran into difficulty in the final over of the match. At this point, Kidmore needed eight runs to win from four balls, and Finch four wickets. So, barring an extraordinary collapse, there were by now only two results possible, a Kidmore win or a draw. The next ball was speared down the leg side, and passed the batsman's feet at yorker length, maybe as much as a foot down the leg side. I was quite clear in my mind that it was a wide, because the batsman was unable to play a normal cricket shot. My decision in isolation was undoubtedly correct. However, the problem was consistency. Had there been other, similar balls that I had not called as wide earlier in the match? Almost certainly, yes. I was fully aware of this when I made my decision, but I felt that my primary duty was to ensure fair play and therefore exercised Law 43. I simply did not think that it was fair for the Finch bowler, in these circumstances, to be allowed to get away with such a delivery. After the game, Kidmore (unsurprisingly) made clear that they agreed with my decision but the Finch captain made clear that he did not. Later, after he had showered and changed, and had a beer in his hand, we had an amicable discussion and he accepted my point of view. However, I think that there will be many people, especially amongst the umpiring fraternity, who will disagree with what I did today. Is my primary duty to apply the laws consistently or to ensure fair play? Sometimes, they are not the same thing. I think the lesson I will learn from today's experience is that I should have been less lenient on wides earlier in the match.

East Woodhay C.C., Sunday, 14th June, 2015

Friendly (40/40). Flashmen 225-6 (40.0), East Woodhay 92 (29.5). Flashmen won by 133 runs.

When one is rained off as a player then that is usually that. However, as an umpire, there is always the possibility of being reassigned elsewhere, and this is what happened to me today. My original match at Ascot Park was rained off so I was instead diverted to this picturesque ground on the outskirts of Newbury. The setting was very rural, with mature trees, including one magnificent oak, surrounding but not tightly enclosing the ground on all sides, and the noise of farm animals in the background.

It was a strange game. The Flashmen were far too strong and made sure of their victory with some quite hostile fast bowling, which seemed a bit out of place for a social match on a Sunday afternoon.

There was one interesting umpiring incident today. After I had given an East Woodhay batsman out caught behind off his glove, he took a long time to leave the crease and then started to talk to the Flashmen fielders. He said that the ball had actually hit his arm and not his glove, so the Flashmen sportingly asked if they could withdraw their appeal. As the batsman had not left the field of play I said that this was fine and duly revoked my decision.[102]

Harlow C.C., Wednesday, 17th June, 2015

I have written previously about not having any downtime as an umpire – you are involved in every ball and therefore

---

[102] Law 27.8, 'Withdrawal of an appeal'.

have no time to switch off and relax.[103] Today I sat and watched the TVCL Representative XI play against the Hertfordshire/Essex League in the Quarter Final of the Sovereign Cup. The TVCL won the match, the ground was attractive and the weather pleasant, and the tea was the best so far this season – delicious sandwiches and homemade cakes. Above all, it was wonderful not to have to concentrate on every ball.

What is this life if, full of care,
We have no time to stand and stare.[104]

Maybe I am umpiring too much at present?

Falkland C.C., Saturday, 20th June, 2015

TVCL Division 1. Kew 279-8 (52.0), Falkland 243-8 (48.0). Match drawn.

There are many beautiful grounds in the TVCL and this is another jewel in its crown. I particularly like the four Poplar trees which today shimmered gently in the breeze, psychologically cooling me on a hot, muggy day. Storms were predicted and apparently biblical just a few miles away, but they missed Newbury.

Interestingly, this, my twenty-second match of the season so far, was the first one that has ended in a draw. To some degree this is a sign of the times, with thirteen of those matches played using the win/lose format, but it is

---

[103] See entry for Chalfont St. Peter C.C., Friday, 20th July, 2012.
[104] Davies, W.H., 'Leisure' in *Songs of joy and others* (London, 1911).

nonetheless surprising that this was the first of my nine traditional matches so far to end in stalemate. It is actually a popular misconception that there are a lot of draws in traditional format league cricket matches. In fact, there are not, primarily because, aside from stopping a rival placed near you in the league table from securing a precious win, there is no tangible benefit in playing negatively for a draw. In most modern league structures (ten teams per division is the norm, often with two up, two down) and points systems, a team's final position is primarily determined by how many matches it wins rather than the number of times it avoids defeat.

Marston Sports Ground, Sunday, 21st June, 2015

Friendly. Oxford University Authentics 220-5 dec. (54.5), Frogs 146 (56.0). Oxford University Authentics won by 74 runs.

This is the second year running that I have umpired this fixture. The Authentics wanted to play the traditional format this time – last year this fixture preceded the win/lose varsity match but this year it came before the three-day game. One of the benefits of the traditional format is that, in an all-day game, you get both a lunch and a tea, which I like and not just for gastronomic reasons – the second break for my aching back is much appreciated! The lunch was interesting: vegetarian and carbohydrate-based, with a choice of spinach pasta (very nice), potato salad (nice again) and couscous (not for me); tea was light and traditional, with sandwiches and cakes. The only disappointment was that they ran out of milk, so rather than a cup of tea it was black coffee or squash. So nice but no cigar.

The cricket was rather slow and uneventful. The overnight rain had slowed down the outfield and runs were quite hard to come by. I made a signalling error, which annoyed me - I realised almost immediately and kicked myself. I called a no ball, but two byes were also run. I called and signalled no ball, and then repeated my signal to the scorers - but forgot to then signal byes. Technically, the scorers should therefore have awarded two runs to the batsman plus one for the no ball.[105] However, when I checked discreetly afterwards, I noticed that they had applied the scorers' equivalent of Law 43 and recorded no ball three. So I smiled quietly to myself and moved on.

Amersham Hill C.C., Tuesday, 23rd June, 2015

ECB Over 60 (45/45). Hampshire 258-6 (45.0), Buckinghamshire 110 (31.0). Hampshire won by 148 runs.

Everything was set up for a good game of cricket today when Buckinghamshire began their reply, but after three early wickets had fallen it was effectively game over. However, the match continued for another hour and a half before Buckinghamshire's last wicket fell and we were all put out of our misery. Win/lose cricket! Ho hum!

I made a silly error today. The umpire is supposed to note down the start time of the match and I normally do so, but today, lulled into a false sense of security because it was an

---

[105] Law 24.13, 'Runs resulting from a no ball - how scored'.

overs match without penalties for slow over rates, I omitted to do so. Alarm bells should have been ringing when Buckinghamshire took the field with only ten players. Then, when the eleventh player arrived 45 minutes after the scheduled start, I had to work out when he could bowl.[106] My colleague had not noted down the start time either but fortunately the scorers had, so after a brief consultation I was able to make the right calculation. I hate getting caught out like this – it does not project an image of competence!

There was another interesting incident when a batsman walked for a catch down the leg side. I have to be honest and say that I was not sure myself – so I would have given him not out if push had come to shove. These senior games are normally played in an excellent spirit.

Harrow School, Wednesday, 24th June, 2015

Friendly. Free Foresters 227-8 dec. (44.2), Harrow School 228-9 (46.2). Harrow School won by 1 wicket.

This was a fantastic game of cricket. With two balls to go, all four results were possible. The Free Foresters are arguably the most famous of all the wandering clubs with a history dating back to 1856. 'Foresters' refers to the forests of Arden and Needwood, and 'Free' to the fact that members were allowed to play *against* as well as *for* the club. Many famous cricketers have turned out for them, including three of my personal favourites, Colin Cowdrey, Frank Worrell and Keith Miller.

---

[106] Law 2.5, 'Fielder absent or leaving the field'.

My colleague today was an elderly gentleman but, although somewhat frail, very sharp. He told me that he had been umpiring for over 40 years and estimated that he had stood in more than 3000 matches in this time. I thought that I had done a lot of umpiring recently – 25 matches and counting this season! – but he (my colleague) told me that he was already past 50. This is just too much, in my opinion – I think you need a break every now and again to recharge your batteries.

Stoke Green C.C., Saturday, 27th June, 2015

TVCL Division 1. Cookham Dean 251-6 dec. (50.0), Stoke Green 119 (36.2). Cookham Dean won by 132 runs.

This was a really hard match to umpire, with two very good spinners bowling most of the overs at my end, and close fielders putting both the batsmen and me under the utmost pressure. I also had a boundary assessment today by the Buckinghamshire ACO Education Officer and, after the match, he picked up on my anxiety at tense moments. He observed that, whereas most of the time my posture remained calm and still, when the pressure was on I started making involuntary movements in my upper body and leaning forward stiffly. This was useful feedback and gives me something to work on. My anxiety when there are spin bowlers operating with close fielders around the bat is because I know that 'thin nicks' will come into play, most especially bat/pad catches.

Somewhat ironically, my two hardest decisions today were LBW appeals from seam bowlers. I turned down one from a Stoke Green bowler against a left-handed Cookham batsman who shouldered arms. I saw the ball shape in and it hit the batsman's front pad in line with off stump. However, I factored in where the bowler was releasing the ball, which was not close to the stumps, and decided that the batsman should have the benefit of doubt that the ball was missing off stump. Then, in the Stoke Green innings, a right-handed batsman got a good stride in but played around the ball. I could see that the ball had hit him in line with off stump, I knew that the bowler was getting in very close to the stumps, I did not think it was going down leg side and nor did I think it was going over. So I gave the batsman out. I am happy with both decisions.

Long Marston C.C., Sunday, 28th June, 2015

ECB Under 17 (50/50 reduced to 42/42). Buckinghamshire 251-8 (42.0), Oxfordshire 227-9 (42.0). Buckinghamshire won by 24 runs.

This was my first visit to Long Marston. It is an attractive ground, enclosed by a variety of mature trees, mainly ash and birch, and with a very large playing area. It has a reputation for excellent teas and did not disappoint today. The scorer, a comfortably built gentleman, lives within walking distance of the ground and yet today contrived to arrive late. Someone observed rather cruelly that he must have passed the sandwich trolley *en route*. However, I must say that he redeemed himself in my eyes with his encyclopaedic knowledge of the competition rain rules when we had a delayed start due to persistent drizzle.

There was an amusing incident today when the Oxfordshire wicketkeeper expertly removed a stump from the ground with ball in hand after he had previously inadvertently knocked the bails off.[107] The only problem was that the batsman had not left his ground. "Nice work", said one of his teammates, sarcastically, "when you've put the wicket back together perhaps you could throw us the ball and we could get on with the game."

RGS High Wycombe, Wednesday, 1st July, 2015

RGS Festival (50/50). RGS Lancaster 337-5 (50.0), RGS Colchester 133 (40.2). RGS Lancaster won by 204 runs.

I played on this ground several times as a schoolboy – I went to Dr. Challoner's and RGS High Wycombe were our main cricketing rivals. Phil Newport was in the RGS team at the time and I remember him being quite quick. I hope that I got into line – I do not remember scoring any runs here and the details of the matches have faded into the annals of time.

Today's match was part of a week-long festival involving the six 'Royal' grammar schools – High Wycombe, Guildford, Colchester, Worcester, Lancaster and Newcastle. Each school takes it in turns to entertain – and this year it was High Wycombe's turn. Cricket can be a cruel game when one team is too strong for the other – and especially so in the win/lose format. If today's match had been played using the traditional format then Lancaster could have declared five or ten overs earlier and put the Colchester fielders out of their misery.

---

107 Law 28.1, 'Wicket put down'.

265

For a while the Colchester fielders trotted out the familiar line – "we don't mind that!" – whenever a Lancaster batsman drove one through the covers or straight down the ground. I was not sure quite what it was that they 'didn't mind' – the ball being struck out of the screws with regularity or the scoreboard showing a lot for not many?

There was an interesting point of law today. The playing regulations stipulate that 'wide will be called for any delivery which passes behind the profile of the striker in his normal guard position'. Late in the Colchester innings, when the result was already a foregone conclusion, the Lancaster captain, a left-arm spinner bowling round the wicket to a right-handed batsman, bowled him behind his legs. By this time the pitch was turning square, and the batsman departed without protest. At this moment I suddenly began to wonder whether I should have called wide ball, because playing regulations generally supersede the Laws of Cricket. However, I later discovered that it was my knowledge of the laws that was lacking, because one should not call a wide until the ball has passed the striker's wicket.[108]

Friday, 3rd July, 2015

In the TVCL the umpires see their marks (and associated comments) from the captains on the Friday after the match. These can be useful and informative; they can also be very frustrating, especially if you feel that you have been marked down unfairly. I had the latter experience today when I saw my marks and comments for last Saturday's game at Stoke

---

[108] Law 25.3, 'Call and signal of wide ball'.

Green. I have the thick skin that all umpires need, but am nonetheless upset.

Some captains are conscientious and fair, but I am afraid that most fall into one of two traps. Winning captains tend to be lazy and too lenient, whereas losing captains can by myopic and vindictive. This is my fifth season as a TVCL panel umpire and last Saturday was my 70th match. I have not yet had better marks from a losing captain than his winning counterpart.

Burnham C.C., Saturday, 4th July, 2015

TVCL Division 2B. Chiswick & Whitton 232-9 dec. (50.0), Burnham II 169 (40.5). Chiswick & Whitton won by 63 runs.

My colleague gave one of the Burnham bowlers today a first and then final warning for running on the protected area of the pitch in his follow through.[109] It was accidental and there was no malice involved, but one needs to be especially vigilant if the wicket is damp and cutting up or, as today, a dustbowl.

The wicket turned square from the start. I had one difficult LBW decision to adjudicate. Burnham's left-arm spinner pitched one on leg stump and straightened it to a right-handed batsman. Normally, this would have been stone dead, but I actually thought it was possibly doing too much and therefore gave the batsman the benefit of doubt that it was turning past off stump.

---

[109] Law 42.12, 'Bowler running on the protected area after delivering the ball'.

An incident was drawn to the attention of my colleague and me during the tea interval today. It proved to be something of nothing. However, it did show that the umpires need to remain alert during the tea interval – and at the time we both had our backs to the playing area. Some years ago when I was still a player I remember an almighty kerfuffle when our groundsman swept, remarked and then rolled the pitch between innings. We were batting second and our captain had legitimately requested that the pitch be rolled.[110] The problem was that our groundsman used a machine, which was both a roller *and* a mower, to do the rolling, and the opposition thought that he was also mowing the pitch, which is not permitted between innings.[111] He was not doing so, and the incident blew over, but I do remember feeling tremendously sorry for the two umpires, who were enjoying a cup of tea and a sandwich and putting their feet up for a few minutes – until all this blew up!

Holmer Green C.C., Sunday, 5th July, 2015

Today I played my first match for five years – a Chalfont Saints reunion game. I scratched around horrendously for seven or eight and then got triggered out LBW to a delivery from a left-arm over the wicket bowler which simply must have pitched outside leg – and if it did not then it certainly did not pitch on and straighten to hit the stumps. Umpires, eh? To be honest, he did me a favour and put me out of my misery. I have now put my kit bag back into the attic where

---

[110] Law 10.1, 'Rolling'.
[111] Law 10.3, 'Mowing'.

it should have remained all along. It was nonetheless a very enjoyable day.

It was a hot day and one of the players was, rather bizarrely, wearing an old-fashioned long-sleeved jumper (as opposed to the fleeces which are more commonplace nowadays). It reminded me of another old Saints teammate who used to do the same thing, on the grounds that he wanted to lose weight. The flaw in his logic, unfortunately, was that he liked a beer after the match. Ten or twelve of them at least. He was one of those chaps who downed rather than supped a pint.

Burnham C.C., Saturday, 11th July, 2015

TVCL Division 2B. Burnham II 292-7 dec. (46.4), High Wycombe II 247-8 (53.0). Match drawn.

This was the second week running that I have umpired Burnham II. This is not something that I normally like to do – I prefer not to see again a team I have umpired for a good few weeks at least. This is because one's decisions from a previous match can linger, whether correct or not. From an umpire's perspective, if you have given a batsman out incorrectly the previous week, or if he did not like the decision, or vice versa you have turned down an appeal from a bowler, it is very hard to blank this out of your mind if you have to make a 'judgement' call involving the same player the next week. Professional umpires have this problem to some extent if they umpire consecutive rubbers in a Test match series – but they are nowadays largely protected from serious errors by the DRS. Anyway, none of those issues materialised today, and I do not think that the Burnham players gave the matter a second thought.

Radley College, Sunday, 12th July, 2015

Friendly. Radley Rangers 266-4 dec. (49.4), Shopwyke Strollers 114 (27.5). Radley Rangers won by 152 runs.

The standard of play today was quite high – with the exception of the Strollers' batting! – and I would say that it was comparable to a TVCL Level 2 match. I had an interesting conversation with one of the players about this during the luncheon interval. He said that he now only played on 'the jazz circuit' (old boys and social matches on Sundays) and had given up Saturday league cricket, primarily because he found the latter rather vulgar – poor player behaviour, putting pressure on umpires, the lack of social interaction between teams. Sadly, I understood only too well what he was saying.

The weather today was pleasantly fresh after the recent hot spell. This pleased me greatly, and I smiled quietly to myself as various people bemoaned the lack of sunshine.

One of the Strollers' bowlers today had a superbly disguised slower ball. He used it twice – on the first occasion bowling a well-set batsman neck and crop, and on the second missing the stumps by a whisker. After this, the batsmen were anticipating another one, but he shrewdly declined to use it again, keeping them guessing to the end. It was good cricket.

Chesham C.C., Tuesday, 14th July, 2015

Friendly (45/45). Chesham 306-5 (45.0), Chairman's XI 199 (38.4). Chesham won by 107 runs.

This is the second year running that I have umpired this fixture, and the first two paragraphs of my diary entry last year could apply just as well to today.[112] The red wine was again flowing at lunchtime and I think that most people, including myself, over-indulged. Chesham's opening bowler was a Muslim observing Ramadan and had been obliged to miss lunch. Coming on to open the bowling after lunch, he gave me his cap and said, "I'm hungry, thirsty and tired but today, for a change, I have the advantage – I am the only sober player on the field!"

There was amusing banter throughout the day. I noticed that one of Chesham's bowlers had acquired the nickname of 'the burglar', presumably because he often gets wickets with bad balls. Later, two near-identical twins/brothers, neither regular bowlers, found themselves bowling in tandem, and there was amusement when the scorer had to come onto the pitch and ask which one was which.

Boyne Hill C.C., Wednesday, 22nd July, 2015

Friendly (40/40). TVCL Representative XI 252-4 (40.0), Boyne Hill 197 (36.4). TVCL Representative XI won by 55 runs.

---

[112] See entry for Chesham C.C., Tuesday, 15th August, 2014.

There was an amusing moment in this match during Boyne Hill's innings. The Rep XI had been one short from the start. Then the wicketkeeper was injured and one of his colleagues had to take him to hospital. So then there were eight. One of the Boyne Hill batsmen then hit a couple of fours over extra cover.

"He's only got one shot!" called out one of the fielders.
"I've only got six fielders", replied the captain.
"Fine", said the fielder, "let's have six deep extra covers!"

Kidmore End C.C., Saturday, 25th July, 2015

TVCL Division 2A. Kidmore End 86 (40.3), Maidenhead & Bray 89-3 (22.5). Maidenhead & Bray won by 7 wickets.

We had a tremendous downpour of rain during Friday and overnight into Saturday morning. The Kidmore guys then worked very hard to get this match on – but received scant reward for their efforts. Bray won the toss – and with it the match as the wicket was virtually unplayable early on. That said, Bray were 14-3 in their reply and at that point it was very much game on.

I had two big decisions to make today and, to be honest, I think that I got both of them wrong. The first was an LBW appeal, which I upheld against Kidmore's opening batsman. I thought that he had been beaten by an *in*-swinging yorker and there is no doubt in my mind that the ball was going to go on and hit the stumps. However, the general consensus of opinion seems to be that he hit it. The thing that annoys me about my mistake here is not so much that I missed the 'thin nick' but that the '*in*-swing' should have given me the vital clue because the bowler was bowling *away*-swingers! I sought out the batsman afterwards and apologised for my mistake, as I always do in such circumstances, and he accepted my apology magnanimously.

My second mistake was to not give a stumping later in the Kidmore innings. At the time I thought that it was too close to call, with the batsman sliding his foot back as the wicketkeeper whipped off the bails, so I gave the benefit of doubt to the batsman and said 'not out'. However, on reflection, I think that it is unlikely that the batsman got his foot back in time. I am happy with my thought process under pressure on this decision even though, with the benefit of hindsight, I think that I probably got it wrong.

High Wycombe C.C., Tuesday, 28th July, 2015

ECB Under 14 (45/45). Buckinghamshire 179-9 (45.0), Staffordshire 183-6 (42.5). Staffordshire won by 4 wickets.

This was a very good game. I had a difficult LBW decision to make late in the Staffordshire innings. The batsman was caught on the back foot about knee high. It was not going over, but I thought that it may have just been sliding down the leg side, so I gave the batsman the benefit of the doubt and said not out. I think that it may have been the decisive moment in the match.

Farnham Common C.C., Thursday, 30th July, 2015

ECB Under 13 (35/35). Buckinghamshire 184-7 (35.0), Inner London 157 (34.1). Buckinghamshire won by 27 runs.

Farnham Common is an unlovely cricket ground. It has a good track, a decent, flat outfield and good clubhouse facilities. But it is very open and the clubhouse is not a cricket pavilion in the traditional sense. I am not sure which came first, the cricket ground or the clubhouse, but one or the other feels like an afterthought. However, I only made one century in my career (with a hard ball[113]), and it was here in 2005, so it does have fond memories for me.

This was a gentle game on a Thursday afternoon, a million miles from the dramatic events at Edgbaston in the Third Ashes Test Match, and I found my concentration wavering at times, especially as quite a few of the parents were listening to *TMS* on the boundary.

Harefield C.C., Friday, 31st July, 2015

Friendly (40/40). TVCL Representative XI 276-7 (40.0), Harefield 271-8 (40.0). TVCL Representative XI won by 5 runs.

This was a cracking match, with the result in doubt until the very last ball. Harefield's number 10 batsman amused me at the start of the last over. His team were eight down at the time and he told me that it was now all down to his colleague

---

[113] Playing with a 'hard ball' is cricketing parlance for it being a 'proper' match.

at the other end –'because I'm a rabbit and the next man in's a ferret'.[114]

Hurst C.C., Saturday, 1st August, 2015

TVCL Division 2B. Hurst 78 (42.2), Henley II 81-4 (25.2). Henley II won by 6 wickets.

My colleague had an interesting dead ball call to make today. The batsman hit the ball to short midwicket, who then rather casually picked it up and threw it in to the wicketkeeper, who also rather casually caught it before seeing that the batsman was out of his ground and promptly removing the bails. My colleague said not out on the basis that the ball was dead – he thought that it had *become settled* in the wicketkeeper's gloves before he removed the bails.[115] We discussed the incident after the match and I said that I would have given the batsman out. In my opinion, the ball was not dead and the batsman had lost concentration – and should not have been out of his ground. However, this is always a subjective call and the law makes clear that 'it is a matter for the umpire alone to decide'.[116]

I also had an interesting 'back foot no ball' situation at my end during the Henley innings. The opening bowler's back foot was landing very close to the return crease each time and I nearly called him on a number of occasions. However, in the end, I did not do so – as far as I could see his back foot

---

[114] Rabbits in cricketing parlance are the weak batsmen at the bottom of the batting order.
[115] Law 23.1, 'Ball is dead'.
[116] Law 23.2, 'Ball finally settled'.

was always either just within the return crease, or his heel was above it.[117] The problem in this situation is transferring one's eyes from the bowler's feet to what is happening at the other end.[118]

Ludgrove School, Sunday, 2nd August, 2015

Friendly: I Zingari 218 (39.5), Flashmen 147 (29.4). I Zingari won by 71 runs.

I reached the school easily enough, but there was no sign of the cricket ground. I asked a couple of workmen and got led down two different garden paths before eventually finding the ground. It felt like being on tour in the old days, before mobile phones and Sat Navs made things easier but considerably less fun. I think that there is a certain Luddite charm to being lost on the way to a new cricket ground.

When I found the ground I realised that the pitch was clearly only 21 yards long. This was not completely unsurprising given that the venue was a prep school, but what was the groundsman thinking? "Fine", said the captains, "we'll make do." The result was, unsurprisingly, a bowler-dominated match

At the start of the match, I Zingari only had ten players and the Flashmen had twelve – although only about half of them had arrived at the ground as there was severe traffic congestion heading out of London. Eventually, the Flashmen had eleven and the match began. I Zingari struggled hugely

---

[117] Law 24.5, 'Fair delivery – the feet'.
[118] See entry for The Oval, Monday, 19th August, 2013.

on the short pitch and were soon 60-7. At this point the Flashmen's twelfth player arrived and promptly volunteered to make up the numbers for I Zingari. He turned out to be a very good batsman and played what proved to be a match-winning innings – and I Zingari ended up winning by 71 runs. It really is a funny old game.

I Zingari are one of the most famous wandering clubs so I was intrigued, as ever, by the origins of the name and their history. I Zingari is an Italian phrase which translates loosely as gypsies and the club was formed in 1845 by a group of Old Harrovians. I really liked their striking black, red and gold caps, which apparently symbolise 'out of darkness, through fire, into light'. There is a stark contrast between this 'jazz circuit' cricket and its hard, uncompromising league counterpart. They both have their place, but the former is definitely doing more to uphold the traditional values and spirit of the game.

I do not think that I had my best ever game as an umpire today. There were two LBW appeals that I turned down and I think that they both could well have been out. On the first one I had no balled a fast bowler several times and was watching his feet carefully. So, for the second day I running I failed to follow Aleem Dar's advice[119] and, fixated by the bowler's front foot, I was not concentrating fully on the business end when the LBW appeal came. On the second one, later in the game, I thought that the batsman had got outside the line, but on reflection I think that he moved after the ball had struck him. The key thing when one has a bad game is to

---

[119] See entry for The Oval, Monday, 19th August, 2013.

learn from one's mistakes and then move on: another day, another match.

Friday, 7th August, 2015

Following on from my recent difficulties with transferring my eyes from the bowler's feet to the batsman's end, there was an interesting conversation on *TMS* today about no balls no longer being called (seemingly) by professional umpires – they just get checked on the DRS if a wicket falls. Jonathan Agnew was scathing in his criticism of the umpires in this respect but I do wonder when he last (if ever) umpired a match? I still think Aleem Dar's advice is spot on. [120]

Jim Maxwell then put forward a new idea that I had not heard before. He suggested that, when the DRS is in operation, the square leg umpire's role is now largely redundant – so he could therefore be more usefully employed at, say, wide extra cover in line with the popping crease to call front foot no balls, leaving the bowler's end umpire free to concentrate on what is happening at the other end. This struck me as a very reasonable idea, but of course it would not be feasible in the recreational game unless three rather than two umpires were appointed.

Tring Park C.C., Saturday, 8th August, 2015

TVCL Division 2A. British Airways 199 (49.1), Tring Park II 200-5 (48.0). Tring Park II won by 6 wickets.

---

[120] See entry for The Oval, Monday, 19th August, 2013.

I have many favourite cricket grounds but I think that Tring Park might just be top of my list. Today was a glorious sunny day and there were lots of cars parked up at the side of the ground, with people setting out deck chairs and picnics to watch the game. Towards the end of the game a hot air balloon floated slowly by and the passengers had a bird's eye view of the climax of the match, although I think that they may have been struggling to read the scoreboard.

There were two bizarre incidents during the BA innings, both involving a batsman who played very well for his 60 odd. Firstly, after he had played and missed, and the wicketkeeper had also missed the ball, he wandered half way down the pitch and then announced that he was not running as he had not played a shot. It was utterly bizarre. Firstly, it was of course my colleague's decision as the bowler's end umpire and not his. Secondly, as the ball had not struck his person, and had run away for byes, the fact that he had not played a shot was irrelevant. Thirdly, according to my colleague who was at the bowler's end at the time, he *had* in fact played a shot. And, fourthly, he was also now out of his ground and the ball was still in play. Tring were bemused and ran him out. My colleague and I consulted and told the Tring captain that if he upheld his appeal we would give the batsman out but suggested that, in the interests of The Spirit of Cricket, he may prefer to withdraw his appeal; to his credit, he took our advice.

In truth, I think that the batsman was a sandwich short of a picnic. Shortly afterwards, he came up to me and asked if he could continue his innings without batting gloves on the grounds that his hands were too hot. I told him that it was his choice alone what protective equipment he chose to wear – but warned him strongly against discarding his batting gloves. Quite aside from risking broken fingers, he was also wearing a ring, which could easily have been pressed into his flesh should he have been struck on it. He ignored my advice. Tring (quite reasonably) promptly brought back their fastest bowlers in response to his action, and soon afterwards he was dismissed. It was all very odd.

The second incident was a 'one bail off' run out scenario similar to the one I had at Ascot Park last season.[121] I was standing at square leg during the Tring innings and clearly saw the BA wicketkeeper dislodge the bails before an incoming throw from the boundary hit the stumps directly with the Tring batsman still out of his ground. So I said not out and thought that I had made a good decision. However, my eagle-eyed friend from BA, now no longer the captain but still my sternest critic[122], came over and informed me that the wicketkeeper had only knocked off one bail. If he was right – and I actually think that he probably was, not least because he had a better view of this aspect from mid on than I had at square leg – then the direct hit would have legally broken the wicket, and I should have given the batsman out.[123] It was too late to reverse my decision, so I just said to him that his understanding of the laws was correct and that if I had seen what he had seen then I would have given the Tring batsman out. He accepted this with good grace.

Eton College, Sunday, 9th August, 2015

---

[121] See entry for Ascott Park, Sunday, 8th June, 2014.
[122] See entry for North Maidenhead C.C., Saturday, 30th May, 2015.
[123] Law 28.2, 'One bail off'.

Friendly: Eton Ramblers 120 (34.2), Cryptics 121-2 (26.1). Cryptics won by 8 wickets.

This was my first visit to Eton College. The match was played on the main Upper Club ground, which is surrounded on all sides by mature trees, including three 'cooling' Poplars[124] in one corner, and has a large flat playing area and a modernised old clubhouse. However, the attractive setting is blighted by the Heathrow flight path. Today, the aeroplanes were taking off to the west and for 15–20 seconds at a time my eardrums were blasted by the roar of the jet engines above. The hot air balloon at Tring yesterday seemed a world away.

The cricket was a little disappointing as the Ramblers' batting collapsed. "At least we made it to lunch", said one of their players, an ironic reference to Australia's first innings at Trent Bridge in the Ashes Test Match a few days ago. However, the hospitality made up for the aeroplanes and the cricket: homemade chicken curry for lunch followed by delicious egg and cucumber sandwiches and lemon drizzle cake for tea.

One of the Cryptics players was disabled. He only had use of his right arm, but bowled a decent spell and memorably held onto a steepler off his own bowling. He settled himself under the catch, raised his good arm perpendicularly skyward and took it as clean as a whistle. Many two-handed players would have dropped it. This actually led to an interesting discussion during the tea interval as to whether or not it is

---

124 See entry for NPL Teddington C.C., Saturday, 2nd July, 2011.

easier to take a catch one-handed. My twopennyworth was that, provided balance is not an issue – and it is not when one is standing underneath a steepler – then it is.

I gave the Ramblers' opening batsman out LBW today shouldering arms. It was a straightforward decision. A right-handed seam bowler was shaping the ball in to a right-handed batsman. It struck him on the left knee roll on or perhaps just outside off stump, and was hitting two thirds of the way up middle and off. After impact, he moved his left leg across towards first slip. Batsmen often do this in an attempt to kid the umpire that the ball was either missing off stump or that they were outside the line. Later, during the luncheon interval, the batsman (politely) suggested to me that it was a harsh decision. I told him what had happened and added that I would have given him the benefit of the doubt of being outside the line if he had played a shot.

As the match finished early and everyone drifted off, I decided to walk across to the second ground at Eton, Agar's Plough. It has a magnificent pavilion, which is visually superior to the one at Upper Club, but the playing area is very open, which is not to my taste.

Aston Rowant C.C., Wednesday, 12th August, 2015

I went to watch a representative match at the magnificent Aston Rowant ground today. I skippered Chalfont St. Peter Sunday 1st XI for four seasons in the mid 1990s and there was one (biennial) fixture when getting a team out was never a problem. Aston Rowant away. It has a superb square and outfield, and a beautiful setting in the Chiltern foothills; and although the clubhouse is rather small it nonetheless has an attractive old world charm. I played my last ever match (as a regular player) here in 2007. I hurt my back, gave away runs in the field and then scratched around horrendously with the bat, which was a microcosm of that whole season for me.

I do have other, happier memories of this ground, including making a fifty here in 2003. It has the hardest track that I ever batted on and, on this particular day, I remember hitting a medium pace dobber on the up through mid off for four. For just a fleeting moment I felt like Graham Gooch! In truth, I wasn't a good enough player to do this sort of thing on a regular basis, and certainly not on the type of tracks that I batted on for most of my career.

I also have another memory from this ground, which will be etched on my mind forever. I was skippering Chalfont St. Peter here in a Sunday 1st XI friendly in 1995. We were fielding second and by the last over our only hope was to salvage a draw. With one over to go, Rowant needed about ten to win with five or six wickets in hand. With two balls to go they still needed three. I put all my fielders on the boundary, and the ball went down to our young fast bowler at fine leg for an easy single but certainly nothing more. He had an arm like an Exocet missile. He charged in at the ball, keen as mustard. "Easy, easy, easy ... hold it ... they're not running!" we all shouted. He did not hear us. In came the ball. Hard, flat and fast. Very hard, flat and fast. The wicketkeeper fumbled. Overthrows. We lost.

Boyne Hill C.C., Saturday, 15th August, 2015

TVCL Division 2B. Boyne Hill 162 (50.1), Chiswick & Whitton 54 (18.1). Boyne Hill won by 108 runs.

The Boyne Hill ground is bowl-shaped, so drainage can be a problem. It had rained the previous day and some dampness had got under the covers. By the time we tossed up it was drying out, but it was still a no-brainer for the winning captain to bowl first. Chiswick won the toss but then firstly let Boyne Hill get too many runs and then batted badly, which perhaps proves that, although the toss can be important, the result of the match depends more on how well a team bats, bowls and fields.

As the pitch was still damp during the first innings, my colleague and I were concerned about players from both sides running on the pitch and causing it to cut up. As a result we issued warnings to both the Boyne Hill batsmen[125] and the Chiswick bowlers[126]. The nature of these warnings are subtly different. For the bowler it is the same as dangerous and unfair bowling – he gets a first warning, a second and final warning and then he is removed from the attack; for the batsman it is a first and final warning that applies not just to him but to all his teammates for the duration of the innings, and any further transgression incurs penalty runs. As an umpire you have to be right on the ball with these laws to do your job properly.

There was an amusing moment during the Chiswick innings. A fielder dropped an easy catch and later on was

---

[125] Law 42.14, 'Batsman damaging the pitch'.
[126] Law 42.12, 'Bowler running on the protected area after delivering the ball'.

asked by his captain to come on to bowl. "*Hand* the ball to him," chirped the disgruntled bowler who was being taken off, "don't throw it!"

North Maidenhead C.C., Saturday, 22nd August, 2015

TVCL Division 2A. North Maidenhead 254-5 dec. (50.0), Kidmore End 238-9 (50.0). Match drawn.

This was a tense match, second versus third in the table and with all to play for. For the first time since my boundary assessment at Stoke Green a couple of months ago I came under real pressure. I was pleased with how I maintained my composure. I have developed a technique whereby I move out of and then back into position after each delivery at the bowler's end. As a result I think that I am keeping my upper body more relaxed when under pressure.

I had an interesting LBW decision to make today in the penultimate over of the match. A right-handed batsman played a reverse sweep. He turned round and was struck on his right (now front) leg. What made this decision tricky is that he was moving very fast. When a batsman does this it is easy to think that he is a left-hander, but for the purposes of the LBW law he is not. So where the ball pitched was irrelevant. I was sure that the ball was going to go on and hit the stumps – so I gave him out.

Grainville, Jersey, Thursday, 27th August, 2015

Rain, rain, rain! I am on tour this week umpiring for Buckinghamshire Under 16s in the Jersey Festival. Well, I was supposed to be. It has rained for four days solid and the week so far has been a complete washout. We have one last chance tomorrow – fingers crossed! I worked here for three years between 2003 and 2006, so I have been able to use the downtime to look up a few old friends and sample the local cuisine – but for the boys cooped up in the hotel it has been dreadful. Such are the trials and tribulations of an English summer.

Maidenhead & Bray C.C., Sunday, 30th August, 2015

Friendly (40/40). Maidenhead & Bray 261-5 (40.0), Jesters 133 (35.0). Maidenhead & Bray won by 128 runs.

Some vandals had attacked the Bray pitch on Friday evening: they had apparently driven a car out onto the square, pulled the covers off, driven across it and then driven off. Fortunately, they did not turn out to be especially bright vandals – they only drove across the square once and not on a length, so both yesterday's and today's matches were played without inconvenience. George Davis and Headingley 1975 it was not.

Chesham C.C., Wednesday, 2nd September, 2015

Tom Orford Trophy (third day of three). Free Foresters 111 (42.3), Buckinghamshire Young Amateurs 113-1 (13.0). Buckinghamshire Young Amateurs won by 9 wickets.

I was called up as a late replacement for this match and was looking forward to it – my first three-day match. However, the first two days were washed out and it was touch and go whether the ground was even playable this morning. The competition rules stipulated that it was now a single innings match. The toss was vital because there was moisture in the pitch early on, but even when you win or lose the toss in such circumstances you still have to adapt and play well – and only one team did. The Buckinghamshire bowlers put the ball in the right place and some of the Foresters' top order batsmen played bad shots. Their late order battled hard from 44–6 but it was all in vain.

I was amused by the notice on the door to the umpires' changing room. It stated the latter in the form of the chart one is asked to read when having one's eyes tested at the opticians – triangular with the letters at the top bigger than the ones at the bottom.

Lord's, Saturday, 5th September, 2015

I was at Lord's today when Ben Stokes was given out obstructed the field (I notice that this is now referred to using the past tense rather than the infinitive). Stokes was facing Mitchell Starc and, advancing down the wicket, hit the ball straight back at the bowler, who fielded it and threw it back at the stumps. Stokes lost his balance and fell to the ground, outside his crease, but then – with his back turned to the ball – put out his left hand and intercepted Starc's throw, which may have been going on to hit his wicket and run him out. The law is quite clear: the batsman is out if he *wilfully* obstructs the field.[127] However, was his action wilful?

---

[127] Law 37.1, 'Out obstructed the field'.

It was a fiendishly difficult decision for the umpires to have to make and opinion amongst pundits and my umpiring friends this evening is divided. My twopennyworth is that, viewed in real time, it looks like he is acting in self-defence – it would certainly be difficult to say, definitively, that his action was *wilful*. However, in slow motion his action looks more culpable. But does slow-motion always tell the true story? Think of the low to the ground catches, which always end up being given not out when referred upstairs. Who would be an umpire?

Eton College, Sunday, 6th September, 2015

Friendly (45/45). Old Amplefordians 100 (33.3), Eton Ramblers 102-5 (27.0). Eton Ramblers won by 5 wickets.

This was a pleasant antidote to the hurly burly of a packed house at Lord's yesterday: attractive surroundings, watery September sunshine, good company, good food and a gentle, social game of cricket. It would have been perfect but for the aeroplanes ...

This is the third time that I have umpired the Ramblers this season and each match has failed to last the distance. Cricket matches cannot be manufactured and the Amplefordians never recovered from a top order batting collapse. Any chance that they might have had of pulling off an unlikely win then foundered on the butterfingers of their wicketkeeper, who dropped two early chances. "Well, at least that's the first two rounds this evening sorted", lamented one of their fielders, clutching at straws for some consolation.

Eversholt C.C., Sunday, 13th September, 2015

Friendly (40/40). Eversholt 215-6 (40.0), Jesters 219-4 (38.0). Jesters won by 6 wickets.

This was the furthest (in time if not mileage) that I have travelled to umpire a match – it took me an hour and twenty minutes each way from my home in Marlow. It was worth it though – a picture postcard village cricket ground, a sunny early autumnal afternoon and a good game.

It was a memorial match for a player who had turned out for both teams, and there were lots of spectators and guests present. Unusually, I felt like an outsider – not because anyone was unfriendly, in fact quite the opposite – but because I did not know the player who was being remembered and therefore could not share in any of the anecdotes and stories, and also, today, I did not have a colleague to stand with either.

The cricket was gentle and I had very little to do. I sometimes amuse myself in these situations by trying to work out nicknames. One fielder was called Chuck so I surmised, correctly as it turned out, that his surname was Berry; as a bowler was marking up his run, a colleague shouted out, "come on, then, Monica", so I surmised, again correctly, that he was going to grunt (like the tennis player, Monica Seles) in his delivery action; and another fielder was referred to as Swanny, so I surmised that he would soon be coming on to bowl some off-spin. However, this time I was wrong – his surname was Swann but there all similarities to the former England off-spinner ended!

Lord's, Monday, 5th October, 2015

Friendly: Cross Arrows v. The Stock Exchange. Match cancelled.

Saving the best for last, my final game of the season today – and the final entry of this diary - was at the home of cricket. I have cracked this joke before[128] except that today it was not a joke. Granted, it was not the main ground – it was on the Nursery Ground! – so I did not exactly walk through the Long Room and out on to the hallowed turf, but this is minor detail and the venue of today's match will be recorded in my personal records as Lord's! Sadly, the recent glorious autumnal weather turned this morning and we were rained off soon after lunch without a ball being bowled.

Cross Arrows C.C. was originally set up to provide an opportunity for MCC staff to play cricket themselves. Nowadays, the club plays a short season of matches at the end of the season on the Nursery Ground against wandering and other notable clubs. The origin of the club name is amusing. Apparently, before one of their early fixtures, when they did not yet have a name, someone asked for directions to the following day's match against Northwood C.C., and was told that, "it's cross 'arrow way" (i.e. somewhere near Harrow) – and the name stuck.

Postscript to the 2015 season

---

[128] See entry for Saturday, 6th October, 2012.

It is funny how cricket seasons sometimes start and end with a whimper rather than a bang. Mine this season started with a fixture c***-up at Harrow School and ended with rain at Lord's, but in between there was a glorious summer and some memorable matches.

Last year I umpired too much and, to be honest, got a little bit stale. This year I was able to rectify that by managing my schedule more selectively. I stood in roughly the same number of matches but, crucially, managed to space them out more effectively.

Acronyms

ACO   Association of Cricket Officials
A&WCL   Airedale and Wharfedale Cricket League
BCB   Buckinghamshire Cricket Board
BSCA   Buckinghamshire Schools Cricket Association
BUCS   British Universities and Colleges Sport
D/L   The Duckworth/Lewis scoring method
ECB   England and Wales Cricket Board
GWL   Ground, weather and light
HCPCL   Home Counties Premier Cricket League
LBW   Leg before wicket
MCC   Marylebone Cricket Club
ODI   One Day International
Tom Smith   Tom Smith's *New Cricket Umpiring and Scoring*
TCSL   Thames & Chilterns Sunday Cricket League
TMS   Test Match Special
TVCL   Thames Valley Cricket League

Bibliography

Tom Smith's *New Cricket Umpiring and Scoring* (London, 2004 [1980])